P9-EFI-282

The 21 Irrefutable
LAWS OF
LEADERSHIP

THE 21 IRREFUTABLE LAWS OF LEADERSHIP

FOLLOW THEM *and* PEOPLE WILL FOLLOW YOU

REVISED & UPDATED
10TH ANNIVERSARY EDITION

JOHN C. MAXWELL

HarperCollins
LEADERSHIP

AN IMPRINT OF HARPERCOLLINS

© 1998 and 2007 by John C. Maxwell

All rights reserved. No portion of this book may be reproduced, stored in a retrieval system, or transmitted in any form or by any means—electronic, mechanical, photocopy, recording, scanning, or other—except for brief quotations in critical reviews or articles, without the prior written permission of the publisher.

Published by HarperCollins Leadership, an imprint of HarperCollins Focus LLC.

Published in association with Yates & Yates, www.yates2.com.

Scripture quotations noted CEV are from THE CONTEMPORARY ENGLISH VERSION. © 1991 by the American Bible Society. Used by permission.

Scripture quotations noted The Message are from *The Message: The New Testament in Contemporary English.* © 1993 by Eugene H. Peterson.

Library of Congress Cataloging-in-Publication Data
Maxwell, John C., 1947–
    The 21 irrefutable laws of leadership : follow them and people will follow you / John C. Maxwell. — 10th anniversary ed.
        p. cm.
    Includes new foreword by Stephen Covey and two new appendices.
    Includes bibliographical references.
    ISBN 978-0-7852-8837-4 (repack)
    ISBN 978-0-7852-8935-7 (IE)
    1. Leadership. 2. Industrial management. I. Title. II. Title: Twenty one irrefutable laws of leadership.
HD57.7.M3937 2007
658.4'092—dc22

2007018067

Printed in China
18 19 20 21 22 DSC 5 4 3 2 1

This book is dedicated to Charlie Wetzel, my writing partner since 1994. Together we've written more than forty books, and I've enjoyed our collaboration on every one. As I have labored to add value to others by identifying and teaching leadership principles, Charlie, you have added value to me and my efforts. Your insights and skills as a wordsmith have been enjoyed by millions of readers. As a result, you have made a greater impact on more people than has anyone else in my inner circle. For that I thank you.

CONTENTS

1. THE LAW OF THE LID   1
Leadership Ability Determines a Person's Level of Effectiveness
Brothers Dick and Maurice came as close as they could to living the
American Dream—without making it. Instead a guy named Ray did it
with the company they had founded. It happened because they didn't
know the Law of the Lid.

2. THE LAW OF INFLUENCE   11
The True Measure of Leadership Is Influence—Nothing More, Nothing Less
Abraham Lincoln started with the rank of captain, but by the time the war
was over, he was a private. What happened? He was a casualty of the Law
of Influence.

3. THE LAW OF PROCESS   23
Leadership Develops Daily, Not in a Day
Theodore Roosevelt helped create a world power, won a Nobel Peace Prize,
and became president of the United States. But today you wouldn't even
know his name if he hadn't known the Law of Process.

Contents

CONTENTS

How did the Confederate army—understaffed and underequipped—stand up so long to the powerful Union army? The Confederates had better generals. Why did they have better generals? The Law of Magnetism makes it clear.

As the new leader, John knew that the most influential person in the organization could torpedo his leadership. So what did he do? He reached out using the Law of Connection.

Lance Armstrong is hailed as the greatest cyclist who ever lived. People credit his toughness. They credit his brutal training. What they miss is the Law of the Inner Circle.

Henry Ford is considered an icon of American business for revolutionizing the automobile industry. So what caused him to stumble so badly that his son feared Ford Motor Company would go out of business? He was held captive by the Law of Empowerment.

Easy Company withstood the German advance at the Battle of the Bulge and dashed Hitler's last hope for stopping the Allies' advance. They were able to do it because their leaders embraced the Law of the Picture.

CONTENTS

Contents

FOREWORD

By Stephen R. Covey

When John Maxwell asked me to write the foreword for this 10th anniversary edition of *The 21 Irrefutable Laws of Leadership*, I was honored and intrigued. During the past two decades, John and I have traveled on parallel paths in our speaking and writing. We have both been called "leadership experts" over the years. We know and respect each other's work. But in spite of the similarities between our messages, we have rarely spoken to the same audience.

So to recommend this book allows me to introduce John Maxwell and his teaching to members of my audience who have not yet read him. And what better book to recommend than this new and improved version of *The 21 Irrefutable Laws of Leadership?* It serves as a sort of manifesto for his teaching and his life. Study this book and you have gotten to know John Maxwell the person as well as his philosophy of leadership.

When *The 21 Laws* was first published in 1998, I could see immediately how practical and applicable the laws were. They still are. For over three decades, John Maxwell has earned his reputation as a communicator. And as he says, communicators "make the complex simple." Rather than an esoteric examination of leadership, this book is more like a foundational instruction manual. With each chapter, you will get to *know* individuals who did—or some who didn't—obey the law in question. The law itself is defined clearly and simply. And—most importantly—John will give you specific steps for applying it to the leadership in your office, community, family, or church.

FOREWORD

John has told me regarding this revision that he was excited about the
opportunity to include the lessons he has learned since *The 21 Laws* was
first written. I know what he means. Leadership is not static, and neither
should be books about it. I believe this revised edition will have an even
greater impact than its predecessor. Laws have been updated, illustrations
refined, and applications enhanced. The foundational leadership concepts
have not been abandoned; rather, they have been updated for a new generation of leaders. As good as the original was, this new edition is even better.

If *The 21 Irrefutable Laws of Leadership* is new to you, let me say that
you are in for a treat. It will change the way you live and lead. As you read,
you will be encouraged and your ability to lead will expand. If you have
read the original book, then you will be thrilled with this new edition. You
will learn many new lessons as well as being reminded of truths that will
serve you well. And by engaging in the new application activities, you will
really sharpen your skills.

I trust that you will enjoy and benefit from reading this book, just as I
did. In it you will find absolutely amazing, inspiring leadership stories!

STEPHEN R. COVEY
author of *The 7 Habits of Highly Effective People,*
The 8th Habit, and *Everyday Greatness*

ACKNOWLEDGMENTS

T hank you to the thousands of leaders around the world who learned and sometimes challenged the laws of leadership, thus sharpening my thinking.

Thank you to the team at Thomas Nelson who gave me the chance to revise and improve this book, and especially to Tami Heim for her strategic leadership and to Victor Oliver who was instrumental in the development of the original concept.

Thank you to Linda Eggers, my executive assistant, and her assistant, Sue Caldwell, for their incredible service and willingness to go the extra mile every day.

Thank you to Charlie Wetzel, my writer, and Stephanie, his wife, without whose work this book would not have been possible.

INTRODUCTION

E very book is a conversation between the author and the individual reading it. Some people pick up a book hoping for a bit of encouragement. Some devour a book's information as if they were attending an intensive seminar. Others find in its pages a mentor they can meet with on a daily, weekly, or monthly basis.

The thing I love about writing books is that it allows me to "talk" to many people I will never personally meet. That's why I made the decision in 1977 to become an author. I had a passion to add value to people that energized me to write. That passion still burns within me today. Few things are more rewarding to me than being on the road and having someone I've never met approach me to say, "Thank you. Your books have really helped me." It's why I write—and intend to continue writing!

Despite the deep satisfaction of knowing that my books help people, there is also a great frustration that comes with being an author. Once a book is published, it freezes in time. If you and I knew each other personally and we met weekly or monthly to talk about leadership, every time we got together I'd share with you something new I'd learned. As a person, I continue to grow. I'm constantly reading. I'm analyzing my mistakes. I'm talking to excellent leaders to learn from them. Each time you and I were to sit down, I'd say, "You won't believe what I just learned."

As a conference and event speaker, I often teach the principles I write about in my books, and I'm constantly updating my material. I use new stories. I refine ideas. And I often gain new insights as I stand in front of an audience. However, when I go back to books that I've previously written, first, I become aware of how I've changed since I've written them. But second, I become frustrated because the books can't grow and change along with me.

That's why I got excited when my publisher, Thomas Nelson, asked if I would like to revise *The 21 Irrefutable Laws of Leadership* for a special tenth anniversary edition. When I originally wrote the book, it was my answer to the question, "If you were to take everything you've learned about leadership over the years and boil it down into a short list, what would it be?" I put on paper the essentials of leadership, communicated as simply and clearly as possible. And soon after the book was published and it appeared on four different bestseller lists, I realized it had the potential to help a lot of people become better leaders.

GROWTH = CHANGE

But now, years later, there are things I am no longer satisfied with in the original edition, and I knew I could improve upon some of the ideas. Some stories had become dated, and I wanted to replace them with new ones. I had also developed new material to better explain and illustrate some of the principles. While teaching the laws for nearly a decade in dozens of countries around the world, I fielded thousands of questions about them. That process advanced my thinking beyond what it was when I first wrote the book. Working on this tenth anniversary edition has allowed me to make those improvements.

By far the biggest change I wanted to make to the original book centered on two of the laws. *What?* you may ask. *How can you* change *one of your* irrefutable *laws?*

First of all, while teaching them I soon discovered that two of the laws were really just subsets of other laws. The Law of E. F. Hutton (When the Real Leader Speaks, People Listen) was really just an aspect of the Law of Influence (The True Measure of Leadership Is Influence—Nothing More,

Nothing Less). When people around a table stop and listen to a leader speak, they are revealing that the speaker has influence. Because the ideas in the Law of E. F. Hutton were part of the Law of Influence, I merged those two chapters. Similarly, I recognized that the Law of Reproduction (It Takes a Leader to Raise Up a Leader) was assumed in the Law of Explosive Growth (To Add Growth, Lead Followers—To Multiply, Lead Leaders). For that reason, I combined them as well.

The other thing that happened was that I began to realize that I had missed some things when writing about the laws of leadership originally. I discovered the first omission as soon as I had taught the laws a few times in developing countries. I found that in many of those places, leadership was focused on position, privilege, and power. In my paradigm of leadership, I took some things for granted. I see leadership primarily as a form of service and had never identified a law to teach that principle. The second oversight had to do with modeling leadership and impacting the culture of an organization. The result is the inclusion of two new laws in this tenth anniversary edition of *The 21 Irrefutable Laws of Leadership*:

The Law of Addition: Leaders Add Value by Serving Others
The Law of the Picture: People Do What People See

From today's perspective I ask myself, *How could I have missed them?* But I did. The good news is that you won't! I feel certain that these two laws will add immeasurably to the book and to your ability to lead. Serving others and showing others the way are two critical components of successful leadership. I wish I could revise each of my books every ten years to include things I missed!

MORE LESSONS LEARNED

There are two other things I've been reminded of as I've taught the 21 Laws these last ten years:

INTRODUCTION

1. Leadership Requires the Ability to Do More Than One Thing Well

Instinctively, successful people understand that focus is important to achievement. But leadership is very complex. During a break at a conference where I was teaching the 21 Laws, a young college student came up to me and said, "I know you are teaching 21 Laws of Leadership, but I want to get to the bottom line." With intensity, he raised his index finger and asked, "What is the one thing I need to know about leadership?"

Trying to match his intensity, I raised my index finger and answered, "The one thing you need to know about leadership is that there is more than one thing you need to know about leadership!" To lead well, we must do 21 things well.

2. No One Does All 21 Laws Well

Despite the fact that we must do 21 things well to be excellent leaders, it is reality that none of us does all of them well. For example, I am average or below average in five of the laws—and I wrote the book! So what is a leader to do? Ignore those laws? No, develop a leadership team.

At the end of this book there is a leadership evaluation. I encourage you to take it to evaluate your aptitude for each law. Once you've discovered in which laws you are average or below, begin looking for team members whose skills are strong where yours are weak. They will complement you and vice versa, and the whole team will benefit. That will make it possible for you to develop an all-star leadership team. Remember, none of us is as smart as all of us.

SOME THINGS NEVER CHANGE

Though I have made adjustments to the laws and updated the ways I teach them, some things have not changed in the last ten years. It's still true that leadership is leadership, no matter where you go or what you do. Times change. Technology marches forward. Cultures differ from place to place. But the principles of leadership are constant—whether you're looking at the citizens of ancient Greece, the Hebrews in the Old Testament, the armies of the modern world, the leaders in the international community, the pastors in local churches, or the businesspeople of today's global economy. Leadership principles are unchanging and stand the test of time.

As you read the following chapters, I'd like you to keep in mind four ideas:

1. **The laws can be learned.** Some are easier to understand and apply than others, but every one of them can be acquired.
2. **The laws can stand alone.** Each law complements all the others, but you don't need one in order to learn another.
3. **The laws carry consequences with them.** Apply the laws, and people will follow you. Violate or ignore them, and you will not be able to lead others.
4. **These laws are the foundation of leadership.** Once you learn the principles, you have to practice them and apply them to your life.

Whether you are a follower who is just beginning to discover the impact of leadership or a natural leader who already has followers, you can become a better leader. As you read about the laws, you may recognize that you already practice some of them very effectively. Other laws may expose weaknesses you didn't know you had. Use your review as a learning experience. In this edition, I've included exercises at the end of each chapter to help you apply each law to your life.

No matter where you are in the leadership process, know this: the greater the number of laws you learn, the better leader you will become. Each law is like a tool, ready to be picked up and used to help you achieve your dreams and add value to other people. Pick up even one, and you will become a better leader. Learn them all, and people will gladly follow you.

Now, let's open the toolbox together.

1

THE LAW OF THE LID

Leadership Ability Determines
a Person's Level of Effectiveness

I often open my leadership conferences by explaining the Law of the Lid because it helps people understand the value of leadership. If you can get a handle on this law, you will see the incredible impact of leadership on every aspect of life. So here it is: leadership ability is the lid that determines a person's level of effectiveness. The lower an individual's ability to lead, the lower the lid on his potential. The higher the individual's ability to lead, the higher the lid on his potential. To give you an example, if your leadership rates an 8, then your effectiveness can never be greater than a 7. If your leadership is only a 4, then your effectiveness will be no higher than a 3. Your leadership ability—for better or for worse—always determines your effectiveness and the potential impact of your organization.

Let me tell you a story that illustrates the Law of the Lid. In 1930, two young brothers named Dick and Maurice moved from New Hampshire to California in search of the American Dream. They had just gotten out of high school, and they saw few opportunities back home. So they headed straight for Hollywood where they eventually found jobs on a movie studio set.

After a while, their entrepreneurial spirit and interest in the entertainment industry prompted them to open a theater in Glendale, a town about five miles northeast of Hollywood. But despite all their efforts, the brothers just couldn't make the business profitable. In the four years they ran the theater, they weren't able to consistently generate enough money to pay the one hundred dollars a month rent that their landlord required.

A NEW OPPORTUNITY

The brothers' desire for success was strong, so they kept looking for better business opportunities. In 1937, they finally struck on something that worked. They opened a small drive-in restaurant in Pasadena, located just east of Glendale. People in Southern California had become very dependent on their cars, and the culture was changing to accommodate that, including its businesses.

The drive-in restaurant was a phenomenon that sprang up in the early thirties, and it was becoming very popular. Rather than being invited into a dining room to eat, customers would drive into a parking lot around a small restaurant, place their orders with carhops, and receive their food on trays right in their cars. The food was served on china plates complete with glassware and metal utensils. It was a timely idea in a society that was becoming faster paced and increasingly mobile.

Dick and Maurice's tiny drive-in restaurant was a great success, and in 1940, they decided to move the operation to San Bernardino, a working-class boomtown fifty miles east of Los Angeles. They built a larger facility and expanded their menu from hot dogs, fries, and shakes to include barbecued beef and pork sandwiches, hamburgers, and other items. Their business exploded. Annual sales reached $200,000, and the brothers found themselves splitting $50,000 in profits every year—a sum that put them in the town's financial elite.

In 1948, their intuition told them that times were changing, and they made modifications to their restaurant business. They eliminated the carhops and started serving only walk-up customers. And they also streamlined everything. They reduced their menu and focused on selling hamburgers. They eliminated plates, glassware, and metal utensils, switching to paper and plastic products instead. They reduced their costs and lowered the prices they charged customers. They also created what they called the Speedy Service System. Their kitchen became like an assembly line, where each employee focused on service with speed. The brothers' goal was to fill each customer's order in thirty seconds or less. And they succeeded. By the mid-1950s, annual revenue hit $350,000, and by then, Dick and Maurice split net profits of about $100,000 each year.

Who were these brothers? Back in those days, you could have found out by driving to their small restaurant on the corner of Fourteenth and E Streets in San Bernardino. On the front of the small octagonal building hung a neon sign that said simply McDonald's Hamburgers. Dick and Maurice McDonald had hit the great American jackpot, and the rest, as they say, is history, right? Wrong. The McDonalds never went any further because their weak leadership put a lid on their ability to succeed.

THE STORY BEHIND THE STORY

It's true that the McDonald brothers were financially secure. Theirs was one of the most profitable restaurant enterprises in the country, and they felt that they had a hard time spending all the money they made. Their genius was in customer service and kitchen organization. That talent led to the creation of a new system of food and beverage service. In fact, their talent was so widely known in food service circles that people started writing them and visiting from all over the country to learn more about their methods. At one point, they received as many as three hundred calls and letters every month.

That led them to the idea of marketing the McDonald's concept. The idea of franchising restaurants wasn't new. It had been around for several decades. To the McDonald brothers, it looked like a way to make money without having to open another restaurant themselves. In 1952, they got started, but their effort was a dismal failure. The reason was simple. They lacked the leadership necessary to make a larger enterprise effective. Dick and Maurice were good single-restaurant owners. They understood how to run a business, make their systems efficient, cut costs, and increase profits.

They were efficient managers. But they were not leaders. Their thinking patterns clamped a lid down on what they could do and become. At the height of their success, Dick and Maurice found themselves smack-dab against the Law of the Lid.

THE BROTHERS PARTNER WITH A LEADER

In 1954, the brothers hooked up with a man named Ray Kroc, who was a leader. Kroc had been running a small company he founded, which sold machines for making milk shakes. He knew about McDonald's. The restaurant was one of his best customers. And as soon as he visited the store, he had a vision for its potential. In his mind he could see the restaurant going nationwide in hundreds of markets. He soon struck a deal with Dick and Maurice, and in 1955, he formed McDonald's Systems, Inc. (later called the McDonald's Corporation).

Kroc immediately bought the rights to a franchise so that he could use it as a model and prototype. He would use it to sell other franchises. Then he began to assemble a team and build an organization to make McDonald's a nationwide entity. He recruited and hired the sharpest people he could find, and as his team grew in size and ability, his people developed additional recruits with leadership skill.

In the early years, Kroc sacrificed a lot. Though he was in his mid-fifties, he worked long hours just as he had when he first got started in business thirty years earlier. He eliminated many frills at home, including his country club membership, which he later said added ten strokes to his golf game. During his first eight years with McDonald's, he took no salary. Not only that, but he personally borrowed money from the bank and against his life insurance to help cover the salaries of a few key leaders he wanted on the team. His sacrifice and his leadership paid off. In 1961, for the sum of $2.7 million, Kroc bought the exclusive rights to McDonald's from the brothers, and he proceeded to turn it into an American institution and global entity. The "lid" in the life and leadership of Ray Kroc was obviously much higher than that of his predecessors.

In the years that Dick and Maurice McDonald had attempted to franchise their food service system, they managed to sell the concept to just fifteen buyers, only ten of whom actually opened restaurants. And even in that size enterprise, their limited leadership and vision were hindrances. For example, when their first franchisee, Neil Fox of Phoenix, told the brothers that he wanted to call his restaurant McDonald's, Dick's response was, "What . . . for? McDonald's means nothing in Phoenix."

In contrast, the leadership lid in Ray Kroc's life was sky high. Between 1955 and 1959, Kroc succeeded in opening 100 restaurants. Four years after that, there were 500 McDonald's. Today the company has opened more than 31,000 restaurants in 119 countries.[1] Leadership ability—or more specifically the lack of leadership ability—was the lid on the McDonald brothers' effectiveness.

SUCCESS WITHOUT LEADERSHIP

I believe that success is within the reach of just about everyone. But I also believe that personal success without leadership ability brings only limited effectiveness. Without leadership ability, a person's impact is only a fraction of what it could be with good leadership. The higher you want to climb, the more you need leadership. The greater the impact you want to make, the greater your influence needs to be.

Whatever you will accomplish is restricted by your ability to lead others.

Let me give you a picture of what I mean. Let's say that when it comes to success, you're an 8 (on a scale from 1 to 10). That's pretty good. I think it would be safe to say that the McDonald brothers were in that range. But let's

The higher you want to climb, the more you need leadership. The greater the impact you want to make, the greater your influence needs to be.

also say that leadership isn't even on your radar. You don't care about it, and you make no effort to develop as a leader. You're functioning as a 1. Your level of effectiveness would look like this:

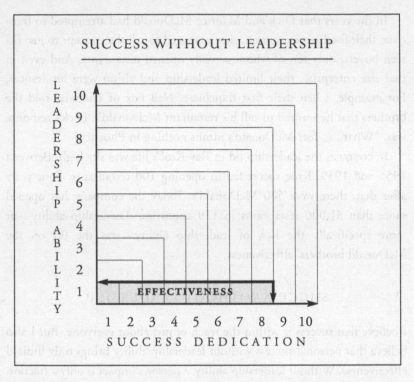

To increase your level of effectiveness, you have a couple of choices. You could work very hard to increase your dedication to success and excellence—to work toward becoming a 10. It's possible that you could make it to that level, though the Law of Diminishing Returns says that the effort it would take to increase those last two points might take more energy than it did to achieve the first eight. If you really killed yourself, you might increase your success by that 25 percent.

But you have another option. You can work hard to increase your level of *leadership*. Let's say that your natural leadership ability is a 4—slightly below average. Just by using whatever God-given talent you have, you already increase your effectiveness by 300 percent. But let's say you become a real student of leadership and you maximize your potential. You take it all the way up to a 7. Visually, the results would look like this:

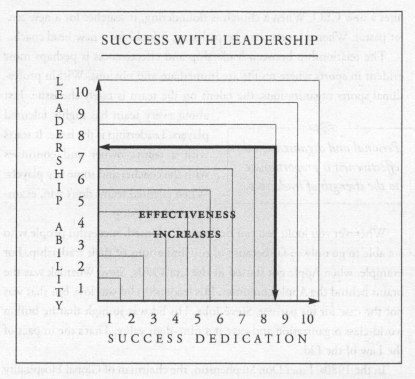

SUCCESS WITH LEADERSHIP

By raising your leadership ability—without increasing your success dedication at all—you can increase your original effectiveness by 600 percent. Leadership has a multiplying effect. I've seen its impact again and again in all kinds of businesses and nonprofit organizations. And that's why I've taught leadership for more than thirty years.

TO CHANGE THE DIRECTION OF THE ORGANIZATION, CHANGE THE LEADER

Leadership ability is always the lid on personal and organizational effectiveness. If a person's leadership is strong, the organization's lid is high. But if it's not, then the organization is limited. That's why in times of trouble, organizations naturally look for new leadership. When the country is experiencing hard times, it elects a new president. When a company is losing money, it hires a new CEO. When a church is floundering, it searches for a new senior pastor. When a sports team keeps losing, it looks for a new head coach.

The relationship between leadership and effectiveness is perhaps most evident in sports where results are immediate and obvious. Within professional sports organizations, the talent on the team is rarely the issue. Just about every team has highly talented players. Leadership is the issue. It starts with a team's owner and continues with the coaches and some key players. When talented teams don't win, examine the leadership.

> *Personal and organizational effectiveness is proportionate to the strength of leadership.*

Wherever you look, you can find smart, talented, successful people who are able to go only so far because of the limitations of their leadership. For example, when Apple got started in the late 1970s, Steve Wozniak was the brains behind the Apple computer. His leadership lid was low, but that was not the case for his partner, Steve Jobs. His lid was so high that he built a world-class organization and gave it a nine-digit value. That's the impact of the Law of the Lid.

In the 1980s, I met Don Stephenson, the chairman of Global Hospitality Resources, Inc., of San Diego, California, an international hospitality advisory and consulting firm. Over lunch, I asked him about his organization. Today he primarily does consulting, but back then his company took over the management of hotels and resorts that weren't doing well financially. His company oversaw many excellent facilities, such as La Costa in Southern California.

Don said that whenever his people went into an organization to take it over, they always started by doing two things. First, they trained all the staff to improve their level of service to the customers, and second, they fired the leader. When he told me that, I was surprised.

"You always fire him?" I asked. "Every time?"

"That's right. Every time," he said.

"Don't you talk to the person first—to check him out to see if he's a good leader?" I said.

"No," he answered. "If he'd been a good leader, the organization wouldn't be in the mess it's in."

And I thought to myself, *Of course. It's the Law of the Lid.* To reach the highest level of effectiveness, you have to raise the lid—one way or another.

The good news is that getting rid of the leader isn't the *only* way. Just as I teach in conferences that there is a lid, I also teach that you can raise it— but that's the subject of another law of leadership.

Applying
THE LAW OF THE LID
To Your Life

1. List some of your major goals. (Try to focus on significant objectives—things that will require a year or longer of your time. List at least five but no more than ten items.) Now identify which ones will require the participation or cooperation of other people. For these activities, your leadership ability will greatly impact your effectiveness.

2. Assess your leadership ability. Complete the leadership evaluation in Appendix A at the back of this book to get an idea of your basic leadership ability.

3. Ask others to rate your leadership. Talk to your boss, your spouse, two colleagues (at your level), and three people you lead about your leadership ability. Ask each of them to rate you on a scale of 1 (low) to 10 (high) in each of the following areas:

- People skills
- Planning and strategic thinking
- Vision
- Results

Average the scores, and compare them to your own assessment. Based on these assessments, is your leadership skill better or worse than you expected? If there is a gap between your assessment and that of others, what do you think is the cause? How willing are you to grow in the area of leadership?

2

THE LAW OF INFLUENCE

*The True Measure of Leadership Is
Influence—Nothing More, Nothing Less*

What do leaders look like? Do they always *look* powerful, impressive, charismatic? And how do you *measure* the effectiveness of a leader? Can you put two people side by side and instantly tell which is the better leader? These are questions people have asked for hundreds of years.

One of the most effective leaders of the late twentieth century was anything but impressive upon first appearance. When most people think of Mother Teresa, they envision a frail little woman dedicated to serving the poorest of the poor. That she was. But she was also a tremendous leader. I say that because she had an amazing amount of influence with others. And if you don't have influence, you will *never* be able to lead others.

SMALL STATURE—BIG IMPACT

Lucinda Vardey, who worked with Mother Teresa on the book *The Simple Path*, described the nun as "the quintessential, energetic entrepreneur, who has perceived a need and done something about it, built an organization against all odds, formulated its constitution, and sent out branches all over the world."

The organization Mother Teresa founded and led is called the Missionaries of Charity. While other vocational orders in the Catholic Church were declining, hers grew rapidly, reaching more than four thousand members during her lifetime (*not* including numerous volunteers). Under her direc-

> If you don't have influence, you will never be able to lead others.

tion, her followers served in twenty-five countries on five continents. In Calcutta alone, she established a children's home, a center for people with leprosy, a home for people who were dying and destitute, and a home for people suffering with tuberculosis or mental disorders. That kind of organizational building can be accomplished only by a true leader.

Mother Teresa's impact reached far beyond her immediate environment. People from all walks of life and from nations around the globe respected her, and when she spoke, people listened. Author and former presidential speechwriter Peggy Noonan wrote about a speech Mother Teresa gave at the National Prayer Breakfast in 1994. It illustrates her level of influence with others. Noonan observed:

The Washington establishment was there, plus a few thousand born-again Christians, orthodox Catholics, and Jews. Mother Teresa spoke of God, of love, of families. She said we must love one another and care for one another. There were great purrs of agreement.

But as the speech continued, it became more pointed. She spoke of unhappy parents in old people's homes who are "hurt because they are forgotten." She asked, "Are we willing to give until it hurts in order to be with our families, or do we put our own interests first?"

The baby boomers in the audience began to shift in their seats. And she continued. "I feel that the greatest destroyer of peace today is abortion," she said, and told them why, in uncompromising terms. For about 1.3 seconds there was silence, then applause swept the room. But not everyone clapped; the President and First Lady [Bill and Hillary Clinton], the Vice President and Mrs. Gore looked like seated statues at Madame Tussaud's, moving not a muscle. Mother Teresa didn't stop there either. When she was finished, there was almost no one she hadn't offended.[1]

At that time if just about any other person in the world had made those statements, people's reactions would have been openly hostile. They would have booed, jeered, or stormed out. But the speaker was Mother Teresa. She was probably the most respected person on the planet at that time. So everyone listened to what she had to say, even though many of them violently disagreed with it. In fact, every time that Mother Teresa spoke, people listened. Why? She was a real leader, and when the real leader speaks, people listen. Leadership is influence—nothing more, nothing less.

LEADERSHIP IS NOT . . .

Leadership is often misunderstood. When people hear that someone has an impressive title or an assigned leadership position, they assume that individual to be a leader. *Sometimes* that's true. But titles don't have much value when it comes to leading.

True leadership cannot be awarded, appointed, or assigned. It comes only from influence, and that cannot be mandated. It must be earned. The only thing a title can buy is a little time—either to increase your level of influence with others or to undermine it.

FIVE MYTHS ABOUT LEADERSHIP

There are plenty of misconceptions and myths that people embrace about leaders and leadership. Here are five common ones:

1. THE MANAGEMENT MYTH

A widespread misunderstanding is that leading and managing are one and the same. Up until a few years ago, books that claimed to be on leadership were often really about management. The main difference between the two is that leadership is about influencing people to follow, while management focuses on maintaining systems and processes. As former Chrysler chairman and CEO Lee Iacocca wryly commented, "Sometimes even the best manager is like the little boy with the big dog, waiting to see where the dog wants to go so that he can take him there."

> *The only thing a title can buy is a little time—either to increase your level of influence with others or to undermine it.*

The best way to test whether a person can lead rather than just manage is to ask him to create positive change. Managers can maintain direction, but often they can't change it. Systems and processes can do only so much. To move people in a new direction, you need influence.

2. The Entrepreneur Myth

Frequently, people assume that all entrepreneurs are leaders. But that's not always the case. Entrepreneurs are skilled at seeing opportunities and going after them. They see needs and understand how to meet them in a way that produces a profit. But not all of them are good with people. Many find it necessary to partner with someone skilled at the people part of the equation. If they can't influence people, they can't lead.

3. The Knowledge Myth

Sir Francis Bacon said, "Knowledge is power." If you believe power to be the essence of leadership, then you might naturally assume that those who possess knowledge and intelligence are therefore leaders. That isn't necessarily true. You can visit any major university and meet brilliant research scientists and philosophers whose ability to think is so high that it's off the charts but whose ability to lead is so low that it doesn't even register on the charts. Neither IQ nor education necessarily equates to leadership.

4. The Pioneer Myth

Another misconception is that anyone who is out in front of the crowd is a leader. But being first isn't always the same as leading. For example, Sir Edmund Hillary was the first man to reach the summit of Mount Everest.

Since his historic ascent in 1953, hundreds of people have "followed" him in achieving that feat. But that doesn't make Hillary a leader. He wasn't even the official leader on the expedition when he reached the summit. John Hunt was. And when Hillary traveled to the South Pole in 1958 as part of the Commonwealth Trans-Antarctic Expedition, he was accompanying another leader, Sir Vivian Fuchs. To be a leader, a person has to not only be out front, but also have people intentionally coming behind him, following his lead, and acting on his vision. Being a trendsetter is not the same as being a leader.

5. THE POSITION MYTH

As mentioned earlier, the greatest misunderstanding about leadership is that people think it is based on position, but it's not. Think about what happened several years ago at Cordiant, the advertising agency formerly known as Saatchi & Saatchi. In 1994, institutional investors of Saatchi & Saatchi forced the board of directors to dismiss Maurice Saatchi, the company's CEO. What was the result? Several executives followed him out. So did many of the company's largest accounts, including British Airways and Mars, the candy maker. Saatchi's

> *"It's not the position that makes the leader; it's the leader that makes the position."*
> —STANLEY HUFFTY

influence was so great that his departure caused the company's stock to fall immediately from $8⅝ to $4 per share.[2] What happened is a result of the Law of Influence. Saatchi lost his title and position, but he continued to be the leader. Stanley Huffty affirmed, "It's not the position that makes the leader; it's the leader that makes the position."

WHO'S THE REAL LEADER?

Many years ago, there was a game show on television called *To Tell the Truth.* Here's how it worked. At the opening of the show, three contestants claimed to be the same person. One of them was telling the truth; the other two were actors. A panel of celebrity judges took turns asking the three people questions, and when time was up, each panelist guessed which person was the real truth-teller. Many times, the actors bluffed well enough to fool the panelists and the members of the audience.

When it comes to identifying a real leader, that task can be much easier. Don't listen to the claims of the person professing to be the leader. Don't examine his credentials. Don't check his title. Check his influence. The proof of leadership is found in the followers.

I personally learned the Law of Influence when I accepted my first job out of college. I went in with all the right credentials. I had the proper college degree. I had a great deal of insight into the work because of the training given to me by my father. I possessed the position and title of leader in the organization. It made for a good-looking résumé—but it didn't make me the real leader. At my first

> *The proof of leadership is found in the followers.*

board meeting, I quickly found out who the real leader was—a farmer named Claude. When he spoke, people listened. When he made a suggestion, people respected it. When he led, others followed. If I wanted to make an impact, I would have to influence Claude. He, in turn, would influence everybody else. It was the Law of Influence at work.

LEADERSHIP IS . . .

The true measure of leadership is influence—nothing more, nothing less. Margaret Thatcher, the former British prime minister, observed, "Being in power is like being a lady. If you have to tell people you are, you aren't." If you watch the dynamics that occur between people in just about every aspect of life, you will see some people leading and others following, and you will notice that position and title often have little to do with who is really in charge.

That being the case, why do some people emerge as leaders while others can't influence people no matter how hard they try? I believe that several factors come into play:

CHARACTER—WHO THEY ARE
True leadership always begins with the inner person. That's why someone like Billy Graham is able to draw more and more followers to him as time goes by. People can sense the depth of his character.

RELATIONSHIPS—WHO THEY KNOW
You're a leader only if you have followers, and that always requires the development of relationships—the deeper the relationships, the stronger the potential for leadership. In my career, each time I entered a new leadership position, I immediately started building relationships. Build enough of the right kinds of relationships with the right people, and you can become the real leader in an organization.

KNOWLEDGE—WHAT THEY KNOW
Information is vital to a leader. You need a grasp of the facts, an understanding of dynamic factors and timing, and a vision for the future. Knowledge alone won't make someone a leader, but without knowledge, no one can become one. Whenever I was new to an organization, I always spent a lot of time doing homework before I tried to take the lead.

INTUITION—WHAT THEY FEEL
Leadership requires more than just a command of data. It demands an ability to deal with numerous intangibles. In fact, that is often one of the main differences between managers and leaders. Leaders seek to recognize and influence intangibles such as energy, morale, timing, and momentum.

EXPERIENCE—WHERE THEY'VE BEEN
The greater the challenges you've faced as a leader in the past, the more likely followers are to give you a chance in the present. Experience doesn't guarantee credibility, but it encourages people to give you a chance to prove that you are capable.

PAST SUCCESS—WHAT THEY'VE DONE

Nothing speaks to followers like a good track record. When I went to my first leadership position, I had no track record. I couldn't point to past successes to help people believe in me. But by the time I went to my second position, I had a positive track record. Every time I extended myself, took a risk, and succeeded, followers had another reason to trust my leadership ability—and to listen to what I had to say.

ABILITY—WHAT THEY CAN DO

The bottom line for followers is what a leader is capable of. They want to know whether that person can lead the team to victory. Ultimately, that's the reason people will listen to you and acknowledge you as their leader. As soon as they no longer believe you can deliver, they will stop listening and following.

LEADERSHIP WITHOUT LEVERAGE

I admire and respect the leadership of my good friend Bill Hybels, the founding pastor of Willow Creek Community Church in South Barrington, Illinois, one of the largest churches in North America. Bill says he believes that the church is the most leadership-intensive enterprise in society. A lot of businesspeople I know are surprised when they hear that statement, but I think Bill is right. What is the basis of his belief? Positional leadership often doesn't work in volunteer organizations. There is no leverage. In other organizations, the person who has position has incredible leverage. In the military, leaders can use rank and, if all else fails, throw people into the brig. In business, bosses have tremendous leverage in the form of salary, benefits, and perks. Most followers are pretty cooperative when their livelihood is at stake.

> *"The very essence of all power to influence lies in getting the other person to participate."*
> —HARRY A. OVERSTREET

But in voluntary organizations the thing that works is leadership in its purest form: influence. Psychologist Harry A. Overstreet observed, "The very essence of all power to influence lies in getting the other person to participate." Followers in voluntary organizations cannot be forced to get on board. If the leader has no influence with them, then they won't follow.

Recently at a meeting where I was speaking to a group of company presidents and CEOs, one participant asked for advice on finding the best leaders in his organization. My advice was to ask candidates to lead a volunteer organization for six months. If those leaders can get people to follow them when they have no leverage—recruiting employees to volunteer, serve the community, work with the United Way, and so on—then you know that they can influence others. That is the mark of true leadership ability.

FROM COMMANDER TO PRIVATE
TO COMMANDER IN CHIEF

One of my favorite stories that illustrates the Law of Influence concerns Abraham Lincoln. In 1832, decades before he became president, young Lincoln gathered together a group of men to fight in the Black Hawk War.

In those days, the person who put together a volunteer company for the militia often became its leader and assumed a commanding rank. In this instance, Lincoln was given the rank of captain. But Lincoln had a problem. He knew nothing about soldiering. He had no prior military experience, and he knew nothing about tactics. He had trouble remembering the simplest military procedures.

> *By the end of his military service, Abraham Lincoln found his rightful place, having achieved the rank of private.*

For example, one day Lincoln was marching a couple of dozen men across a field and needed to guide them through a gate into another field. But he couldn't manage it. Recounting the incident later, Lincoln said, "I could not for the life of me remember the proper word of command for getting my company endwise. Finally, as we came near [the gate] I shouted:

'This company is dismissed for two minutes, when it will fall in again on the other side of the gate.'"[3]

As time went by, Lincoln's level of influence with others in the militia actually *decreased.* While other officers proved themselves and gained rank, Lincoln found himself going in the other direction. He began as a captain, but *title and position* did him little good. He couldn't overcome the Law of Influence. By the end of his military service, Abraham Lincoln had found his rightful place, having achieved the rank of private.

Fortunately for Lincoln—and for the fate of the United States—he overcame his inability to influence others. Lincoln followed his time in the military with undistinguished stints in the Illinois state legislature and the U.S. House of Representatives. But over time and with much effort and personal experience, he became a person of remarkable influence and impact, and one of the nation's finest presidents.

I love the leadership proverb that says, "He who thinks he leads, but has no followers, is only taking a walk." If you can't influence people, then they will not follow you. And if people won't follow, you are not a leader. That's the Law of Influence. No matter what anybody else may tell you, remember that leadership is influence—nothing more, nothing less.

Applying
THE LAW OF THE INFLUENCE
To Your Life

1. Which of the myths in the chapter have you bought into in the past: management, entrepreneur, knowledge, pioneer, or position? Why have you been susceptible to that myth? What does that say about your perception of leadership up until now? What must you change in your current thinking to make you more open to improving your leadership in the future?

2. What do you usually rely upon most to persuade people to follow you? Rate yourself on a scale of 1 to 10 for each of the seven factors named in the chapter (a 1 means it's not a factor while a 10 means you rely on it continually):

- Character—who you are
- Relationships—who you know
- Knowledge—what you know
- Intuition—what you feel
- Experience—where you've been
- Past success—what you've done
- Ability—what you can do

How can you optimize or better utilize the ones with low scores?

3. Find an organization for which to volunteer. Pick something you believe in—for example, a school, soup kitchen, or community project—and offer your time and energy. If you believe you have leadership ability, then try leading. You will learn to lead through influence.

3

THE LAW OF PROCESS

Leadership Develops Daily, Not in a Day

A nne Scheiber was 101 years old when she died in January 1995. For
years she had lived in a tiny, run-down, rent-controlled studio apart-
ment in Manhattan. The paint on the walls was peeling, and the old book-
cases that lined the walls were covered in dust. Rent was four hundred
dollars a month.

Scheiber lived on Social Security and a small monthly pension, which
she started receiving in 1943 when she retired as an auditor for the Internal
Revenue Service. She hadn't done very well at the IRS. More accurately, the
agency hadn't done right by her. Despite having a law degree and doing
excellent work, she was never promoted. And when she retired at age fifty-
one, she was making only $3,150 a year.

"She was treated very, very shabbily," said Benjamin Clark, who knew
her as well as anyone did. "She really had to fend for herself in every way.
It was really quite a struggle."

Scheiber was the model of thrift. She didn't spend money on herself.
She didn't buy new furniture as the old pieces she owned became worn out.
She didn't even subscribe to a newspaper. About once a week, she used to
go to the public library to read the *Wall Street Journal.*

WINDFALL!

Imagine the surprise of Norman Lamm, the president of Yeshiva University in New York City, when he found out that Anne Scheiber, a little old lady whose name he had never heard—and who had never attended Yeshiva—left nearly her entire estate to the university.

"When I saw the will, it was mind blowing, such an unexpected windfall," said Lamm. "This woman has become a legend overnight."

The estate Anne Scheiber left to Yeshiva University was worth $22 million![1]

How in the world did a spinster who had been retired for fifty years build an eight-figure fortune? The answer is, she did it one day at a time.

By the time she retired from the IRS in 1943, Anne Scheiber had managed to save $5,000. She invested that money in stocks. By 1950, she had made enough profit to buy 1,000 shares of Schering-Plough Corporation stock, then valued at $10,000. And she held on to that stock, letting its value build. By the time she died, those original shares split enough times to produce 128,000 shares, worth $7.5 million.[2]

The secret to Scheiber's success was that she spent most of her life building her worth. Whether her stock's values went up or down, she didn't sell it off with the thought, *I'm finished building; now it's time to cash out.* She was in for the long haul, the *really* long haul. When she earned dividends—which kept getting larger and larger—she reinvested them in additional stocks. She spent her whole lifetime building. While other older people worry that they may run out of funds before the end of their lives, the longer she lived, the wealthier she became. When it came to finances, Scheiber understood and applied the Law of Process.

LEADERSHIP IS LIKE INVESTING—IT COMPOUNDS

Becoming a leader is a lot like investing successfully in the stock market. If your hope is to make a fortune in a day, you're not going to be successful. There are no successful "day traders" in leadership development. What matters most is what you do day by day over the long haul. My friend Tag Short maintains, "The secret of our success is found in our daily agenda." If you continually invest in your leadership development, letting your "assets" compound, the inevitable result is growth over time. What can you see when you look at a person's daily agenda? Priorities, passion, abilities, relationships, attitude, personal disciplines, vision, and influence. See what a person is doing every day, day after day, and you'll know who that person is and what he or she is becoming.

When I teach leadership at conferences, people inevitably ask me if leaders are born. I always answer, "Yes, of course they are . . . I've yet to meet an unborn leader! How else would you expect them to come into the world?" We all laugh, and then I answer the real question—whether leadership is something a person either is born with and possesses or is not born with and doesn't.

Although it's true that some people are born with greater natural gifts than others, the ability to lead is really a collection of skills, nearly all of which can be learned and improved. But that

> *Becoming a leader is a lot like investing successfully in the stock market. If your hope is to make a fortune in a day, you're not going to be successful.*

process doesn't happen overnight. Leadership is complicated. It has many facets: respect, experience, emotional strength, people skills, discipline, vision, momentum, timing—the list goes on. As you can see, many factors that come into play in leadership are intangible. That's why leaders require so much seasoning to be effective. That's why I felt that only after reaching age fifty was I truly beginning to understand the many aspects of leadership with clarity.

LEADERS ARE LEARNERS

In a study of ninety top leaders from a variety of fields, leadership experts Warren Bennis and Burt Nanus made a discovery about the relationship between growth and leadership: "It is the capacity to develop and improve their skills that distinguishes leaders from their followers." Successful leaders are learners. And the learning process is ongoing, a result of self-discipline and perseverance. The goal each day must be to get a little better, to build on the previous day's progress.

> *"It is the capacity to develop and improve their skills that distinguishes leaders from their followers."*
> —BENNIS AND NANUS

The problem is that most people overestimate the importance of events and underestimate the power of processes. We want quick fixes. We want the compounding effect that Anne Scheiber received over fifty years, but we want it in fifty minutes.

Don't get me wrong. I appreciate events. They can be effective catalysts. But if you want lasting improvement, if you want power, then rely on a process. Consider the difference between the two:

AN EVENT	A PROCESS
Encourages decisions	Encourages development
Motivates people	Matures people
Is a calendar issue	Is a culture issue
Challenges people	Changes people
Is easy	Is difficult

If I need to be inspired to take steps forward, then I'll attend an event. If I want to improve, then I'll engage in a process and stick with it.

THE PHASES OF LEADERSHIP GROWTH

What does the leadership growth process look like? Every person's is different. However, whether or not you possess great natural ability for leadership, your development and progress will probably occur according to the following five phases:

PHASE 1: I DON'T KNOW WHAT I DON'T KNOW

Many people fail to recognize the value of leadership. Some don't recognize its importance. Others believe that leadership is only for a few—for the people at the top of the corporate ladder. They have no idea of the opportunities they're passing up when they don't learn to lead. This point was driven home for me when a college president shared with me that only a handful of students signed up for a leadership course offered by the

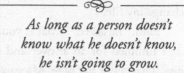

As long as a person doesn't know what he doesn't know, he isn't going to grow.

school. Why? Only a few thought of themselves as leaders. If they had understood that leadership is influence, and that in the course of each day most individuals usually try to influence at least four other people, their desire might have been sparked to learn more about the subject. It's unfortunate because as long as a person doesn't know what he doesn't know, he isn't going to grow.

PHASE 2: I KNOW THAT I NEED TO KNOW

At some point in life, many people find themselves placed in a leadership position only to look around and discover that no one is following them. When that happens, we realize that we need to *learn* how to lead. And of course, that's when it's possible for the process to start. Benjamin Disraeli, former British prime minister, wisely commented, "To be conscious that you are ignorant of the facts is a great step to knowledge."

That's what happened to me when I took my first leadership position in 1969. I had captained sports teams all my life and had been the student government president in college, so I already thought I was a leader. But when I tried to lead people in the real world, I found out the awful truth. Being put in charge is not the same as being a leader.

PHASE 3: I KNOW WHAT I DON'T KNOW

I struggled for a while in that first leadership position. To be honest, I relied on my extremely high energy and whatever charisma I possessed. But there came a moment when I realized that leadership was going to be the key to my professional career. If I didn't get better at leadership, my career would eventually bog down, and I would never reach the goals I had set for myself. Fortunately at that time, I had breakfast with Kurt Kampmeir of Success Motivation, Inc. At that breakfast, he asked a question that would change my life.

"John," he asked, "what is your plan for personal growth?"

I fumbled for an answer and then finally admitted that I didn't have one. That night my wife, Margaret, and I decided to make financial sacrifices so that I could get on the program Kurt offered. That was an intentional step toward growth. From that day to now, I have made it a practice to read books, listen to tapes, and go to conferences on leadership.

Around the time I met with Kurt, I also had another idea: I wrote to the top ten leaders in my field and offered them one hundred dollars for a half hour of their time so that I could ask them questions. (That was quite a sum for me back then.) For the next several years, Margaret and I planned every vacation around where those people lived. If a great leader in Cleveland said yes to my request, then that year we vacationed in Cleveland so that I could meet him. I can't explain how valuable those experiences were for me. Those leaders shared insights with me that I could have learned no other way.

PHASE 4: I KNOW AND GROW, AND IT STARTS TO SHOW
When you recognize your lack of skill and begin the daily discipline of personal growth, exciting things start to happen.

Several years ago I was teaching leadership to a group of people in Denver, and in the crowd I noticed a really sharp nineteen-year-old named Brian. For a couple of days, I watched as he eagerly took notes. I observed him interacting with others. And I talked to him a few times during breaks. When I got to the part of the seminar where I teach the Law of Process, I asked Brian to stand up so that I could talk to him, and I wanted everyone else in the audience to listen in.

"Brian, I've been watching you here," I said, "and I'm very impressed with how hungry you are to learn and glean and grow. I want to tell you a secret that will change your life." Everyone in the whole auditorium seemed to lean forward.

"I believe that in about twenty years, you can be a *great* leader. I want to encourage you to make yourself a lifelong learner of leadership. Read books, listen to tapes regularly, and keep attending seminars. And whenever you come across a golden nugget of truth or a significant quote, file it away for the future.

"It's not going to be easy," I said. "But in five years, you'll see progress as your influence becomes greater. In ten years, you'll develop a competence that makes your leadership highly effective. And in twenty years, when you're only thirty-nine years old, if you've continued to learn and grow, others will likely start asking you to teach them about leadership. And some will be amazed. They'll look at each other and say, 'How did he suddenly become so wise?'

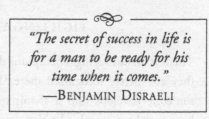

"The secret of success in life is for a man to be ready for his time when it comes."
—BENJAMIN DISRAELI

"Brian," I concluded, "you can be a great leader, but it won't happen in a day. Start paying the price now." What's true for Brian is also true for you. Start developing your leadership today, and someday you will experience the effects of the Law of Process.

PHASE 5: I SIMPLY GO BECAUSE OF WHAT I KNOW

When you're in phase four, you can be pretty effective as a leader, but you have to think about every move you make. However, when you reach phase five, your ability to lead becomes almost automatic. You develop great instincts. And that's when the payoff is incredible. But the only way to get there is to obey the Law of Process and pay the price.

TO LEAD TOMORROW, LEARN TODAY

Leadership is developed daily, not in a day. That is the reality dictated by the Law of Process. Benjamin Disraeli asserted, "The secret of success in life is for a man to be ready for his time when it comes." What a person does on a disciplined, consistent basis gets him ready, no matter what the goal.

You can see the effect of the Law of Process in any walk of life. NBA Hall of Fame player Larry Bird became an outstanding free-throw shooter by practicing five hundred shots each morning before he went to school. Demosthenes of ancient Greece became the greatest orator by reciting verses with pebbles in his mouth and speaking over the roar of the ocean's waves—and he did it despite having been born with a speech impediment. You need to have the same dedication. To become an excellent leader, you need to work on it every day.

FIGHTING YOUR WAY UP

There is an old saying: champions don't become champions in the ring—they are merely recognized there. That's true. If you want to see where someone develops into a champion, look at his daily routine. Former heavyweight champ Joe Frazier stated, "You can map out a fight plan or a life plan. But when the action starts,

> *Champions don't become champions in the ring—they are merely recognized there.*

you're down to your reflexes. That's where your road work shows. If you cheated on that in the dark of the morning, you're getting found out now under the bright lights."[3] Boxing is a good analogy for leadership development because it is all about daily preparation. Even a person with natural talent has to prepare and train to become successful.

One of this country's greatest leaders was a fan of boxing: President Theodore Roosevelt. In fact, one of his most famous quotes uses a boxing analogy:

> It is not the critic who counts, not the man who points out how the strong man stumbled, or where the doer of deeds could have done them better. The credit belongs to the man who is actually in the arena; whose face is

marred by dust and sweat and blood; who strives valiantly; who errs and comes short again and again; who knows the great enthusiasms, the great devotions, and spends himself in a worthy cause; who, at best, knows in the end the triumph of high achievement; and who, at the worst, if he fails, at least fails while daring greatly, so that his place shall never be with those cold and timid souls who know neither victory nor defeat.

Roosevelt, a boxer himself, was the ultimate man of action. Not only was he an effective leader, but he was one of the most flamboyant of all U.S. presidents. British historian Hugh Brogan described him as "the ablest man to sit in the White House since Lincoln; the most vigorous since Jackson; the most bookish since John Quincy Adams."

A MAN OF ACTION

TR (Roosevelt's nickname) is remembered as an outspoken man of action and proponent of the vigorous life. While in the White House, he was known for regular boxing and judo sessions, challenging horseback rides, and long, strenuous hikes. A French ambassador who visited Roosevelt used to tell about the time that he accompanied the president on a walk through the woods. When the two men came to the banks of a stream that was too deep to cross by foot, TR stripped off his clothes and expected the dignitary to do the same so that they could swim to the other side. Nothing was an obstacle to Roosevelt.

At different times in his life, Roosevelt was a cowboy in the Wild West, an explorer and big-game hunter, and a rough-riding cavalry officer in the Spanish-American War. His enthusiasm and stamina seemed boundless. As the vice presidential candidate in 1900, he gave 673 speeches and traveled 20,000 miles while campaigning for President McKinley. And years after his presidency, while preparing to deliver a speech in Milwaukee, Roosevelt was shot by a would-be assassin. With a broken rib and a bullet in his chest, Roosevelt insisted on delivering his one-hour speech before allowing himself to be taken to the hospital.

ROOSEVELT STARTED SLOW

Of all the leaders this nation has ever had, Roosevelt was one of the toughest—both physically and mentally. But he didn't start that way. America's cowboy president was born in Manhattan to a prominent wealthy family. As a child, he was puny and very sickly. He had debilitating asthma, possessed very poor eyesight, and was painfully thin. His parents weren't sure he would survive.

When he was twelve, young Roosevelt's father told him, "You have the mind, but you have not the body, and without the help of the body the mind cannot go as far as it should. You must *make* the body." Make it he did. He lived by the Law of Process.

TR began spending time *every day* building his body as well as his mind, and he did that for the rest of his life. He worked out with weights, hiked, ice-skated, hunted, rowed, rode horseback, and boxed. In later years, Roosevelt assessed his progress, admitting that as a child he was "nervous and timid. Yet," he said, "from reading of the people I admired . . . and from knowing my father, I had a great admiration for men who were fearless and who could hold their own in the world, and I had a great desire to be like them."[4] By the time TR graduated from Harvard, he *was* like them, and he was ready to tackle the world of politics.

NO OVERNIGHT SUCCESS

Roosevelt didn't become a great leader overnight, either. His road to the presidency was one of slow, continual growth. As he served in various positions, ranging from New York City police commissioner to president of the United States, he kept learning and growing. He improved himself, and in time he became a strong leader. That was further evidence that he lived by the Law of Process.

Roosevelt's list of accomplishments is remarkable. Under his leadership, the United States emerged as a world power. He helped the country develop a first-class navy. He saw that the Panama Canal was built. He negotiated peace between Russia and Japan, winning a Nobel Peace Prize in the process. And when people questioned TR's leadership—since he had first become president when McKinley was assassinated—he campaigned and was reelected by the largest majority of any president up to his time.

Ever the man of action, when Roosevelt completed his second term as president in 1909, he immediately traveled to Africa where he led a scientific expedition sponsored by the Smithsonian Institution. A few years later, in 1913, he co-led a group to explore the uncharted River of Doubt in Brazil. It was a learning adventure he said he could not pass up. "It was my last chance to be a boy," he later admitted. He was fifty-five years old.

On January 6, 1919, at his home in New York, Theodore Roosevelt died in his sleep. Then Vice President Marshall said, "Death had to take him sleeping, for if Roosevelt had been awake, there would have been a fight." When they removed him from his bed, they found a book under his pillow. Up to the very last, TR was still striving to learn and improve himself. He was still practicing the Law of Process.

If you want to be a leader, the good news is that you can do it. Everyone has the potential, but it isn't accomplished overnight. It requires perseverance. And you absolutely cannot ignore the Law of Process. Leadership doesn't develop in a day. It takes a lifetime.

Applying
THE LAW OF PROCESS
To Your Life

1. What is your personal plan for growth? If you are like I was when Kurt Kampmeir asked me this question, you have a vague intention to grow, not a specific plan. Write out a plan. I recommend that you read one book a month, listen to at least one CD, tape, or streaming message a week, and attend one conference a year. Select the materials in advance, set aside time for growth on your calendar, and start immediately. If developing a plan from scratch seems difficult, you may want to read my book *Today Matters*. It contains the personal growth plan I have used for years.

2. One thing that separates great leaders from good leaders is the way they invest in those who follow them. Just as you need a growth plan to improve, so do those who work for you. You can take groups of employees through books, bring in trainers, mentor people one-on-one—anything that works. Make providing opportunities for growth your responsibility.

3. If you are the leader of a business, an organization, or a department, you can create a culture of growth. When people in your sphere of influence know that personal growth and leadership development are valued, resourced, and rewarded, then growth will explode. And the environment you created will begin attracting high achievers and people with great potential.

4

THE LAW OF NAVIGATION

Anyone Can Steer the Ship, but It
Takes a Leader to Chart the Course

In 1911, two groups of explorers set off on an incredible mission. Though they used different strategies and routes, the leaders of the teams had the same goal: to be the first in history to reach the South Pole. Their stories are life-and-death illustrations of the Law of Navigation.

One group was led by Norwegian explorer Roald Amundsen. Ironically, Amundsen had not originally intended to go to Antarctica. His desire was to be the first man to reach the *North* Pole. But when he discovered that Robert Peary had beaten him there, Amundsen changed his goal and headed toward the other end of the earth. North or south—he knew his planning would pay off.

AMUNDSEN CAREFULLY CHARTED HIS COURSE

Before his team ever set off, Amundsen had painstakingly planned his trip. He studied the methods of the Eskimos and other experienced Arctic travelers and determined that their best course of action would be to transport all their equipment and supplies by dogsled. When he assembled his team, he chose expert skiers and dog handlers. His strategy was simple. The dogs would do most of the work as the group traveled fifteen to twenty miles in a six-hour period each day. That would afford both the dogs and the men plenty of time for daily rest prior to the following day's travel.

Amundsen's forethought and attention to detail were incredible. He located and stocked supply depots all along the intended route. That way they would not have to carry every bit of their supplies with them the whole trip. He also equipped his people with the best gear possible. Amundsen had carefully considered every possible aspect of the journey, thought it through, and planned accordingly. And it paid off. The worst problem they experienced on their trip was an infected tooth that one man had to have extracted.

SCOTT VIOLATED THE LAW OF NAVIGATION

The other team of people was led by Robert Falcon Scott, a British naval officer who had previously done some exploring in the Antarctic area. Scott's expedition was the antithesis of Amundsen's. Instead of using dogsleds, Scott decided to use motorized sledges and ponies. Their problems began when the motors on the sledges stopped working only five days into the trip. The ponies didn't fare well either in those frigid temperatures. When they reached the foot of the Transantarctic Mountains, all of the poor animals had to be killed. As a result, the team members themselves ended up hauling the two-hundred-pound sledges. It was arduous work.

Scott hadn't given enough attention to the team's other equipment either. Their clothes were so poorly designed that all of the men developed frostbite. One team member required an hour every morning just to get his boots onto his swollen, gangrenous feet. Everyone became snowblind because of the inadequate goggles Scott had supplied. On top of everything else, the team was always low on food and water. That was also due to Scott's poor planning. The depots of supplies Scott established were inadequately stocked, too far apart, and often poorly marked, which made them very difficult to find. Because they were continually low on fuel to melt snow, everyone became dehydrated. Making things even worse was Scott's last-minute decision to take along a fifth man, even though they had prepared enough supplies for only four.

After covering a grueling eight hundred miles in ten weeks, Scott's exhausted group finally arrived at the South Pole on January 17, 1912. There they found the Norwegian flag flapping in the wind and a letter from Amundsen. The other well-led team had beaten them to their goal by more than a month!

IF YOU DON'T LIVE BY THE LAW OF NAVIGATION . . .

Scott's expedition to the Pole is a classic example of a leader who could not navigate for his people. But the trek back was even worse. Scott and his men were starving and suffering from scurvy, yet Scott, unable to navigate to the very end, was oblivious to their plight. With time running out and the food supply desperately low, Scott insisted that they collect thirty pounds of geological specimens to take back—more weight to be carried by the worn-out men.

The group's progress became slower and slower. One member of the party sank into a stupor and died. Another, Lawrence Oates, a former army officer who had originally been brought along to take care of the ponies, had frostbite so severe that he had trouble doing anything. Because he believed he was endangering the team's survival, he purposely walked out into a blizzard to keep from hindering the group. Before he left the tent and headed into the storm, he said, "I am just going outside; I may be some time."

Scott and his final two team members made it only a little farther north before giving up. The return trip had already taken two months, and still they were 150 miles from their base camp. There they died. We know their story only because they spent their last hours updating their diaries. Some of Scott's last words were these: "We shall die like gentlemen. I think this will show that the Spirit of pluck and

> *Because Robert Falcon Scott was unable to live by the Law of Navigation, he and his companions died by it.*

power to endure has not passed out of our race."[1] Scott had courage but not leadership. Because he was unable to live by the Law of Navigation, he and his companions died by it.

Followers need leaders able to effectively navigate for them. When they're facing life-and-death situations, the necessity is painfully obvious. But even when consequences aren't as serious, the need is also great. The truth is that nearly anyone can steer the ship, but it takes a leader to chart the course. That is the Law of Navigation.

NAVIGATORS SEE THE TRIP AHEAD

Former General Electric chairman Jack Welch asserts, "A good leader remains focused . . . Controlling your direction is better than being controlled by it." Welch is right, but leaders who navigate do even more than control the direction in which they and their people travel. They see the whole trip in their minds before they leave the dock. They have vision for getting to their destination, they understand what it will take to get there, they know who they'll need on the team to be successful, and they rec-

> "A leader is one who sees more than others see, who sees farther than others see, and who sees before others do."
> —LEROY EIMS

ognize the obstacles long before they appear on the horizon. Leroy Eims, author of *Be the Leader You Were Meant to Be*, writes, "A leader is one who sees more than others see, who sees farther than others see, and who sees before others do."

The larger the organization, the more clearly the leader has to be able to see ahead. That's true because sheer size makes midcourse corrections more difficult. And if there are errors in navigation, many more people are affected than when a leader is traveling alone or with only a few people. The disaster shown in James Cameron's 1997 film *Titanic* was a good example of that kind of problem. The crew could not see far enough ahead to avoid the iceberg altogether, and they could not maneuver enough to change course once the object was in view because of the size of the ship. The result was that more than one thousand people lost their lives.

WHERE THE LEADER GOES . . .

First-rate navigators always have in mind that other people are depending on them and their ability to chart a good course. I read an observation by James A. Autry in *Life and Work: A Manager's Search for Meaning* that illustrates this idea. He writes that occasionally you hear about the crash of four military planes flying together in a formation. The reason for the loss of all four is this: When jet fighters fly in groups of four, one pilot—the leader—designates where the team will fly. The other three planes fly on the leader's wing, watching him and following him wherever he goes. Whatever moves he makes, the rest of his team will make along with him. That's true whether he soars in the clouds or smashes into a mountaintop.

Before good leaders take their people on a journey, they go through a process in order to give the trip the best chance of being a success:

Navigators Draw on Past Experience

Every past success and failure you've experienced can be a valuable source of information and wisdom—if you allow it to be. Successes teach you what you're capable of doing and give you confidence. However, your failures often teach greater lessons. They reveal wrong assumptions, character flaws, errors in judgment, and poor working methods. Ironically, many people hate their failures so much that they quickly cover them up instead of analyzing them and learning from them. As I explain in my book *Failing Forward*, if you fail to learn from your mistakes, you're going to fail again and again.

Why do I even mention something that seems so basic? Because most natural leaders are activists. They tend to look forward—not backward—make decisions, and move on. I know this because that is my tendency. But for leaders to become good navigators, they need to take time to reflect and learn from their experiences. That's why I have developed the discipline of reflective thinking. I write about it in detail in my book *Thinking for a Change*, but allow me to give you some advantages of reflective thinking here. Reflective thinking

- gives you true perspective,
- gives emotional integrity to your thought life,
- increases your confidence in decision making,
- clarifies the big picture, and
- takes a good experience and makes it a valuable experience.[2]

Each benefit gives a leader a great advantage when planning next steps for a team or organization.

NAVIGATORS EXAMINE THE CONDITIONS BEFORE MAKING COMMITMENTS

Drawing on experience means looking inward. Examining conditions means looking outward. No good leader plans a course of action without paying close attention to current conditions. That would be like setting sail against the tide or plotting a course into a hurricane. Good navigators count the cost *before* making commitments for themselves and others. They examine not only measurable factors such as finances, resources, and talent, but also intangibles such as timing, morale, momentum, culture, and so on. (I'll discuss this more in the Laws of Intuition and Timing.)

> No matter how much you learn from the past, it will never tell you all you need to know for the present.

NAVIGATORS LISTEN TO WHAT OTHERS HAVE TO SAY

No matter how much you learn from the past, it will never tell you all that you need to know for the present. No matter how good a leader you are, you yourself will not have all the answers. That's why top-notch navigators gather information from many sources. For example, before Roald Amundsen's expedition to the South Pole, he had learned from a group of Native Americans in Canada about warm clothing and Arctic survival techniques. Those skills and practices meant the difference between failure and success for his team in Antarctica.

Navigating leaders get ideas from many sources. They listen to members of their leadership team. They talk to the people in their organization to find out what's happening on the grassroots level. And they spend time with leaders from outside the organization who can mentor them. They always think in terms of relying on a team, not just themselves.

NAVIGATORS MAKE SURE THEIR CONCLUSIONS REPRESENT BOTH FAITH AND FACT

Being able to navigate for others requires a leader to possess a positive attitude. You've got to have faith that you can take your people all the way. If you can't confidently make the trip in your mind, you're not going to be able to take it in real life.

On the other hand, you also have to be able to see the facts realistically. You can't minimize obstacles or rationalize your challenges and still lead effectively. If you don't go in with your eyes wide open, you're going to get blindsided. As Bill Easum, president of Easum, Bandy, and Associates, observes, "Realistic leaders are objective enough to minimize illusions. They understand that self-deception can cost them their vision."

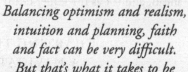

Balancing optimism and realism, intuition and planning, faith and fact can be very difficult. But that's what it takes to be effective as a navigating leader.

Jim Collins confirmed this balance between faith and fact in his 2001 book *Good to Great*. He calls it the Stockdale Paradox. He writes, "You must retain faith that you will prevail in the end *and* you must also confront the most brutal facts of your current reality."[3] Balancing optimism and realism, intuition and planning, faith and fact can be very difficult. But that's what it takes to be effective as a navigating leader.

A LESSON IN NAVIGATION

I remember the first time I really understood the importance of the Law of Navigation. I was twenty-eight years old, and I was leading the second church in my pastoral career. Before my arrival there in 1972, the church had experienced a decade-long plateau in its growth. But by 1975, our attendance had gone from four hundred to more than a thousand. I knew we could keep growing and helping more people, but only if we built a new auditorium.

The good news was that I already had some experience leading a construction project because I had taken my first church through the process. The bad news was that the first one was really

> If the leader can't navigate the people through rough waters, he is liable to sink the ship.

small in comparison to the second one. This was going to be a multimillion-dollar project more than twenty times larger than my first one. But even that was not the greatest obstacle.

Right before I came on board as leader of the church, there had been a huge battle over another building proposal, and the debate had been vocal, divisive, and bitter. For that reason, I knew that I would experience genuine opposition to my leadership for the first time. There were rough waters ahead, and if I as the leader didn't navigate us well, I could sink the ship.

CHARTING THE COURSE WITH
A NAVIGATION STRATEGY

I should probably confess at this point that I am not a strong navigator. I don't take joy in getting into details, and I tend to go with my gut instinct—sometimes a little too quickly for my own good. In the last fifteen to twenty years, I've often staffed my weaknesses and hired good navigating leaders to help my organizations. For example, for many years when I was a church leader, Dan Reiland was on my staff as executive pastor. He is an excellent navigator. Currently at EQUIP, the nonprofit organization I founded in 1996, John Hull works as its president, and he is a fantastic navigating leader. However, back in 1975, I had to take responsibility for the navigation process myself. To help me do that, I developed a strategy that I have used repeatedly in my leadership. I wrote it as an acrostic so that I would always be able to remember it:

Predetermine a course of action.
Lay out your goals.
Adjust your priorities.
Notify key personnel.
Allow time for acceptance.
Head into action.
Expect problems.
Always point to the successes.
Daily review your plan.

That became my blueprint as I prepared to navigate this change for my organization.

I had a strong sense of what our course of action needed to be. If we were going to keep growing, we needed to build a new auditorium. I had looked at every possible alternative, and I knew that was the only viable solution. My goal was to design and build the facility, pay for it in ten years, and unify all the people in the process—no small feat.

Any plan I introduced would have to be voted on in a congregational meeting, so I scheduled one a couple of months ahead to give me time to get everything ready. The next thing I did was direct our board members and a group of key financial leaders to conduct a twenty-year analysis of our growth and financial patterns. It covered the previous ten years and projections for the next ten years. Based on that, we determined the requirements of the facility.

We then formulated a ten-year budget that carefully explained how we would handle financing. I also asked that all of the information we were gathering be put into a twenty-page report to be given to the members of the congregation. I knew that major barriers to successful planning are fear of change, ignorance, uncertainty about the future, and lack of imagination. I was going to do everything I could to prevent those factors from hindering us.

My next step was to notify the key leaders. I started with the ones who had the most influence, meeting with them individually and sometimes in small groups. Over the course of several weeks, I met with about a hundred leaders. I cast the vision for what we needed to do and fielded their questions. And any time I could sense that a person was hesitant about the project, I planned to meet individu-

> *Major barriers to successful planning are fear of change, ignorance, uncertainty about the future, and lack of imagination.*

ally with him again. Then I allowed time for those key leaders to influence the rest of the people and help them accept the coming changes.

When the time arrived for the congregational meeting, we were ready to head into action. I took two hours to present the project to the people. I handed out my twenty-page report with the floor plans, financial analysis, and budgets. I tried to answer every question the people would have before they even had a chance to ask it. I also asked some of the most influential people in the congregation to speak.

I had expected opposition, but when I opened the floor for questions, I was shocked. There were only two questions: one person wanted to know about the placement of the building's water fountains, and the other asked about the number of restrooms. That was when I knew we had navigated the tricky waters successfully. When it was time for the motion asking everyone to vote, the church's most influential layperson made it. And I had already asked a leader who had previously opposed the building project to be the one to second the motion. When the final count was tallied, 98 percent of the people had voted in favor.

Once we navigated through this tricky part of the process, the rest of the project was pretty straightforward. I continually kept the vision in front of the people by giving them good news reports. I made sure we celebrated successes. And I periodically reviewed our plans and their results to make sure we were on track. The course had been charted. All we had to do was steer the ship.

That was a wonderful learning experience for me. Above everything else, I found out that the secret to the Law of Navigation is preparation. When you prepare well, you convey confidence and trust to people. Lack of prepara- tion has the opposite effect. In the end, it's not the size of the project that determines its acceptance, sup- port, and success—it's the size of the leader. That's why I say that anyone

In the end, it's not the size of the project that determines its acceptance, support, and success. It's the size of the leader.

can *steer* the ship, but it takes a leader to chart the course. Leaders who are good navigators are capable of taking their people just about anywhere.

Applying
THE LAW OF NAVIGATION
To Your Life

1. Do you make it a regular practice to reflect on your positive and negative experiences? If not, you will miss the potential lessons they have to offer. Do one of two things: Set aside a time to reflect every week, examining your calendar or journal to jog your memory. Or build reflection time into your schedule immediately after every major success or failure. In either case, write down what you learn during that discovery process.

2. Navigating leaders do their homework. For some project or major task that you are currently responsible for, draw on your past experience, hold intentional conversations with experts and team members to gather information, and examine current conditions that could impact the success of your endeavor. Only after taking these steps should you create your action plan.

3. Which way do you naturally lean—toward facts or faith? Rarely is a leader especially talented in both areas. (I'm a faith person. I am highly visionary and believe that anything is possible. I often rely on my brother, Larry, to help me with realistic thinking.) Yet good navigators must be able to do both.

To successfully practice the Law of Navigation, you must know your own bent. If you're not sure, ask trusted friends and colleagues. Then make sure you have someone with the opposite bent on your team so that you can work together.

5

THE LAW OF ADDITION

Leaders Add Value by Serving Others

In a world where many political leaders enjoy their power and prestige and where CEOs of large corporations make astronomical incomes, work and live in luxury, and appear to be most concerned with what's in it for them, Jim Sinegal is an oddity.

Sinegal is the cofounder and CEO of Costco, the fourth largest retailer in the United States and the ninth largest in the world. He doesn't seem much interested in perks. He works in an unremarkable office comprised primarily of folding tables and chairs. If he invites someone to meet him at the corporate offices, he goes down to the lobby to meet his guest. He answers his own phone. And he takes a salary of only $350,000 a year, which puts him in the bottom 10 percent of CEOs of large corporations.

Sinegal's path to corporate leadership wasn't typical either. He didn't attend an Ivy League school. He isn't a lawyer or a CPA. As a teenager, he thought of becoming a doctor, but his high school grades were less than stellar. So he went off to community college and earned an associate's degree. While he was attending San Diego State College (now University), he helped a friend unload mattresses at a new local retail store called Fed-Mart. That one day of work turned into a regular job. When he received a promotion, he discontinued his studies. He had found his career. In time, he had also found a mentor, Sol Price, Fed-Mart's chairman. Under Price's guidance, Sinegal rose to the post of executive vice president for merchandising. Sinegal later helped Price found Price Club and then went on to cofound Costco in 1983 with Jeffrey H. Brotman. The company's growth was rapid. Costco purchased and merged with Price Club ten years later.

ADDING PROFITS BY ADDING VALUE

Retail experts give a lot of attention to Sinegal's formula for success: offer a limited number of items, rely on high volume sales, keep costs as low as possible, and don't spend money on advertising. But there is something that separates him from the competitors who employ similar strategies: the way he treats his employees. He believes in paying his employees well and offering them good benefit packages. Costco employees are paid an average of 42 percent more than the company's chief rival. And Costco employees pay a fraction of the national average for health care. Sinegal believes that if you pay people well, "You get good people and good productivity."[1] You also get employee loyalty. Costco has by far the lowest employee turnover rate in all of retailing.

But Sinegal's leadership style of adding value doesn't end with employee compensation. He goes out of his way to show Costco workers that he cares about them. He maintains an open-door policy with everyone. He wears an employee name tag, is on a first-name basis with everyone, and makes sure to visit every single Costco store at least once a year.

"No manager and no staff in any business feels very good if the boss is not interested enough to come and see them," says Sinegal. And when he shows up, his people are always glad to see him. "The employees know that I want to say hello to them, because I like them."[2]

Sinegal once flew from Texas to the San Francisco area when he heard that a Costco executive was hospitalized for emergency surgery. It came as no surprise to the executive. It was consistent with the way Sinegal always leads.

The Law of Addition

LEADERSHIP LESSONS LEARNED EARLY

Sol Price, Sinegal's one-time mentor, says, "Jim has done a very good job in balancing the interests of the shareholders, the employees, the customers, and the managers. Most companies tilt too much one way or another." Many of the lessons Sinegal learned came from Price, who believed in treating people well and giving them credit. In a meeting at Fed-Mart, Sinegal noted that a manager was quick to take the credit and to place blame on others. But Price saw through him.

"To teach us all a lesson," recalls Sinegal, "Sol used a weekly meeting to purposely raise hell about something that was wrong in one of the stores. I wondered why he did it. But when he saw that this manager let two of his employees take the blame, he fired him within a week.

"It's improper for one person to take credit when it takes so many people to build a successful organization," asserts Sinegal. "When you try to be top dog, you don't create loyalty. If you can't give credit (and take blame), you will drown in your inability to inspire."[3]

The only real criticism of Sinegal comes from Wall Street. Analysts there believe that Sinegal is too kind and generous to his people. They would like to see him pay employees less and squeeze them more. But Sinegal wouldn't think of it. He believes that if you treat the employees and customers right, profits will follow. "On Wall Street," he observes, "they're in the business of making money between now and next Thursday. I

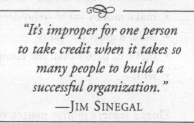

"It's improper for one person to take credit when it takes so many people to build a successful organization."
—JIM SINEGAL

don't say that with any bitterness, but we can't take that view. We want to build a company that will still be here fifty and sixty years from now."[4]

Others outside the organization appreciate his approach to business. Nell Minow, an expert on corporate governance, remarked, "I would love to clone him. Of the 2,000 companies in our database, he has the single shortest CEO employment contract." It's less than a page long. "And [it's] the only one which specifically says he can be—believe it or not—'terminated for cause.'"[5]

When it comes down to it, Sinegal is more focused on adding value to people by serving them than on serving himself or making himself richer with an exorbitant salary. He lives by the Law of Addition. "I just think that if you're going to try to run an organization that's very cost-conscious, then you can't have those disparities. Having an individual who is making 100 or 200 or 300 times more than the average person working on the floor is wrong."[6]

Sinegal sums it up this way: "This is not altruistic. This is good business." He could also say it's good leadership!

DO MOTIVES MATTER?

Why should leaders lead? And when they do, what is their first responsibility? If you were to ask a lot of leaders, you might hear a variety of responses. You might hear that a leader's job is to:

- be in charge,
- make the organization run smoothly,
- make money for shareholders,
- build a great company,
- make us better than the competition, and
- win.

Does a leader's motive matter, or is it simply getting the job done that's important? What's the bottom line?

I didn't give it much thought until the last ten years. I vividly remember teaching leadership to a group of government officials in a developing nation a few years ago and teaching that leaders add value by serving others. I could see that many of the audience members looked very uncomfortable as I talked about it. When I finished speaking and mentioned what I observed to one of my hosts, he said, "Yes, I'm sure they did look uncomfortable. What you have to realize is that probably more than half of those people killed someone to obtain their current position of power." I've seen and heard a lot of things around the world, but I must admit I was shocked. In that moment, I realized that I could not take for granted why leaders lead and how they go about doing it.

DO THE MATH

Many people view leadership the same way they view success, hoping to go as far as they can, to climb the ladder, to achieve the highest position possible for their talent. But contrary to conventional thinking, I believe the bottom line in leadership isn't how far we advance ourselves but how far we advance others. That is achieved by serving others and adding value to their lives.

> *The bottom line in leadership isn't how far we advance ourselves but how far we advance others.*

The interaction between every leader and follower is a relationship, and all relationships either add to or subtract from a person's life. If you are a leader, then trust me, you are having either a positive or a negative impact on the people you lead. How can you tell? There is one critical question: *Are you making things better for the people who follow you?* That's it. If you cannot answer with an unhesitant yes, and give some evidence that backs it up, then you may very well be a subtractor. Often subtractors don't realize they are subtracting from others. I would say that 90 percent of all people who subtract from others do so unintentionally. They don't recognize their negative impact on others. And when a leader is a subtractor and doesn't change his ways, it's only a matter of time before his impact on others goes from subtraction to division.

In contrast, 90 percent of all people who add value to others do so intentionally. Why do I say that? Because human beings are naturally selfish. I'm selfish. Being an adder requires me to get out of my comfort zone every day and think about adding value to others. But that's what it takes to be a leader whom others want to follow. Do that long enough, and you not only add value to others—you begin to multiply it.

The people who make the greatest difference seem to understand this. If you think about some of the people who have won the Nobel Peace Prize, for example, Albert Schweitzer, Martin Luther King Jr., Mother Teresa, and Bishop Desmond Tutu, you see leaders who were less interested in their position and more interested in their positive impact on others. If you read their writings or, more important, study their lives, you notice that they wanted to make things better for others, to add value to people's lives. They didn't set out to receive the Nobel Prize; they desired to engage in noble service to their fellow human beings. A servant's mind-set pervades their thinking. The 1952 prize winner, Albert Schweitzer, advised, "Seek always to do some good, somewhere. Every man has to seek in his own way to realize his true worth. You must give some time to your fellow man. For remember, you don't live in a world all your own. Your brothers are here too."

Adding value to others through service doesn't just benefit the people being served. It allows the leaders to experience the following:

- Fulfillment in leading others
- Leadership with the right motives
- The ability to perform significant acts as leaders
- The development of a leadership team
- An attitude of service on a team

The best place for a leader isn't always the top position. It isn't the most prominent or powerful place. It's the place where he or she can serve the best and add the most value to other people.

Albert Einstein, who was awarded the Nobel Prize for physics in 1921, asserted, "Only a life lived in the service of others is worth living." Great leadership means great service. How do leaders serve their people? Jim Sinegal pays good wages and treats employees with respect. Martin Luther King Jr. marched for civil rights. Mother Teresa cared for the sick and established places where others could do the same. The specifics depend on the vision, the type of work, and the organization. But the intention is always the same—to add value. When you add value to people, you lift them up, help them advance, make them a part of something bigger than themselves, and assist them in becoming who they were made to be. Often their leader is the only person able to help them to do those things.

ADDING VALUE, CHANGING LIVES

I have developed four guidelines to help me add value to others. Three of them are fundamental and can be used by anyone desiring to practice the Law of Addition. The fourth is based on my faith. If that might offend you or you don't have interest in that area, then simply skip it.

1. WE ADD VALUE TO OTHERS WHEN WE . . .
TRULY VALUE OTHERS

Darryl Hartley-Leonard, who retired as chairman of the board of Hyatt Hotels Corporation and is currently chairman and chief executive officer of Production Group International, says, "When a person moves into a position of authority, he or she gives up the right to abuse people." I believe that is true. But that is only the beginning of good leadership. Effective leaders go beyond not harming others, and they intentionally help others. To do that, they must value people and demonstrate that they care in such a way that their followers know it.

> "When a person moves into a position of authority, he or she gives up the right to abuse people."
> —DARRYL HARTLEY-LEONARD

Dan Reiland, who was my right-hand man for many years, is an excellent leader and values people highly. But when he first came to work for me, he didn't show it. One day when he was new on the job, I was chatting with some people in the lobby, and Dan came in, briefcase in hand. Dan walked right past all of us without saying a word and went straight down the hall toward his office. I was astounded. How could a leader walk right by a group of people he worked with and not even say hello to them? I quickly excused myself from the conversation I was having and followed Dan to his office.

"Dan," I asked after greeting him, "how could you walk right past everybody like that?"

"I've got a lot of work to do today," Dan answered, "and really want to get started."

"Dan," I said, "you just walked past your work. Never forget that leadership is about people." Dan cared about people and wanted to serve them as a leader. He just didn't show it.

I'm told that in American Sign Language, the sign for serving is to hold the hands out in front with the palms up and to move them back and forth between the signer and the signee. And really, that is a good metaphor for the attitude that servant leaders should possess: they should be open, trusting, caring, offering their help, and willing to be vulnerable. Leaders who add value by serving believe in their people before their people believe in them and serve others before they are served.

2. We Add Value to Others When We . . .
Make Ourselves More Valuable to Others

The whole idea of adding value to other people depends on the idea that you have something of value to add. You can't give what you do not possess. What do you have to give others? Can you teach skills? Can you give opportunities? Can you give insight and perspective gained through experience? None of these things comes without a price.

If you have skills, you gained them through study and practice. If you have opportunities to give, you acquired them through hard work. If you possess wisdom, you gained it by intentionally evaluating the experiences you've had. The more intentional you have been in growing personally, the more you have to offer. The more you continue to pursue personal growth, the more you will continue to have to offer.

3. WE ADD VALUE TO OTHERS WHEN WE . . .
KNOW AND RELATE TO WHAT OTHERS VALUE

Management consultant Nancy K. Austin says that once when she looked under the bed in her room at one of her favorite hotels, she was surprised to find a card. It said, "Yes, we clean under here too!" Austin said, "I don't remember the lobby, or the number of chandeliers, or how many square feet of marble they cobbled together to make our underfoot experience pleasant." What she remembered was that card. The housekeeping staff had anticipated what was important to her and had served her well.

We think of that as good customer service, and when we are clients or guests, we expect to receive it. But as leaders, we don't automatically expect to give it. But it is a key to effective leadership. As leaders, how do we know and relate to what our people value? We listen.

Inexperienced leaders are quick to lead before knowing anything about the people they intend to lead. But mature leaders listen, learn, and then lead. They *listen* to their people's stories. They find out about their hopes and dreams. They become acquainted with their aspirations. And they pay attention to their emotions. From those things, they *learn* about their

> *Inexperienced leaders are quick to lead before knowing anything about the people they intend to lead. But mature leaders listen, learn, and then lead.*

people. They discover what is valuable to them. And *then* they *lead* based upon what they've learned. When they do that, everybody wins—the organization, the leader, and the followers.

4. WE ADD VALUE TO OTHERS WHEN WE . . .
DO THINGS THAT GOD VALUES

I already mentioned that you may want to skip this final point, but for me it's a non-negotiable. I believe that God desires us not only to treat people with respect, but also to actively reach out to them and serve them. Scripture provides many examples and descriptions of how we should conduct ourselves, but here is my favorite, captured by Eugene Peterson's *The Message*:

When he finally arrives, blazing in beauty and all his angels with him, the Son of Man will take his place on his glorious throne. Then all the nations will be arranged before him and he will sort the people out, much as a shepherd sorts out sheep and goats, putting sheep to his right and goats to his left.

Then the King will say to those on his right, "Enter, you who are blessed by my Father! Take what's coming to you in this kingdom. It's been ready for you since the world's foundation. And here's why:

I was hungry and you fed me,
I was thirsty and you gave me a drink,
I was homeless and you gave me a room,
I was shivering and you gave me clothes,
I was sick and you stopped to visit,
I was in prison and you came to me."

Then those "sheep" are going to say, "Master, what are you talking about? When did we ever see you hungry and feed you, thirsty and give you a drink? And when did we ever see you sick or in prison and come to you?" Then the King will say, "I'm telling the solemn truth: Whenever you did one of these things to someone overlooked or ignored, that was me—you did it to me."[7]

That standard for my conduct influences everything I do, not just including my leadership, but especially my leadership. Because the more power I have, the greater my impact on others—for better or worse. And I always want to be someone who adds value to others, not takes it away.

IT'S NOT JUST ABOUT THE CHICKEN

When I moved my companies and my family to Atlanta in 1997, it wasn't long before I received a call from Dan Cathy, the president of Chick-fil-A, the privately held national restaurant chain. He had a question for me: "John, how can we help you and your organization?"

I was surprised. How often does a company that's bigger and stronger than you come seemingly out of the blue and offer a hand to help? But that's what Dan did. He brought together two hundred top businesspeople from the Atlanta area and hosted a lunch where he introduced me and offered me a chance to speak to them for forty minutes. It gave me instant credibility that it would have taken me years to earn—if indeed I could have earned it at all without his help. He added tremendous value to me and my organization.

What I discovered as I got to know Dan, Truett Cathy (his father and founder of Chick-fil-A), and their entire organization is that an attitude of service pervades everything they do. And for that reason, along with their dedication to excellence, I have to say that Chick-fil-A is one of the companies that I most greatly admire and respect.

In 2005 when I hosted Exchange, a weekend leadership growth experience for executives, I took the participants to Chick-fil-A's headquarters south of Atlanta. Everyone got to see the company's operations, meet Truett Cathy, and hear Dan Cathy speak about the organization. He shared many eye-opening comments that revealed their dedication to service and adding value to their employees and customers. For example, Dan was preparing that day to camp out with customers for the nineteenth time on the eve of a new restaurant opening. He said that he has gotten to know customers and their desires in a way he never could before he started that practice.

Dan also talked about the company's desire to give "second-mile service." Because Chick-fil-A is a privately held company and is much smaller than McDonald's, KFC, and many of its other competitors, he believes the company will compete and win, not through strength, but through service. For that reason, the company is teaching etiquette to its employees, many of whom are teenagers. Dan joked, "There's evidence that the words etiquette and fast food have never been mentioned in the same sentence before."

But Dan's approach to leadership became clear when he prepared to give every person at Exchange what he called a leadership relationship development tool. Dan said,

Now this is a nine-inch, 100 percent horsehair shoe brush. This is an industrial-strength shoe brush. It's the best you can get from the Johnston and Murphy Shoe Company. I'm going to present all of these, one to each of you here. And, John, why don't you come over here just for a moment. I made a commitment I'd never give one of these leadership relationship development tools to anybody without first showing you how to use it, so, John, step up here so they can see you here. And I'm going to challenge you to watch closely. This really has substance and real meaning when it's practiced with people that you really know, that you really work with a lot. So if you'll let me show you how this happens, I'll tell you how it works.

Dan sat me down, kneeled at my feet, and began cleaning my shoes with the brush.

Now this works whether the person's got tennis shoes, Nike, Reebok, it will work on any type of shoe, so don't worry about what kind of shoes the person has on. You don't say anything—that's one of the real keys here. And you're in no big hurry as you do this. Then [when you're done] you give them a big hug.

At this point Dan stood up, gave me a big hug, and then turned to address the crowd once again:

I find that, in the right setting when you have enough time to do this and to really talk about this, this can have a powerful impact on people's lives. I believe what this does is it "cleans out the closet" in our relationships with other people.[8]

Such a big part of good leadership is having no unresolved relational conflict with other people. Serving others who follow you really purifies your motives and helps you gain perspective. And it also brings to the surface any impure motives of followers. Anytime you can remove wrong agendas from a leadership relationship, you clear the way for fantastic achievement.

When Truett Cathy answered some questions at the end of our time with them, he quoted Ben Franklin as saying, "The handshake of the host affects the taste of the roast." Another way to say it would be that the attitude of the leader affects the atmosphere of the office. If you desire to add value by serving others, you will become a better leader. And your people will achieve more, develop more loyalty, and have a better time getting things done than you ever thought possible. That is the power of the Law of Addition.

Applying
THE LAW OF ADDITION
To Your Life

1. Do you have a servant's attitude when it comes to leadership? Don't be too quick to say yes. Here's how you can tell. In situations where you are required to serve others' needs, how do you respond? Do you become impatient? Do you feel resentful? Do you believe that certain tasks are beneath your dignity or position? If you answer yes to any of those questions, then your attitude is not as good as it could be. Make it a practice to perform small acts of service for others without seeking credit or recognition for them. Continue until you no longer resent doing them.

2. What do the people closest to you value? Make a list of the most important people in your life—from home, work, church, hobbies, and so on. After making the list, write what each person values most. Then rate yourself on a scale of 1 (poorly) to 10 (excellently) on how well you relate to that person's values. If you can't articulate what someone values or you score lower than an 8 in relating to that person, spend more time with him or her to improve.

3. Make adding value part of your lifestyle. Begin with those closest to you. How could you add value to the people on your list related to what *they* value? Start doing it. Then do the same with all the people you lead. If there are only a few, add value individually. If you lead large numbers of people, you may have to think of ways to serve groups as well as individuals.

6

THE LAW OF SOLID GROUND

Trust Is the Foundation of Leadership

How important is trust for a leader? It is *the most important thing*. Trust is the foundation of leadership. It is the glue that holds an organization together. Leaders cannot repeatedly break trust with people and continue to influence them. It just doesn't happen.

As a nation, we have seen our trust in leaders go up and down during the last several decades. Watergate certainly took its toll on the American people's confidence in leadership. Trust in President Richard Nixon became so low that he had no choice but to resign; he had lost his ability to influence. Bill Clinton was a remarkably gifted leader, but questions of trust undermined his leadership. The corporate scandals of the 1990s shook people's confidence in business leadership. Reports of sexual harassment at the military academies undermined confidence in leadership in the armed services. And the incidents of abuse in the Catholic Church disillusioned many people with its leadership. Leaders cannot lose trust and continue to influence others. Trust is the foundation of leadership. That's the Law of Solid Ground.

IT WASN'T THE DECISIONS—IT WAS THE LEADERSHIP

I personally learned the power of the Law of Solid Ground when I was the senior pastor of Skyline Church in the San Diego area. In the fall of 1989, we had several new programs starting at the church, preparations for our exhausting Christmas show season were in full swing, and I was traveling quite a bit as a speaker. It was very hectic. Because I was so busy, I let my choleric nature get the better of me and made a big mistake. I very quickly made three major decisions and implemented them: I changed some components of the Christmas show, I permanently discontinued our Sunday evening service, and I fired a staff member.

What's interesting is that none of my three decisions was wrong. The change in the Christmas program was beneficial. The Sunday evening service, though enjoyed by a few of the older members of the congregation, wasn't serving a need that wasn't already being met better elsewhere. And the staff member I fired had to go, and it was important that I not delay in dismissing him. My mistake was the way I made those three decisions. In an organization made up of many volunteers, decisions need to be processed correctly.

Because everything in the church was going so well, I thought I could take a shortcut. I was wrong. Ordinarily, I would gather my leaders, cast vision for them, answer questions, and guide them through the issues. Then I would give them time to exert their influence with the next level of leaders in the church. And finally, once the timing was right, I would make a general announcement to everyone, giving plenty of reassurance and encouraging people to be a part of the new vision. But I didn't do any of those things, and I should have known better.

THE RESULT WAS MISTRUST

It wasn't long before I began to sense unrest among the people and to hear rumblings. At first, my attitude was that everyone should get over it and move on. But then I realized that the problem wasn't them. It was me. I had been too impatient. On top of that, my attitude wasn't very positive— not good when you're the guy who writes books on attitude! That's when I realized that I had broken the Law of Solid Ground. For the first time in my career, my people were questioning me. Our relationship of trust was beginning to erode.

As soon as I realized I was wrong, I publicly apologized to my people and asked for their forgiveness. Your people know when you make mistakes. The real question is whether you're going to fess up. If you do, you can often regain their trust. Fortunately, that's what happened with me. From then on, I was more careful to correctly process decisions. I learned firsthand that when it comes to leadership, you just can't take shortcuts, no matter how long you've been leading your people.

Trust is like change in a leader's pocket. Each time you make good leadership decisions, you earn more change. Each time you make poor decisions, you pay out some of your change to the people. All leaders have a certain amount of change in their pocket when they start in a new leadership position. Whatever they do either builds up their change or depletes it. If leaders make one bad decision after another, they keep paying out change. Then one day, after making one last

> *When it comes to leadership, you just can't take shortcuts, no matter how long you've been leading your people.*

bad decision, they suddenly—and irreparably—run out of change. It doesn't even matter if the last blunder was big or small. At that point it's too late. When you're out of change, you're out as the leader.

In contrast, leaders who keep making good decisions and keep recording wins for the organization build up change. Then even if they make a huge blunder, they still have plenty of change left over. That's the kind of history I had at Skyline. For eight years I had made good decisions and earned the people's trust. That is why I was able to regain their trust very quickly.

TRUST IS THE FOUNDATION OF LEADERSHIP

Trust is the foundation of leadership. How does a leader build trust? By consistently exemplifying competence, connection, and character. People will forgive occasional mistakes based on ability, especially if they can see that you're still growing as a leader. And they will give you some time to connect. But they won't trust someone who has slips in character. In that area, even occasional lapses are lethal. All effective leaders know this truth. Craig Weatherup, who retired as founding chairman and CEO of the Pepsi Bottling Group, acknowledges, "People will tolerate honest mistakes, but if you violate their trust you will find it very difficult to ever regain their confidence. That is one reason that you need to treat trust as your most precious asset. You may fool your boss but you can never fool your colleagues or subordinates."

> To build trust, a leader must exhibit competence, connection, and character.

General H. Norman Schwarzkopf points to the significance of character: "Leadership is a potent combination of strategy and character. But if you must be without one, be without strategy." Character and leadership credibility always go hand in hand. Anthony Harrigan, president of the U.S. Business and Industrial Council, said,

The role of character always has been the key factor in the rise and fall of nations. And one can be sure that America is no exception to this rule of history. We won't survive as a country because we are smarter or more sophisticated but because we are—we hope—stronger inwardly. In short, character is the only effective bulwark against internal and external forces that lead to a country's disintegration or collapse.

Character makes trust possible. And trust makes leadership possible. That is the Law of Solid Ground.

CHARACTER COMMUNICATES

Whenever you lead people, it's as if they consent to take a journey with you. The way that trip is going to turn out is predicted by your character. With good character, the longer the trip is, the better it seems. But if your character is flawed, the longer the trip is, the worse it gets. Why? Because no one enjoys spending time with someone he doesn't trust.

A person's character quickly communicates many things to others. Here are the most important ones:

CHARACTER COMMUNICATES CONSISTENCY

Leaders without inner strength can't be counted on day after day because their ability to perform changes constantly. NBA great Jerry West commented, "You can't get too much done in life if you only work on the days when you feel good." If your people don't know what to expect from you as a leader, at some point they won't look to you for leadership.

When I think of leaders who epitomize consistency of character, the first person who comes to mind is Billy Graham. Regardless of personal religious beliefs, everybody trusts him.

> *Character makes trust possible. And trust makes leadership possible. That is the Law of Solid Ground.*

Why? Because he has modeled high character for more than half a century. He lives out his values every day. He never makes a commitment unless he is going to keep it. And he goes out of his way to personify integrity.

CHARACTER COMMUNICATES POTENTIAL

British politician and writer John Morley observed, "No man can climb out beyond the limitations of his own character." Weak character is limiting. Who do you think has the greater potential to achieve great dreams and have a positive impact on others: someone who is honest, disciplined, and hardworking, or someone who is deceitful, impulsive, and lazy? It sounds obvious when it's phrased that way, doesn't it?

Talent alone is never enough. It must be bolstered by character if a person desires to go far. Think about someone like the NFL's Terrell Owens. Few football players have his talent. Yet he seems unable to get along with his teammates, wherever he plays. If he keeps going on the same track, he will never fulfill his potential as a player.

Poor character is like a time bomb ticking away. It's only a matter of time before it blows up a person's ability to perform and the capacity to lead. Why?

Because people with weak character are not trustworthy, and trust is the foundation of leadership. Craig Weatherup explains, "You don't build trust by talking about it. You build it by achieving results, always with integrity and in a manner that shows real personal regard for the people with whom you work."[1]

When a leader's character is strong, people trust him, and they trust in his ability to release their potential. That not only gives his followers hope for the future, but it also promotes a strong belief in themselves and their organization.

CHARACTER COMMUNICATES RESPECT

When you don't have character within, you can't earn respect without. And respect is absolutely essential for lasting leadership. How do leaders earn respect? By making sound decisions, by admitting their mistakes, and by putting what's best for their followers and the organization ahead of their personal agendas.

Years ago a movie was made about the Fifty-fourth Massachusetts Infantry regiment and its colonel, Robert Gould Shaw. The film was called *Glory*, and though some of its plot was fictionalized, the Civil War story of Shaw's journey with his men—and of the respect he earned from them—was real.

> *How do leaders earn respect? By making sound decisions, by admitting their mistakes, and by putting what's best for their followers and the organization ahead of their personal agendas.*

The movie recounted the formation of this unit in the Union army, which was the first to be composed of African American soldiers. Shaw, a white officer, took command of the regiment, oversaw recruiting, selected the (white) officers, equipped the men, and trained them as soldiers. He drove them hard, knowing that their performance in battle would either vindicate or condemn the value of black people as soldiers and citizens in the minds of many white Northerners. In the process, the soldiers and Shaw earned one another's respect.

A few months after their training was complete, the men of the Fifty-fourth got the opportunity to prove themselves in the Union assault on

Confederate Fort Wagner in South Carolina. Shaw's biographer Russell Duncan said of the attack: "With a final admonition to 'prove yourselves men,' Shaw positioned himself in front and ordered, 'forward.' Years later, one soldier remembered that the regiment fought hard because Shaw was in front, not behind."

Almost half of the six hundred men from the Fifty-fourth who fought that day were wounded, captured, or killed. Though they fought valiantly, they were unable to take Fort Wagner. And Shaw, who had courageously led his men to the top of the fort's parapet in the first assault, was killed alongside his men.

Shaw's actions on that final day solidified the respect his men already had for him. Two weeks after the battle, Albanus Fisher, a sergeant in the Fifty-fourth, said, "I still feel more Eager for the struggle than I ever yet have, for I now wish to have Revenge for our galant Curnel [sic]."[2] J. R. Miller once observed, "The only thing that walks back from the tomb with the mourners and refuses to be buried is the character of a man. This is true. What a man is survives him. It can never be buried." Shaw's character, strong to the last, had communicated a level of respect to his men that lived beyond him.

> "*The only thing that walks back from the tomb with the mourners and refuses to be buried is the character of a man. This is true. What a man is survives him. It can never be buried.*"
> —J. R. MILLER

A leader's good character builds trust among his followers. But when a leader breaks trust, he forfeits his ability to lead. That's the Law of Solid Ground.

THE BEGINNING OF THE END OF TRUST

Earlier I mentioned Watergate and the various public scandals that have undermined the public's confidence in leaders during the last thirty years. But the event that I believe began to erode the public's faith in the nation's leaders and developed strong skepticism in the country was the war in

Vietnam. The actions taken by members of the Johnson administration, the mistakes made by Robert McNamara, and their unwillingness to face and admit those mistakes broke trust with the American people. They violated the Law of Solid Ground, and the United States has been suffering from the repercussions ever since.

Vietnam was already at war when President Kennedy and Robert McNamara, his secretary of defense, took office in January of 1961. The Vietnam region had been a battleground for decades, and the United States got involved in the mid-1950s when President Eisenhower sent a small number of U.S. troops to Vietnam as advisors. When Kennedy took office, he continued Eisenhower's policy. It was always his intention to let the South Vietnamese fight and win their own war, but over time, the United States became increasingly involved. Before the war was over, more than half a million American troops at one time served in Vietnam.

If you experienced those war years, you may be surprised to know that in the beginning American support for the war was very strong, even as the number of troops being sent overseas rapidly increased and the casualties mounted. By 1966, more than two hundred thousand Americans had been sent to Vietnam, yet two-thirds of all Americans surveyed by Louis Harris believed that Vietnam was the place where the United States should "stand and fight communism." And most people expressed the belief that the United States should stay until the fight was finished.

FIRST TRUST, THEN SUPPORT

But support eventually eroded. The Vietnam War was being handled very badly. On top of that, our leaders continued the war even after they realized that we couldn't win it. But the worst mistake of all was that McNamara and President Johnson weren't honest with the American people about it. And because trust is the foundation of leadership, it ultimately destroyed the administration's leadership.

In his book *In Retrospect*, McNamara recounts that he repeatedly minimized American losses and told only half-truths about the war. For example, he says, "Upon my return to Washington [from Saigon] on December 21, [1963,] I was less than candid when I reported to the press . . . I said, 'We observed the results of a very substantial increase in Vietcong activity' (true); but I then added, 'We reviewed the plans of the South Vietnamese and we have every reason to believe they will be successful' (an overstatement at best)."

For a while, nobody questioned McNamara's statements because there was no reason to mistrust the country's leaders. But in time, people recognized that his words and the facts weren't matching up. And that's when the American public began to lose faith. Years later, McNamara admitted his failure: "We of the Kennedy and Johnson administrations who participated in the decisions on Vietnam acted according to what we thought were the principles and traditions of this nation. We made our decisions in light of those values. Yet we were wrong, terribly wrong."[3]

BY THEN, IT WAS TOO LATE

Many would argue that McNamara's admission came thirty years and fifty-eight thousand lives too late. The cost of Vietnam was high, and not just in human lives. As the American people's trust in their leaders deteriorated, so did their willingness to follow them. Protests led to open rebellion and to society-wide turmoil. The era that had begun with the hope and idealism characterized by John F. Kennedy ultimately ended with the mistrust and cynicism associated with Richard Nixon.

Whenever a leader breaks the Law of Solid Ground, he pays a price in his leadership. McNamara and President Johnson lost the trust of the American people, and their ability to lead suffered as a result. Eventually, McNamara resigned as secretary of defense. Johnson, the consummate politician, recognized his weakened position, and he didn't run for reelection. But the repercussions of broken trust didn't end there. The American people's distrust for politicians has continued to this day.

No leader can break trust with his people and expect to keep influencing them. Trust is the foundation of leadership. Violate the Law of Solid Ground, and you diminish your influence as a leader.

Applying
THE LAW OF SOLID GROUND
To Your Life

1. How trustworthy would your followers say you are? How can you measure their trust? By how open they are with you. Do they openly share opinions with you—even negative ones? Do they give you bad news as readily as good news? Do they let you know what's going on in their areas of responsibility? If not, they may not trust your character.

How about your colleagues and your leader? Do they consistently put their trust in you? How do you measure their trust? By how much responsibility they entrust to you. If you regularly carry weighty responsibilities, that is a good sign that you are trustworthy. If not, then you need to find out whether they doubt your competence or your character.

2. Most high achievers spend time developing their professional skills. They seek to be highly competent. Fewer focus on their character. What are you currently doing to develop your character?

I recommend that you focus on three main areas: integrity, authenticity, and discipline. To develop your integrity, make a commitment to yourself to be scrupulously honest. Don't shave the truth, don't tell white lies, and don't fudge numbers. Be truthful even when it hurts. To develop authenticity, be yourself with everyone. Don't play politics, role play, or pretend to be anything you're not. To strengthen your discipline, do the right things every day regardless of how you feel.

3. If you have broken trust with others in the past, then your leadership will always suffer until you try to make things right. First, apologize to whomever you have hurt or betrayed. If you can make amends or restitution,

then do so. And commit to work at re-earning their trust. The greater the violation, the longer it will take. The onus is not on them to trust. The onus is on you to earn it. (And if you have broken trust at home, start there before working to repair professional relationships.)

7

THE LAW OF RESPECT

People Naturally Follow Leaders Stronger Than Themselves

I f you had seen her, your first reaction might not have been respect. She wasn't a very impressive-looking woman—just a little over five feet tall, in her late thirties, with dark brown weathered skin. She couldn't read or write. The clothes she wore were coarse and worn. When she smiled, she revealed that her top two front teeth were missing.

She lived alone. The story was that she had abandoned her husband when she was twenty-nine. She gave him no warning. One day he woke up, and she was gone. She talked to him only once after that, years later, and she never mentioned his name again afterward.

Her employment was erratic. Most of the time she took domestic jobs in small hotels: scrubbing floors, making up rooms, and cooking. But just about every spring and fall she would disappear from her place of employment, come back broke, and work again to scrape together what little money she could. When she was present on the job, she worked hard and seemed physically tough, but she also was known to suddenly fall asleep—sometimes in the middle of a conversation. She attributed her affliction to a blow to the head she had taken during a teenage fight.

Who would respect a woman like that? The answer is the more than three hundred slaves who followed her to freedom out of the South—they recognized and respected her leadership. So did just about every abolitionist in New England. The year was 1857. The woman's name was Harriet Tubman.

A LEADER BY ANY OTHER NAME

While she was only in her thirties, Harriet Tubman came to be called Moses because of her ability to go into the land of captivity and bring so many of her people out of slavery's bondage. Tubman started life as a slave. She was born in 1820 and grew up in the farmland of Maryland. When she was thirteen, she received the blow to her head that troubled her all her life. She was in a store, and a white overseer demanded her assistance so that he could beat an escaping slave. When she refused and blocked the overseer's way, the man threw a two-pound weight that hit Tubman in the head. She nearly died, and her recovery took months.

At age twenty-four, she married John Tubman, a free black man. But when she talked to him about escaping to freedom in the North, he wouldn't hear of it. He said that if she tried to leave, he'd turn her in. When she resolved to take her chances and go north in 1849, she did so alone, without a word to him. Her first biographer, Sarah Bradford, said that Tubman told her: "I had reasoned this out in my mind: there was one of two things I had a *right* to, liberty or death. If I could not have one, I would have the other, for no man should take me alive. I should fight for my liberty as my strength lasted, and when the time came for me to go, the Lord would let them take me."

Tubman made her way to Philadelphia, Pennsylvania, via the Underground Railroad, a secret network of free blacks, white abolitionists, and Quakers who helped escaping slaves on the run. Though free herself, she vowed to return to Maryland and bring her family out. In 1850, she made her first return trip as an Underground Railroad "conductor"—someone who retrieved and guided out slaves with the assistance of sympathizers along the way.

A LEADER OF STEEL

Each summer and winter, Tubman worked as a domestic, scraping together the funds she needed to make return trips to the South. And every spring and fall, she risked her life by going south and returning with more people. She was fearless, and her leadership was unshakable. Hers was extremely dangerous work, and when people in her charge wavered or had second thoughts, she was strong as steel. Tubman knew escaped slaves who returned would be beaten and tortured until they gave information about those who had helped them. So she never allowed any people she was guiding to give up. "Dead folks tell no tales," she would tell a fainthearted slave as she put a loaded pistol to his head. "You go on or die!"

Between 1850 and 1860, Harriet Tubman guided out more than three hundred people, including many of her family members. She made nineteen trips in all and was very proud of the fact that she never once lost a single person under her care. "I never ran my train off the track," she said, "and I never lost a passenger." At the time, Southern whites put a $12,000 price on her head—a fortune. By the start of the Civil War, she had brought more people out of slavery than any other American in history—black or white, male or female.

INCREASING RESPECT

Tubman's reputation and influence commanded respect, and not just among slaves who dreamed of gaining their freedom. Influential Northerners of both races sought her out. She spoke at rallies and in homes throughout Philadelphia, Pennsylvania; Boston, Massachusetts; St. Catharines, Canada; and Auburn, New York, where she eventually settled. People of prominence sought her out, such as Senator William Seward, who later became Abraham Lincoln's secretary of state, and outspoken abolitionist and former slave Frederick Douglass. Tubman's advice and leadership were also requested by John Brown, the famed revolutionary abolitionist. Brown always referred to the former slave as "General Tubman," and he was quoted as saying she "was a better officer than most whom he had seen, and could command an army as successfully as she had led her small parties of fugitives."[1] That is the essence of the Law of Respect.

A TEST OF LEADERSHIP

Harriet Tubman would appear to be an unlikely candidate for leadership because the deck was certainly stacked against her. She was uneducated. She began life as a slave. She lived in a culture that didn't respect African Americans. And she labored in a country where women didn't have the right to vote yet. Despite her circumstances, she became an incredible leader. The reason is simple: people naturally follow leaders stronger than themselves. Everyone who came in contact with her recognized her strong leadership ability and felt compelled to follow her. That's how the Law of Respect works.

IT'S NOT A GUESSING GAME

People don't follow others by accident. They follow individuals whose leadership they respect. People who are an 8 in leadership (on a scale from 1 to 10, with 10 being the strongest) don't go out and look for a 6 to follow—they naturally follow a 9 or 10. The less skilled follow the more highly skilled and gifted. Occasionally, a strong leader may choose to follow someone weaker than himself. But when that happens, it's for a reason. For example, the stronger leader may do it out of respect for the person's office or past accomplishments. Or he may be following the chain of command. In general, though, followers are attracted to

> *The more leadership ability a person has, the more quickly he recognizes leadership—or its lack—in others.*

people who are better leaders than themselves. That is the Law of Respect.

When people get together for the first time in a group, take a look at what happens. As they start interacting, the leaders in the group immediately take charge. They think in terms of the direction they desire to go and who they want to take with them. At first, people may make tentative moves in many different directions, but after the people get to know one another, it doesn't take long for them to recognize the strongest leaders and to start following them.

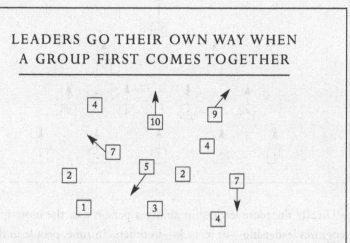

LEADERS GO THEIR OWN WAY WHEN
A GROUP FIRST COMES TOGETHER

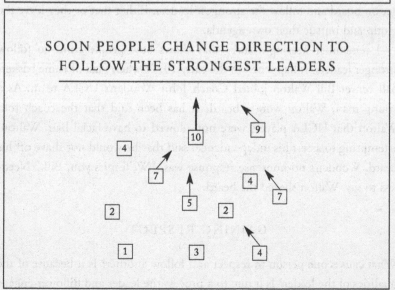

SOON PEOPLE CHANGE DIRECTION TO
FOLLOW THE STRONGEST LEADERS

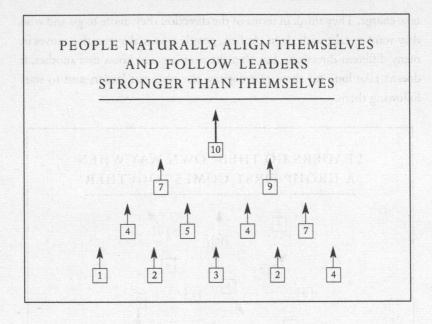

PEOPLE NATURALLY ALIGN THEMSELVES
AND FOLLOW LEADERS
STRONGER THAN THEMSELVES

Usually the more leadership ability a person has, the more quickly he recognizes leadership—or its lack—in others. In time, people in the group get on board and follow the strongest leaders. Either that or they leave the group and pursue their own agenda.

I remember hearing a story that shows how people come to follow stronger leaders. It happened in the early 1970s when Hall of Fame basketball center Bill Walton joined Coach John Wooden's UCLA team. As a young man, Walton wore a beard. It has been said that the coach told Walton that UCLA players were not allowed to have facial hair. Walton, attempting to assert his independence, said that he would not shave off his beard. Wooden's no-nonsense response was, "We'll miss you, Bill." Needless to say, Walton shaved the beard.

GAINING RESPECT

What causes one person to respect and follow another? Is it because of the qualities of the leader? Is it due to a process the leader and follower engage in? Does it occur because of the circumstances? I believe all of those factors can come into play. Based on my observations and personal experience, here are the top six ways that leaders gain others' respect:

1. NATURAL LEADERSHIP ABILITY

First and foremost is leadership ability. Some people are born with greater skills and ability to lead than others. All leaders are not created equal. However, as I've stated in the Law of the Lid and the Law of Process, every person can become a better leader.

If you possess natural leadership ability, people will want to follow you. They will want to be around you. They will listen to you. They will become excited when you communicate vision. However, if you do not exhibit some of the additional practices and charac-

> *When people respect you as a person, they* admire *you. When they respect you as a friend, they* love *you. When they respect you as a leader, they* follow *you.*

teristics listed below, you will not reach your leadership potential, and people may not continue to follow you. One of the greatest potential pitfalls for natural leaders is relying on talent alone.

2. RESPECT FOR OTHERS

Dictators and other autocratic leaders rely on violence and intimidation to get people to do what they want. That's not really leadership. In contrast, good leaders rely on respect. They understand that all leadership is voluntary. When leaders show respect for others—especially for people who have less power or a lower position than theirs—they gain respect from others. And people *want* to follow people they respect greatly.

Gaining respect from others follows a pattern:

When people respect you as a person, they *admire* you.
When they respect you as a friend, they *love* you.
When they respect you as a leader, they *follow* you.

If you continually respect others and consistently lead them well, you will continue to have followers.

3. COURAGE

One thing that caused everyone to respect Harriet Tubman so much was her tremendous courage. She was determined that she was going to succeed, or she was going to die trying. She didn't care about the danger. Her mission was clear, and she was absolutely fearless.

> *"A leader does not deserve the name unless he is willing occasionally to stand alone."*
> —HENRY KISSINGER

Former U.S. secretary of state Henry Kissinger remarked, "A leader does not deserve the name unless he is willing occasionally to stand alone." Good leaders do what's right, even at the risk of failure, in the face of great danger and under the brunt of relentless criticism. I can't think of even one great leader from history who was without courage. Can you? A leader's courage has great value: it gives followers hope.

4. SUCCESS

Success is very attractive. People are naturally drawn to it. It's one reason that people in our society are so focused on celebrities' lives, cheer for their favorite sports team, and follow the careers of rock stars.

Success is even more important when it applies to the people who lead us. People respect others' accomplishments. And it's hard to argue with a good track record. When leaders are successful in their own endeavors, people respect them. When they succeed in leading the team to victory, then followers believe they can do it again. As a result, followers follow them because they want to be part of success in the future.

5. LOYALTY

We live in an era of free agency. Professional athletes hop from team to team, looking for the best deal. CEOs negotiate ridiculously high financial packages and then bail out as millionaires when things go wrong. The average worker, according to one source, will change occupations ten times by the time he reaches age thirty-six.[2]

In a culture of constant change, turnover, and transition, loyalty is an asset. When leaders stick with the team until the job is done, remain loyal to the organization when the going gets rough, and look out for followers even when it hurts them, followers respect them and their actions.

6. VALUE ADDED TO OTHERS

Perhaps the greatest source of respect for a leader comes from his or her dedication to adding value to others. Because I've already discussed this extensively in the Law of Addition, I probably don't need to say much here. But you can be sure that followers value leaders who add value to them. And their respect for them carries on long after the relationship has ended.

MEASURE YOUR LEVEL OF RESPECT

If you want to measure how much respect you have as a leader, the first thing you should do is to look at who you attract. Dennis A. Peer remarked, "One measure of leadership is the caliber of people who choose to follow you." The second thing you should do is to see how your people respond when you ask for commitment or change.

When leaders are respected and they ask for commitment, their people step up and sign up. They are ready to take risks, charge the hill, put in long hours, or do whatever else is necessary to get the job done. Likewise, when respected leaders ask

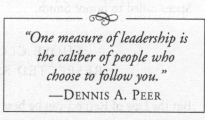

"One measure of leadership is the caliber of people who choose to follow you."
—DENNIS A. PEER

for change, followers are willing to embrace it. But when leaders who are not respected ask for commitment or change, people doubt, they question, they make excuses, or they simply walk away. It is very hard for a leader who hasn't earned respect to get other people to follow.

A RESPECTED LEADER STEPS DOWN

In October of 1997, college basketball saw the retirement of a great leader, someone who engendered respect as he spent more than thirty years of his life pouring himself into others. His name is Dean Smith, and he was the head basketball coach of the University of North Carolina. He compiled a remarkable record while leading the Tar Heels and is considered one of the best to coach at any level. In thirty-two years as head coach at North Carolina, he won a remarkable 879 games.[3] His teams recorded twenty-seven consecutive twenty-win seasons. They won thirteen Atlantic Coast Conference titles, played in eleven Final Fours, and won two national championships.

> *"The leader must know, must know he knows, and must be able to make it abundantly clear to those about him that he knows."*
> —Clarence B. Randall

The respect Smith has earned among his peers is tremendous. When he scheduled the press conference to announce his retirement, people such as Hall of Fame coaches John Thompson, whom Smith beat for the national championship in 1982, and Larry Brown came to show their support. Michael Hooker, the chancellor of the University of North Carolina, gave Smith an open invitation to do just about anything he wanted at the school in the coming years. Even the president of the United States called to honor Smith.

THOSE CLOSEST TO HIM
RESPECTED SMITH THE MOST

But the Law of Respect can be best seen in Smith's career by looking at the way his players interacted with him. They respected him for many reasons. He taught them much about basketball as well as life. He pushed them to achieve academically, with nearly every player earning a degree. He made them winners. And he showed them incredible loyalty and respect. Charlie Scott, who played for Smith and graduated from North Carolina in 1970, advanced to play pro basketball and then went on to work as marketing director for Champion Products. Concerning his time with Smith, he said,

> As one of the first black college athletes in the ACC, I experienced many difficult moments during my time at North Carolina, but Coach Smith was always there for me. On one occasion, as we walked off the court following a game at South Carolina, one of their fans called me a "big black baboon." Two assistants had to hold Coach Smith back from going after the guy. It was the first time I had ever seen Coach Smith visibly upset, and I was shocked. But more than anything else, I was proud of him.[4]

During his time at North Carolina, Smith made quite an impact. His leadership not only won games and the respect of his players but also helped produce a remarkable forty-nine men who went on to play professional basketball. Included in that list are greats such as Bob McAdoo, James Worthy, and of course, Michael Jordan—not only one of the best players ever to dribble a basketball, but also a fine leader in his own right.

James Jordan, Michael's father, credited Smith and his leadership for a lot of his son's success. Before a play-off game in Chicago in 1993, the elder Jordan observed:

> People underestimate the program that Dean Smith runs. He helped Michael realize his athletic ability and hone it. But more important than that, he built character in Michael that took him through his career. I don't think Michael was privileged to any more teaching than anyone else. He had the personality to go with the teaching, and at Carolina he was able to blend the two of them together. That's the only way I can look at it, and I think that's what made Michael the player he became.[5]

Michael Jordan understood what it meant to follow a good leader. During the waning years of his career, he was adamant about his desire to play for only one coach—Phil Jackson, the man he believes is the best in the business. It made sense. A leader like Jordan wanted to follow a strong leader—one stronger than himself. That's the Law of Respect. It's just possible that Jordan's desire got its seed when the young North Carolinian, still developing, was being led and mentored by his strong coach, Dean Smith.

If you ever become frustrated because the people you want to follow you are reluctant to, it very well may be that you are trying to lead people whose leadership is stronger than yours. That creates a difficult situation. If you're a 7 as a leader, 8s, 9s, and 10s aren't likely to follow you—no matter how compelling your vision is or how well thought-out a plan you've devised.

Mathematician André Weil observed, "A first-rate man will try to surround himself with his equals, or better if possible. The second-rate man will surround himself with third-rate men. The third-rate man will surround himself with fifth-rate men." That's not necessarily by design or because weaker leaders are insecure. It's because of the Law of Respect. Like it or not, that's just the way leadership works.

So what can you do about it? Become a better leader. There's always hope for a leader who wants to grow. People who are naturally a 7 may never become a 10—but they can become a 9. There is always room to grow. And the more you grow, the better the people you will attract. Why? Because people naturally follow leaders stronger than themselves.

~~~

Applying
THE LAW OF RESPECT
To Your Life

1. Think about the last time you asked employees, followers, or volunteers for a commitment to something you were leading or to changing something they were doing. What was their response? In general, how readily do people rally to you in either of those situations? That can be used as a fairly accurate gauge of your leadership level.

2. Take a look at the qualities that help a leader to gain respect:

- Leadership ability (natural ability)
- Respect for others
- Courage
- Success record
- Loyalty
- Value added to others

Evaluate yourself in each area on a scale of 1 (low) to 10 (high). One of the best ways to raise your "leadership number" is to improve in each individual area. In one sentence for each, write a practice, habit, or goal that will help you to improve in that area. Then work for a month on each to make it a regular part of your life.

3. One of my favorite definitions of success is having the respect of those closest to me. I believe that if my family (who knows me the best) and my closest coworkers (who work with me every day) have respect for me, then I am a success and my leadership will be effective.

If you have the courage, ask the people in your life who are closest to you what they respect most about you. And ask them to tell you in which areas you most need to grow. Then determine to improve based on their honest feedback.

8

—❧—

THE LAW OF INTUITION

Leaders Evaluate Everything with a Leadership Bias

During the decade that I've spoken to audiences about the 21 Laws of Leadership, I've found that the Law of Intuition is the most difficult to teach. When I talk about it, natural leaders get it instantly, learned leaders get it eventually, and non-leaders just look at me blankly.

Leaders look at things differently than others do. They evaluate everything according to their leadership bias. They possess leadership intuition that informs everything they do. It is an inseparable part of who they are.

EVERYBODY IS INTUITIVE

Not all people are intuitive in the area of leadership, but every person possesses intuition. Why do I say that? Because people are intuitive in their area of strength. I'll give you an example. Because I am a communicator and do a lot of public speaking, people occasionally want to hear from my wife, Margaret, and she receives an invitation to speak at an event. As the date approaches, Margaret works on her presentation and puts together her notes, but we inevitably end up having a conversation something like this:

"John, how do you think I should start?" she asks.

"It depends," I answer.

"That's not much help."

"Margaret, I'm not trying to be difficult. Every speaking situation is different."

"Okay, but what would you do?"

"Well, I'd go out and talk to many of the attendees before the event to try to get a feel for who they are—you know, just check out the room. And I'd listen to what the host said and to the people who spoke before me to get an idea if I should play off something they said or that happened earlier. I'd find a way to really connect with the audience."

> *People are intuitive in their area of strength.*

"That doesn't help me," she answers in frustration.

To be honest, her questions frustrate me as much as my answers frustrate her. I have a hard time explaining what I would do because communication is intuitive for me; it's one of my greatest strengths.

TURNING THE TABLES

I'm not picking on Margaret. She is more highly talented than I am in so many areas. To give you an idea, when I'm getting ready to speak at an event and I'm trying to pick out my clothes, I'm worthless. One of two things usually happens: I stand in the closet, paralyzed and drooling, totally incapable of figuring out what goes together. Or I pick something out, put it on, go into the bedroom, and Margaret says, "Oh, John, you're not going to wear *that*, are you?"

"Uh, I, uh, no, of course not," I answer. "What do *you* think I should wear?"

At that, Margaret strolls into the closet and looks around for about two seconds. "I haven't seen you in this jacket yet, so how about this?" she says as she starts grabbing things. "And if you wear this shirt and this tie, it will really pop." As she picks the slacks, I try to be helpful and pick out shoes. "No, you can't wear those shoes with this," she says. "Here, wear these and this belt."

When I am at the event, I hear compliments about how I'm dressed, so when I return home, I hang that whole outfit together in the closet because I know it goes together. Then the next time I get ready to leave for a speaking engagement, I put it on and walk confidently into the bedroom. Margaret says, "You can't wear *that* again," and off we go through the whole routine again.

Margaret has incredible instincts when it comes to *anything* artistic. She has a great sense of style and a fantastic eye for color. She can paint, arrange flowers, design, hunt down fine antiques, garden, decorate—you name it. She is intuitive in the areas of her strengths. Thanks to her, our homes have always been gorgeous. She could easily hold her own against any decorator on HGTV. I'm lucky because I benefit from her talent.

MORE THAN FACTS

Intuition is so difficult to explain because it's not concrete. It doesn't rely on just empirical evidence. If you've ever seen reruns of the old show *Dragnet* on TV Land (or if you're my age and saw them when new), you probably know the phrase Jack Webb made famous: "Just the facts, ma'am, just the facts." The Law of Intuition depends on so much *more than just the facts.* The Law of Intuition is based on facts plus instinct plus other intangible factors, such as employee morale, organizational momentum, and relational dynamics.

Colin Powell, retired army general and former secretary of state, provides a good explanation of the use of leadership intuition and its importance. He observes that many leaders have trouble if they desire to have an exhaustive amount of data or wait to have all their questions answered before making decisions. Powell says that his practice is to make a leadership decision after gathering only 40 to 60 percent of the information that can be obtained, and then he uses his experience to make up the difference. In other words, he bases his leadership decisions as much on intuition as on facts. He relies on the Law of Intuition. And that often separates the great leaders from the merely good ones.

LEADERSHIP IS THEIR BIAS

Good leaders see everything with a leadership bias, and as a result, they instinctively, almost automatically, know what to do when it comes to leading. This read-and-react instinct is evident in the best leaders. For example, consider the career of another former U.S. Army general: H. Norman Schwarzkopf. Time after time, he was assigned commands that others avoided, but he was able to turn the situations around as the result of his exceptional leadership intuition and ability to act. Leaders are often able to do similar things.

When Schwarzkopf had been in the army seventeen years, he finally got his chance to command a battalion. It occurred in December 1969 during his second tour of Vietnam as a lieu-tenant colonel. The command, which nobody wanted, was of the First Battalion of the Sixth Infantry, the "First of the Sixth." But because the group had such a horrible reputa-tion, it was nicknamed the "worst of the Sixth." Confirming this was the fact that as he took command, Schwarzkopf was told that the battalion had just flunked its annual inspection with an abysmal score—only sixteen out of a possible one hundred points. He had only thirty days to whip his men into shape.

> *Schwarzkopf was repeatedly able to turn bad situations around as the result of his exceptional leadership intuition.*

SEEING THROUGH A LEADERSHIP LENS

After the change-in-command ceremony, Schwarzkopf met the outgoing commander. Before the man left, he told Schwarzkopf, "This is for you," handing him a bottle of Scotch. "You're gonna need it. Well, I hope you do better than I did. I tried to lead as best I could, but this is a lousy battalion. It's got lousy morale. It's got a lousy mission. Good luck to you."

Schwarzkopf anticipated a terrible situation, but it was even worse than he expected. His predecessor hadn't known the first thing about leadership.

The man had never ventured outside the safety of the base camp to inspect his troops. And the results were appalling. The entire battalion was in chaos. The officers were indifferent, the most basic military security procedures weren't being followed, and soldiers were dying needlessly. The departing commander was right: it was a lousy battalion with lousy morale. But he didn't realize that it was largely his fault.

During the next few weeks, Schwarzkopf's leadership intuition kicked in, and he took action. He implemented procedures, retrained the troops, developed his leaders, and gave the men direction and a sense of purpose. When it was time for the thirty-day inspection, they achieved a passing score. And the men started to think to themselves, *Hey, we can do it right. We can be a success. We're not the worst of the Sixth anymore.* As a result, fewer men died, morale rose, and the battalion started to become effective in its mission. The battalion's turnaround was so strong that just a few months after Schwarzkopf took it over, it was selected to perform more difficult missions—the kind that could be carried out only by a disciplined, well-led group with strong morale.

WHO YOU ARE DETERMINES WHAT YOU SEE

How was Schwarzkopf able to turn around this group of soldiers? The same way he overcame difficult assignments again and again: the Law of Intuition. Other officers had the same training and access to the same resources. And Schwarzkopf wasn't necessarily smarter than his counterparts either. What he brought to the table was strong leadership intuition. He saw everything with a leadership bias.

Who you are dictates what you see. A scene from the movie *The Great Outdoors* illustrates this perfectly. In the movie, Chet, played by John Candy, is vacationing with his family at a small lake community in the woods. He is unexpectedly visited by his sister-in-law and her husband, Roman, played by Dan Aykroyd. As the two men sit on the porch of their cabin overlooking the lake and miles of beautiful forest, they start to talk. And Roman, a fast-talking wheeler-dealer, shares his vision with Chet: "I'll tell you what I see when I look out there . . . I see the underdeveloped resources of northern Minnesota, Wisconsin, and Michigan. I see a syndicated development consortium exploiting over a billion and a half dollars in forest products. I see a paper mill and—if the strategic metals are there—a mining operation; a green belt between the condos on the lake and a waste management facility . . . Now I ask you, what do you see?"

> *Who you are dictates what you see.*

"I, uh, I just see trees," answers Chet.

"Well," says Roman, "nobody ever accused you of having a grand vision."

Chet saw trees because he was there to enjoy the scenery. Roman saw business opportunities because he was someone whose desire was to make money. How you see the world around you is determined by who you are.

HOW LEADERS THINK

Because of their intuition, leaders evaluate everything with a leadership bias. People born with natural leadership ability are especially strong in the area of leadership intuition. Others have to work hard to develop and hone it. But either way, intuition comes from two things: the combination of natural ability, which comes in a person's areas of strength, and learned skills. It is an informed intuition, and it causes leadership issues to jump out to a leader in a way that they don't with others.

I regard leadership intuition as the ability of a leader to read what's going on. For that reason, I say that leaders are readers:

LEADERS ARE READERS OF THEIR SITUATION

Today I wear many hats. I write, speak, mentor, and network. I also own two companies. Although I speak with the presidents of my companies on a weekly basis, they run the day-to-day operations, and I go to the office only occasionally.

Recently John Hull, the president and CEO of EQUIP, commented, "John, when you come in to the office, you reenter our world very easily." I thought that was an interesting choice of words, so I asked what he meant.

"You are very aware of the atmosphere and environment," he explained. "You ask good questions and quickly fall in step with us on our journey. It's never awkward when you return to the office." As I reflected, I realized what he was describing was my use of leadership intuition.

In all kinds of circumstances, leaders pick up on details that might elude others. They "tune in" to leadership dynamics. Many leaders describe this as an ability to "smell" things in their organization. They can sense people's attitudes. They are able to detect the chemistry of a team. They can tell when things are humming and when they're winding down or getting ready to grind to a halt. They

> *Natural ability and learned skills create an informed intuition that makes leadership issues jump out at leaders.*

don't need to sift through stats, read reports, or examine a balance sheet. They know the situation *before* they have all the facts. That is the result of their leadership intuition.

Leaders Are Readers of Trends

Most followers are focused on their current work. They think in terms of tasks at hand, projects, or specific goals. That is as it should be. Most managers are concerned with efficiency and effectiveness. They often possess a broader view than employees, thinking in terms of weeks, months, or even years. But leaders take an even broader view. They look years, even decades ahead.

Everything that happens around us does so in the context of a bigger picture. Leaders have the ability—and responsibility—to step back from what's happening at the moment and to discern not only where the organization has been but also where it is headed. Sometimes they can accomplish this through analysis, but often the best leaders sense it first and find data to explain it later. Their intuition tells them that something is happening, that conditions are changing, and that trouble or opportunity is coming. Leaders must always be a few steps ahead of their best people, or they're not really leading. They can do that only if they are able to read trends.

LEADERS ARE READERS OF THEIR RESOURCES

A major difference between leaders and everyone else is the way they see resources. A good worker encounters a challenge and thinks, *What can I do to help?* A high achiever asks, *How can I solve this problem?* A peak performer wonders, *What must I do to reach the next level so that I can overcome this?*

> *Leaders who want to succeed maximize every asset and resource they have for the benefit of their organization.*

Leaders think differently. They think in terms of resources and how to maximize them. They see a challenge, problem, or opportunity, and they think, *Who is the best person to take this on? What resources—raw materials, technology, information, and so forth—do we possess that will help us? What will this take financially? How can I encourage my team to achieve success?*

Leaders see everything with a leadership bias. Their focus is on mobilizing people and leveraging resources to achieve their goals rather than on using their own individual efforts. Leaders who want to succeed maximize every asset and resource they have for the benefit of their organization. For that reason, they are continually aware of what they have at their disposal.

LEADERS ARE READERS OF PEOPLE

President Lyndon Johnson once said that when you walk into a room, you don't belong in politics if you can't tell who's for you and who's against you. That statement also applies to any other kind of leader. Intuition helps leaders sense what's happening among people and know their hopes, fears, and concerns. They can sense what's happening in a room—whether there's curiosity, doubt, reluctance, anticipation, or relief.

Reading people is perhaps the most important intuitive skill leaders can possess. After all, if what you are doing doesn't involve people, it's not leadership. And if you aren't persuading people to follow, you aren't really leading.

LEADERS ARE READERS OF THEMSELVES

Finally, good leaders develop the ability to read themselves. Poet James Russell Lowell observed, "No one can produce great things who is not thoroughly sincere in dealing with himself." Leaders must know not only their own strengths and blind spots, skills and weaknesses, but also their current state of mind. Why? Because leaders can hinder progress just as easily as they can help create it. In fact, it's easier to damage an organization than it is to build one. We've all seen excellent organizations that took generations to build begin falling apart in a matter of years.

When leaders become self-centered, pessimistic, or rigid in their thinking, they often hurt their organizations because they are likely to fall into the trap of thinking they cannot or should not change. And once that happens, the organization has a hard time becoming better. Its decline is inevitable.

THREE LEVELS OF LEADERSHIP INTUITION

If you're saying to yourself, *I'd like to be able to read these dynamics in my organization, but I just don't see things intuitively*, don't despair. The good news is that you can improve your leadership intuition, even if you are not a natural-born leader. As I've already mentioned, leadership intuition is *informed* intuition. The less natural leadership talent you have, the more you will need to make up for it by developing skills and gaining experience. They can help you to develop thinking patterns, and thinking patterns can be learned.

I've found that all people fit into three major intuition levels:

1. THOSE WHO *NATURALLY* UNDERSTAND LEADERSHIP

Some people are born with exceptional leadership gifts. They instinctively understand people and know how to move them from point A to point B. Even when they're kids, they act as leaders. Watch them on the playground, and you can see other kids following them. People with natural leadership intuition can build upon it and become world-class leaders of the highest caliber.

2. THOSE WHO CAN BE *NURTURED* TO UNDERSTAND LEADERSHIP

Most people fall into this category. They have adequate people skills, and if they are teachable, they can develop intuition. Leadership can be learned. However, people who don't try to improve their leadership and never work to develop their intuition are condemned to being blindsided in their leadership for the rest of their lives.

3. THOSE WHO WILL *NEVER* UNDERSTAND LEADERSHIP

I believe nearly everyone is capable of developing leadership skills and intuition. But occasionally, I run across someone who doesn't seem to have a leadership bone in his body *and* who has no interest in developing the skills necessary to lead. This isn't you because these people never pick up a leadership book.

DEVELOPING INTUITION
BY CHANGING YOUR THINKING

Several years ago I gained insight into college football and about how quarterbacks are trained to think when I was invited to the University of Southern California. Their coach at that time was Larry Smith. He asked me to speak to the Trojans football team before a big game and also allowed me to visit the team's offensive war room.

On chalkboards covering every wall, the coaches had mapped out every possible situation their team could be in—according to down, yardage, and place on the field. And for every situation, the coaches had planned a specific play designed to succeed, based on their years of experience and their intuitive knowledge of the game.

While I was there, I noticed a cot against one of the walls. When I asked what it was for, the offensive coordinator said, "I always spend Friday night here to make sure that I know all the plays, too."

"Yeah, but you've got all of them written down on that sheet that you'll carry with you tomorrow on the sidelines," I said. "Why don't you just use that?"

"I can't rely on that," he answered. "There isn't time. You see, by the time the ball carrier's knee touches the ground, I have to know what play to call next based on the situation. There's no time to fumble around deciding what to do." It was his job to put the coaching staff's intuition into action in an instant.

But the coaches didn't stop there. The three USC quarterbacks had to memorize every one of those plays. The night before the game, I watched as the coaches grilled those young

> *A leader has to read the situation and know instinctively what play to call.*

men, firing one situation after another at them. The job of the quarterbacks was to recite which play was right for the situation. The coaches wanted those players to be so well informed, so ready, that their intuition would take over during crunch time. It would help them to effectively lead the team.

LEADERS SOLVE PROBLEMS USING THE LAW OF INTUITION

Whenever leaders face a problem, they automatically measure it—and begin solving it—using the Law of Intuition. They evaluate everything with a leadership bias. For example, leadership intuition came into play in recent years at Apple Computer. Just about everybody knows the success story of Apple. The company was created in 1976 by Steve Jobs and Steve Wozniak in a garage. Just four years later, the business went public, opening at twenty-two dollars a share and selling 4.6 million shares. It made more than forty employees and investors millionaires overnight.

But Apple's story hasn't been all positive. Since those early years, Apple's success, stock value, and ability to capture customers have fluctuated wildly. Jobs left Apple in 1985, having been pushed out in a battle with CEO John Sculley, the former Pepsi president whom Jobs had recruited in 1983. Sculley was followed by Michael Spindler in 1993 and then Gilbert Amelio in 1996. None of them was able to reestablish Apple's previous success. In its glory days, Apple had sold 14.6 percent of all personal computers in the United

> *Whenever leaders face a problem, they automatically measure it—and begin solving it—using the Law of Intuition.*

States. By 1997, sales were down to 3.5 percent. That was when Apple again looked to the leadership of its original founder, Steve Jobs, for help. The failing company believed he could save it.

REINVENTING APPLE

Jobs intuitively reviewed the situation and immediately took action. He knew that improvement was impossible without a change in leadership, so he quickly dismissed all but two of the previous board members and installed new ones. He made changes in the executive leadership. And he fired the company's ad agency and held a competition for the account among three firms.

He also refocused the company. Jobs wanted to get back to the basics of what Apple had always done best: use its individuality to create products that made a difference. At the time Jobs said, "We've reviewed the road map of new products and axed more than 70 percent of the projects, keeping the 30 percent that were gems. Plus we're adding new ones that are a whole new paradigm of looking at computers."[1]

None of those actions was especially surprising. But Jobs also did something that really showed the Law of Intuition in action. He read Apple's situation and made a leadership decision that went absolutely against the grain of Apple's previous thinking. It was an incredible intuitive leadership leap. Jobs created a strategic alliance with the man whom Apple employees considered to be their archenemy—Bill Gates. Jobs explained,

"I called Bill and said Microsoft and Apple should work more closely together, but we have this issue to resolve, this intellectual-property dispute. Let's resolve it."

They negotiated a deal quickly, which settled Apple's lawsuit against Microsoft. Gates promised to pay off Apple and invest $150 million in non-voting stock. That cleared the way for future partnership and brought much-needed capital to the company. It was something only an intuitive leader would have done. Apple's stock value immediately went up 33 percent. And in time, Apple regained some of the prestige it had lost over the years.

REVOLUTIONIZING MUSIC

In 2001, Jobs made another leadership move based on his intuition. While other computer manufacturers were pursuing PDAs, he was looking at music. And when an independent contractor and hardware expert named Tony Fadell approached Apple with an idea for an MP3 player and a music sales company, Apple embraced it, even though several other companies had rejected it. Fadell was hired on, and they began working on what would eventually be known as the iPod.

> *Improvement is impossible without change.*

Jobs's involvement with the iPod is an indication of his leadership intuition. Ben Knauss, who was on the inside of the project, says, "The interesting thing about the iPod is that since it started, it had 100 percent of Steve Jobs's time. Not many projects get that. He was heavily involved in every single aspect of the project."[2] Why did Jobs do that? Because his intuition as a leader made him understand the impact that the device could make. It was consistent with his vision for creating a digital lifestyle.

Jobs has been right on. Sales have been phenomenal and have exceeded the company's computer sales. Apple was making a profit while other technology companies suffered. By spring of 2002, Apple had shipped more than 10 million units.[3] By the end of 2005, Apple possessed 75 percent of the world market for digital music players![4]

Jobs's story is a reminder that leadership is really more art than science. The principles of leadership are constant, but the application changes with every leader and every situation. That's why it requires intuition. Without it, leaders get blindsided, and that's one of the worst things that can happen to a leader. If you want to lead long, lead well, and stay ahead of others, you've got to obey the Law of Intuition.

Applying
THE LAW OF INTUITION
To Your Life

1. How are you when it comes to trusting your intuition? Are you a facts or feelings person? To become better at the Law of Intuition, you must first be willing to *trust* your intuition. Begin by working within your areas of greatest strength.

First, determine which is your strongest natural talent. Second, participate in that talent, paying attention to your feelings, instincts, and intuition. When do you know something is "right" before you have evidence? How can you tell when you're "on"? Do your instincts in this area ever betray you? If so, when and why? Get to know your aptitude for intuition where you are strong before trying to develop it in leadership.

2. One of the most important abilities in leadership is reading people. How would you rate yourself in this area? Can you tell what others are feeling? Can you sense when people are upset? Happy? Confused? Angry? Do you anticipate what others are thinking?

If this is not an area of strength for you, then work on improving by doing these things:

• Read books on relationships.
• Engage more people in conversations.
• Become a people watcher.

3. Train yourself to think in terms of mobilizing people and harnessing resources. Think about current projects or goals. Now imagine how you can accomplish them *without* doing any of the work yourself except for recruiting, empowering, and motivating others.

You may even want to write the following on a note card and keep it in your pocket or organizer:

- Who is the best person to take this on?
- What resources do we possess that can help us?
- What will this take financially?
- How can I encourage my team to achieve success?

THE LAW OF MAGNETISM

Who You Are Is Who You Attract

E ffective leaders are always on the lookout for good people. I think each of us carries around a mental list of what kind of people we would like to have in our organization or department. Think about it. Do you know who you're looking for right now? What is your profile of perfect employees? What qualities would they possess? Would you want them to be aggressive and entrepreneurial? Are you looking for leaders? Do you care whether they are in their twenties, forties, or sixties? Stop right now, take a moment, and make a list of the qualities you'd like in the people on your team. Find a pencil or pen, and do it now before you read any farther.

My People Would Have These Qualities:

_____

_____

_____

Now, what will determine whether the people you want are the people you get and whether they will possess the qualities you desire? You may be surprised by the answer. Believe it or not, who you attract is not determined by what you *want*. It's determined by who you *are*.

Go back to the list you just made, and for each characteristic you identified, decide whether you possess that quality. For example, if you wrote that you would like "great leaders" and you are an excellent leader, that's a match. Put a check (✓) by it. But if your leadership is no better than average, put an X and write "only average leader" next to it. If you wrote that you want people who are "entrepreneurial" and you possess that quality, put a check. Otherwise, mark it with an X, and so on. Now review the whole list.

> *Who you attract is not determined by what you want. It's determined by who you are.*

If you see a whole bunch of Xs, then you're in trouble, because the people you describe are not the type who will want to follow you. In most situations, unless you take strong measures to counteract it, you draw people to you who possess the same qualities you do. That's the Law of Magnetism: who you are is who you attract.

FROM MUSICIANSHIP TO LEADERSHIP

When I was a kid, my mother used to tell me that birds of a feather flock together. I thought that was a wise saying when I was spending time with my older brother, Larry, and playing ball. He was a good athlete, so I figured that made me one, too. As I grew up, I think I instinctively recognized that good students spent time with good students, people who only wanted to play stuck together, and so on. But I don't think I really understood the impact of the Law of Magnetism until I moved to San Diego, California, and became the leader of the last church I pastored.

My predecessor at Skyline Church was Dr. Orval Butcher. He is a wonderful man with many admirable qualities. One of his best is his musicianship. He plays piano and has a beautiful Irish tenor voice, even today in his eighties. At the time I arrived in 1981, Skyline had a solid reputation for fine music and was nationally known for its outstanding musical productions. In fact, the church was filled with talented musicians and vocalists. And in the twenty-seven years Dr. Butcher led the church, only two music directors worked for him—an unbelievable track record. (In comparison, during my fourteen years there, I employed five people in that capacity.)

Why were there so many exceptional musicians at Skyline? The answer lies in the Law of Magnetism. People with musical talent were naturally attracted to Dr. Butcher. They respected him and understood him. They shared his motivation and values. They were on the same page with him. Leaders help to shape the culture of their organizations based on who they are and what they do. Music was valued. It was practiced and performed with excellence. It was used to reach out to the community. It was deeply ingrained in the culture of the organization.

In contrast, I enjoy music, but I am not a musician. It's funny, but when I interviewed for the position at Skyline, one of the first questions they asked me was whether I could sing. They were very disappointed when I told them no. After I came on board at the church, the number of new musicians arriving at the church declined quickly. We still had more than our share because Dr. Butcher had created momentum and a wonderful legacy in that area. But do you know what kind of people started coming instead? Leaders. I valued leadership, modeled it, trained people in it, and rewarded it. Leadership was woven into the fabric of the organization. By the time I left Skyline, not only was the church filled with hundreds of excellent leaders, but the church had raised up and sent out hundreds of leaders. The reason was the Law of Magnetism. Our organization became a magnet for people with leadership ability.

WHERE DO THEY MATCH UP?

Maybe you've started thinking about the people that you have attracted in your organization. You might say to yourself, *Wait a minute. I can name twenty things that make my people different from me.* And my response would be, "Of course you can." We're all individuals. But the people who are drawn to you probably have more similarities than differences, especially in a few key areas.

Take a look at the following characteristics. If you have recruited and hired a staff, you will probably find that you and the people who follow you share common ground in several of these key areas:

GENERATION

Most organizations reflect the characteristics of their key leaders, and that includes their age. During the dot-com boom of the 1990s, thousands of companies were founded by people in their twenties and early thirties. And who did they hire? Others in their twenties and thirties. In just about any type of organization, most of the time the people who come on board are similar in age to the leaders who hire them. Often that occurs within departments. Sometimes it occurs company-wide.

> *If you think your people are negative, then you'd better check your attitude.*

ATTITUDE

Rarely have I seen positive and negative people attracted to one another. People who view life as a series of opportunities and exciting challenges don't want to hear others talk about how bad things are all the time. I know that's true for me. And not only do people attract others with similar attitudes, but their attitudes tend to become alike. Attitude is one of the most contagious qualities a human being possesses. People with good attitudes tend to make people around them feel more positive. Those with a terrible attitude tend to bring others down.

BACKGROUND

In the chapter on the Law of Process, I wrote about Theodore Roosevelt. One of his memorable accomplishments is his daring charge up San Juan Hill with the Rough Riders during the Spanish-American War. Roosevelt personally recruited that all-volunteer cavalry company, and it was said to be a remarkably peculiar group of people. It was comprised primarily of two types of men: wealthy aristocrats from the Northeast and cowboys from the Wild West. Why? Because TR was an aristocratic-born, Harvard-educated New Yorker who turned himself into a real-life cowboy and big-game hunter in the Dakotas of the West. He was a strong and genuine leader in both worlds, and as a result, he attracted both kinds of people.

People attract—and are attracted to—others of similar background. Blue-collar workers tend to stick together. Employers tend to hire people of the same race. People with education tend to respect and value others who are also well educated. This natural magnetism is so strong that organizations that value diversity have to fight against it.

In the NFL, for example, the team owners are white, and for decades, all the head coaches were white. But because members of the league valued racial diversity, they put into place a diversity policy requiring teams to include at least one minority candidate in the interview process when hiring head coaches. That policy has helped more highly qualified African American head coaches to be hired. (But other than in the area of race, the *background* of all the coaches remains strikingly similar.)

VALUES

People are attracted to leaders whose values are similar to their own. Think about the people who flocked to President John F. Kennedy after he was elected in 1960. He was a young idealist who wanted to change the world, and he attracted people with a similar profile. When he formed the Peace Corps and called people to service, saying, "Ask not what your country can do for you; ask what you can do for your country," thousands of young, idealistic people stepped forward to answer the challenge.

It doesn't matter whether the shared values are positive or negative. Either way, the attraction is equally strong. Think about someone like Adolf Hitler. He was a very strong leader (as you can judge by his level of influence). But his values were rotten to the core. What kinds of people did he attract? Leaders with similar values: Hermann Goering, founder of the Gestapo; Joseph Goebbels, a bitter anti-Semite who ran Hitler's propaganda machine; Reinhard Heydrich, second in command of the Nazi secret police, who ordered mass executions of Nazi opponents; and Heinrich Himmler, chief of the SS and director of the Gestapo, who initiated the systematic execution of Jews. They were all strong leaders, and they were all utterly evil men. The Law of Magnetism is powerful. Whatever character you possess is what you will likely find in the people who follow you.

ENERGY
It's a good thing that people with similar levels of energy are attracted to one another because when you pair a high-energy person with a low-energy person and ask them to work closely together, they can drive one another crazy. The high-energy person thinks the low-energy one is lazy, and the low-energy person thinks the high-energy one is insane.

GIFTEDNESS
People do not go out looking for mediocre leaders to follow. People are attracted to talent and excellence, especially in their area of giftedness. They are most likely to respect and follow someone who possesses their kind of talent. Businesspeople want to follow bosses with skill in building an organization and making a profit. Football players want to follow coaches with great football talent. Creative people want to follow leaders who are willing to think outside the box. Like attracts like. That may seem pretty obvious. Yet I've met many leaders who expect highly talented people to follow them, even though they neither possess nor express value for those people's giftedness.

LEADERSHIP ABILITY
Finally, the people you attract will have leadership ability similar to your own. As I said in discussing the Law of Respect, people naturally follow leaders stronger than themselves. But you also have to factor in the Law of Magnetism, which states that who you are is who you attract. If you are a 7 when it comes to leadership, you are more likely to draw 5s and 6s to you than 2s and 3s. The leaders you attract will be similar in style and ability to you.

LIVING LEADERSHIP

Al McGuire, former head basketball coach of Marquette University, once said, "A team should be an extension of the coach's personality. My teams were arrogant and obnoxious." It's more than a matter of "should be"—teams cannot help being an extension of their leader's personality.

In 1996, I founded my nonprofit organization, EQUIP, which exists to train leaders internationally. Guess what kinds of donors are attracted to EQUIP? Leaders! Men and women who lead others and understand the value and impact that come from training leaders are continually attracted to EQUIP.

GOING AGAINST THE GRAIN

As you read this chapter, you may find yourself in one of two situations. You may be saying to yourself, *I'm not crazy about the people I'm attracting. Am I stuck with my situation?* The answer is no. If you are dissatisfied with the leadership ability of the people you are attracting, then embrace the Law of Process and work to increase your leadership skill. If you want to grow an organization, grow the leader. If you find the people you attract to be unreliable or untrustworthy, then examine your character. Developing stronger character can be a more difficult road, but the payoff is huge. Good character improves every aspect of a person's life.

On the other hand, you may be saying, *I like who I am, and I like the kind of people I attract.* That's great! Now, take the next step in effective leadership. Work at recruiting people who are different from you to staff your weaknesses. If you don't, important organizational tasks are likely to be overlooked, and the organization will suffer as a result. An organization will never fulfill its potential if everyone in it is a visionary or if everyone is an accountant.

It is possible for a leader to go out and recruit people unlike himself, but those are not the people he will naturally attract. Attracting people unlike yourself requires a high degree of intentionality. To succeed at it, people

THE 21 IRREFUTABLE LAWS OF LEADERSHIP

must believe in you, and the vision you share must be compelling. You can learn more about that in the Law of Buy-In.

HISTORY CHANGES COURSE

Once you understand the Law of Magnetism, you can see it at work in just about any kind of situation: business, government, sports, education, the military, and more. As you read history, look for its clues. One of the most vivid examples of the Law of Magnetism is found in American history among the military leaders of the Civil War. When the Southern states seceded, there were questions about which side many of the generals would fight for. Robert E. Lee was considered the best general in the nation, and President Lincoln actually offered him command of the Union army. But Lee would never consider fighting against his native Virginia. He declined the offer and joined the Confederacy—and the best generals in the land followed him.

> *The better leader you are, the better leaders you will attract.*

If Lee had chosen to lead an army for the Union instead, many other good generals would have followed him north. As a result, the war probably would have been much shorter. Some speculate that it might have lasted two years instead of five—and hundreds of thousands of lives would have been saved. It just goes to show you that the better leader you are, the better leaders you will attract. And that has an incredible impact on everything you do.

How do the people you are currently attracting to your organization or department look to you? Are they the strong, capable, potential leaders you desire? Or could they be better? Remember, their quality does not ultimately depend on a hiring process, a human resources department, or even what you consider to be the quality of your area's applicant pool. It depends on you. Who you are is who you attract. That is the Law of Magnetism. If you want to attract better people, become the kind of person you desire to attract.

— 110 —

Applying

THE LAW OF MAGNETISM

To Your Life

1. If you skipped the exercise of writing down the qualities you desire in your followers, then do it now. Once you are finished (or if you already completed it), think about *why* you desire the qualities you listed. When you wrote them, did you think you were describing people like you or different from you? If there is a disparity between your image of yourself and of your employees, then your level of self-awareness may be low, and it may be hindering your personal development. Talk to a trusted colleague or friend who knows you well to help you identify your blind spots.

2. Based on who you are attracting, you may need to grow in the areas of character and leadership. Find mentors willing and able to help you grow in each area. Good candidates as a character mentor could be a pastor or spiritual advisor, a professional whose ability you respect, or a professional coach. Ideally, your leadership mentor should work in the same or a similar profession and be several steps ahead of you in his or her career.

3. If you are already attracting the kinds of people you desire, then it's time to take your leadership to the next level. Work at staffing your weaknesses and recruiting people who will complement your leadership in the area of skills. Write a list of your five greatest strengths when it comes to skills. Then write your five greatest weaknesses.

Now it's time to create a profile of who you are looking for. Start with giftedness that corresponds to your weaknesses. Add to that values and attitudes that are similar to yours. Also consider whether age, background, and education are factors. Will it help if they are different? Finally, look for someone who is potentially a good leader or at the very least understands and appreciates how leadership works. Few things are more frustrating to a good leader than a partner with a bureaucratic mindset.

10

&

THE LAW OF CONNECTION

Leaders Touch a Heart Before They Ask for a Hand

There are incidents in the lives and careers of leaders that become defining moments for their leadership. In the perception of followers, the general public, and historians, those moments often represent who those leaders are and what they stand for. Here's an example of what I mean. I believe the presidency of George W. Bush can be summed up by two defining moments that he experienced during his time in office.

A CONNECTION MADE

The first moment occurred early in his first term, and it defined that entire term in office. On September 11, 2001, the United States was attacked by terrorists who crashed planes into the World Trade Center and Pentagon. People in the United States were angry. They were fearful. They were uncertain about the future. And they were in mourning for the thousands of people who lost their lives to the terrorists.

Just four days after the collapse of the World Trade Center towers, Bush went to Ground Zero. He spent time there with the firefighters, police officers, and rescue workers. He shook hands. He listened. He took in the devastation. He thanked the people working there and told them, "The nation sends its love and compassion to everybody who's here." Reports said that the spirits of the tired searchers lifted when the president arrived and started shaking hands.

Cameras captured Bush standing in the wreckage with his arm around firefighter Bob Beckwith. When some members of the crowd shouted that they couldn't hear him, Bush called back, "I can hear you. The rest of the world hears you. And the people who knocked these buildings down will hear all of us soon."[1] The people cheered. They felt validated. They felt understood. Bush had connected with them in a way no one had seen him do prior to that moment.

NOBODY'S HOME

The second incident came during Bush's second four years in office, and it defined that second term. It occurred on August 31, 2005, just two days after the landfall of Hurricane Katrina. After the levees in New Orleans broke and water flooded into the city, instead of visiting the city as he did in New York after 9/11, Bush flew over New Orleans in Air Force One, peering through one of the jet's small windows to see the damage. To the people of the Gulf Coast, it was a picture of indifference.

As the tragedy unfolded, no one in authority at any level of government connected with the people of New Orleans: not the president, not the governor, not the mayor. By the time Mayor Ray Nagin ordered the city's evacuation, it was too late for many poor residents to leave. He sent people to the Superdome, advising them to eat before they went because the local government had made no provisions for them. Meanwhile, he held press conferences and complained that he wasn't getting any help. And the people most affected by the problems felt abandoned, forgotten, and betrayed.

After the worst of the tragedy was over, no matter what President Bush said or how much help he provided, he was unable to regain the people's confidence and trust. It's true that when democratic Mayor Nagin was reelected less than a year after the disaster, he thanked Bush for "delivering for the citizens of New Orleans." And Donna Brazile, another Democrat, has since described

Bush as "very much engaged" in the rebuilding process and praised him for prompting Congress to dedicate money to rebuilding the levees.[2] But by then Bush could not undo the image of indifference he had created. He had failed to connect with the people. He had broken the Law of Connection.

THE HEART COMES FIRST

When it comes to working with people, the heart comes before the head. That's true whether you are communicating to a stadium full of people, leading a team meeting, or trying to relate to your spouse. Think about how you react to people. If you listen to a speaker or teacher, do you want to hear a bunch of dry statistics or a load of facts? Or would you rather the speaker engaged you on a human level—maybe with a story or joke? If you've been on any kind of winning team in business, sports, or service, you know that the leader didn't simply give instructions and then send you on your way. No, he or she connected with you on an emotional level.

> *You can't move people to action unless you first move them with emotion. . . . The heart comes before the head.*

For leaders to be effective, they need to connect with people. Why? Because you first have to touch people's hearts before you ask them for a hand. That is the Law of Connection. All great leaders and communicators recognize this truth and act on it almost instinctively. You can't move people to action unless you first move them with emotion.

An outstanding orator and African American leader of the nineteenth century was Frederick Douglass. It's said that he had a remarkable ability to connect with people and move their hearts when he spoke. Historian Lerone Bennett said of Douglass, "He could make people *laugh* at a slave owner preaching the duties of Christian obedience; could make them *see* the humiliation of a Black maiden ravished by a brutal slave owner; could make them *hear* the sobs of a mother separated from her child. Through him, people could cry, curse, and *feel*; through him they could *live* slavery."

THE GREAT CONNECTOR

Good leaders work at connecting with others all of the time, whether they are communicating to an entire organization or working with a single individual. The stronger the relationship you form with followers, the greater the connection you forge—and the more likely those followers will be to want to help you.

I used to tell my staff, "People don't care how much you know until they know how much you care." They would groan because they heard me say it so much, but they recognized that it was true nonetheless. You develop credibility with people when you connect with them and show that you genuinely care and want to help them. And as a result, they usually respond in kind and want to help you.

> *The stronger the relationship and connection between individuals, the more likely the follower will want to help the leader.*

An excellent example of a leader who was able to connect with both audiences and individuals was President Ronald Reagan. His ability to develop rapport with an audience is reflected in the nickname he received as president: the Great Communicator. But he also had the ability to touch the hearts of the individuals close to him. He really could have been called the Great Connector.

Former Reagan speechwriter Peggy Noonan said that when Reagan used to return to the White House from long trips and the staff heard his helicopter landing on the lawn, everyone would stop working, and staff member Donna Elliott would say, "Daddy's home!" They couldn't wait to see him. Some employees dread it when their boss shows up. Reagan's people felt encouraged because he connected with them.

CONNECT WITH PEOPLE ONE AT A TIME

One key to connecting with others is recognizing that even in a group, you have to relate to people as individuals. General Norman Schwarzkopf remarked, "I have seen competent leaders who stood in front of a platoon and all they saw was a platoon. But great leaders stand in front of a platoon and see it as forty-four individuals, each of whom has aspirations, each of whom wants to live, each of whom wants to do good."[3]

I've had the opportunity to speak to some wonderful audiences during the course of my career. The largest have been in stadiums with more than sixty thousand people in attendance. Some of my colleagues who also speak for a living have asked me, "How in the world do you speak to that many people?" The secret is simple. I don't try to talk to the thousands. I focus on talking to one person. That's the only way to connect

> *To connect with people in a group, relate to them as individuals.*

with people. It's the same way when writing a book. I don't think of the millions of people who have read my books. I think of *you*. I believe that if I can connect with you as an individual, then what I have to offer might be able to help you. If I'm not connecting, you'll stop reading and go do something else.

How do you connect? Whether you're speaking in front of a large audience or chatting in the hallway with an individual, the guidelines are the same:

1. CONNECT WITH YOURSELF
You must know who you are and have confidence in yourself if you desire to connect with others. People don't heed the call of an uncertain trumpet. Be confident and be yourself. If you don't believe in who you are and where you want to lead, work on that before doing anything else.

2. COMMUNICATE WITH OPENNESS AND SINCERITY
People can smell a phony a mile away. Legendary NFL coach Bill Walsh observed, "Nothing is more effective than sincere, accurate praise, and nothing is more lame than a cookie-cutter compliment." Authentic leaders connect.

3. KNOW YOUR AUDIENCE

When you work with individuals, knowing your audience means learning people's names, finding out about their histories, asking about their dreams. When you communicate to an audience, you learn about the organization and its goals. You want to speak to what *they* care about, not just what you care about.

4. LIVE YOUR MESSAGE

Perhaps the most important thing you can do as a leader and communicator is to practice what you preach. That's where credibility comes from. Plenty of people out in the marketplace are willing to say one thing to an audience but do something else. They don't last.

5. GO TO WHERE THEY ARE

As a communicator, I dislike any kind of barrier to communication. I don't like to be too far from my audience or too high above them on a stage. And I definitely don't want any physical barriers between me and the people. But a person's *method* of communication can also be a barrier. Whether I'm speaking from a stage or sitting across from someone in my office, I try to speak the other person's language, to go to that person. I try to be attuned to others' culture, background, education, and so on. I adapt to others; I don't expect them to adapt to me.

6. FOCUS ON THEM, NOT YOURSELF

If you got on an elevator with me and asked me to tell you the secret to good communication before I got off at the next floor, I'd tell you to focus on others, not yourself. That is the number one problem of inexperienced speakers, and it is also the number one problem of ineffective leaders. You will always connect faster when your focus is not on yourself.

7. BELIEVE IN THEM

It's one thing to communicate to people because you believe you have something of value to say. It's another to communicate with people because you believe they have value. People's opinion of us has less to do with what they see in us than it does with what we can help them see in themselves.

8. OFFER DIRECTION AND HOPE

People expect leaders to help them get where they want to go. But good leaders do that and more. French general Napoleon Bonaparte said, "Leaders are dealers in hope." That is so true. When you give people hope, you give them a future.

IT'S THE LEADER'S JOB

Some leaders have problems with the Law of Connection because they believe that connecting is the responsibility of followers. That is especially true of positional leaders. They often think, *I'm the boss. I have the position. These are my employees. Let them come to me.* But successful leaders who obey the Law of Connection are always initiators. They take the first step with others and then make the effort to continue building relationships. That's not always easy, but it's important to the success of the organization. A leader has to do it, no matter how many obstacles there might be.

> *It's one thing to communicate to people because you believe you have something of value to say. It's another to communicate with people because you believe they have value.*

I learned this lesson in 1972 when I was faced with a very difficult situation. I was moving to Lancaster, Ohio, to accept the leadership of a church there. It was going to be a big step up in responsibility for me. Before I accepted the position, I learned that the church had just gone through a big battle related to a building project. Heading up one of the factions was the number one influencer in the church, a man named Jim. I also heard that Jim had a reputation for being negative and something of a maverick. He liked to use his influence to move the people in directions that didn't always help the organization.

Because the previous leader of the church had faced opposition from Jim more than a few times, I knew that I needed to win him over. Otherwise, I would always have conflict with him. If you want someone on your side, don't try to convince him—connect with him. That's what I was determined to do. So the first thing I did when I got to my new position was to make an appointment to meet Jim in my office.

I admit I was not looking forward to meeting Jim. He was a big man—six feet four inches tall and about 250 pounds. He was very intimidating. Further, he was sixty-five years old, and I was only twenty-five. The meeting had the potential to go ugly.

"Jim," I said as he sat in my office, "I know you're the influencer in this church, and I want you to know that I've decided I'm going to do everything in my power to build a good relationship with you. I'd like to meet with you every Tuesday for lunch at the Holiday Inn to talk through issues. While I'm the leader here, I'll never take any decision to the people without first discussing it with you. I really want to work with you.

"But I also want you to know that I've heard you're a very negative person," I continued, "and that you like to fight battles. If you decide to work against me, I guess we'll just have to be on opposite sides. And because you have so much influence, I know you'll win most of the time, at least in the beginning. But I'm going to develop relationships with people and draw new people to this church. This church will grow, and someday I'll have greater influence than you.

> *It's the leader's job to initiate connection with the people.*

"But I don't want to battle you," I confided. "You're sixty-five years old right now. Let's say you've got another ten to fifteen years of good health and productivity ahead of you. If you want, you can make these years your very best and make your life count.

"We can do a lot of great things together at this church," I summed up, "but the decision is yours."

When I finished, Jim didn't say a word. He got up from his seat, walked into the hall, and stopped to take a drink at the water fountain. I followed him out and waited. I didn't know whether he was going to dress me down, declare war, or tell me to take a hike.

After a long time, Jim stood up straight and turned around. When he did, I could see that tears were rolling down his cheeks. And then he gave me a great big bear hug and said, "You can count on me to be on your side."

And Jim did get on my side. As it turned out, he did live about another ten years, and because he was willing to help me, a young kid with a vision, we accomplished many positive things together. But it never would have happened if I hadn't had the courage to try to make a connection with him that first day in my office.

THE TOUGHER THE CHALLENGE,
THE GREATER THE CONNECTION

Never underestimate the power of making connections and building relationships with people before asking them to follow you. If you've ever studied the lives of notable military commanders, you have probably noticed that the best ones practiced the Law of Connection. I read that during World War I in France, General Douglas MacArthur told a battalion commander before a daring charge, "Major, when the signal comes to go over the top, I want you to go first, before your men. If you do, they'll follow." Then MacArthur removed the Distinguished Service Cross from his uniform and pinned it on the major. He had, in effect, awarded him for heroism before asking him to exhibit it. And of course, the major led his men, they followed him over the top, and they achieved their objective.

Not all military examples of the Law of Connection are quite so dramatic, but they are still effective. For example, it's said that Napoleon made it a practice to know every one of his officers by name and to remember where they lived and which battles they had fought with him. Robert E. Lee was known to visit the men at their campsites the night before any major battle. Often he met the next day's challenges without having slept. More recently, I read about how Norman Schwarzkopf connected with his troops during the first Persian Gulf War. On Christmas in 1990, he spent the day in the mess halls among the men and women who were so far away from their families. In his autobiography, he says,

> I shook hands with everyone in the line, went behind the serving counter to greet the cooks and helpers, and worked my way through the mess hall, hitting every table, wishing everyone Merry Christmas. Then I went into the second and third dining facilities and did the same thing. I came back to the first mess tent and repeated the exercise, because by this time there was an entirely new set of faces. Then I sat down with some of the troops and had my dinner. In the course of four hours, I must have shaken four thousand hands.[4]

Schwarzkopf was a general. He didn't have to do that, but he did. He used one of the most effective methods for connecting with others, something I call *walking slowly through the crowd*. It may sound corny, but it's really true: people don't care how much you know until they know how much you care. As a leader, find times to make yourself available to people. Learn their names. Tell them how much you appreciate them. Find out how they're doing. And most important, listen. Leaders who relate to their people and really connect with them are leaders that people will follow to the ends of the earth.

> It may sound corny, but it's really true: people don't care how much you know until they know how much you care.

THE RESULT OF CONNECTION

When a leader truly has done the work to connect with his people, you can see it in the way the organization functions. Employees exhibit loyalty and a strong work ethic. The vision of the leader becomes the aspiration of the people. The impact is incredible.

One of the companies I admire is Southwest Airlines. The company has been successful and profitable while other airlines have filed for bankruptcy and folded. The person responsible for the initial success of the organization and the creation of its culture is Herb Kelleher, the company's founder and current executive chairman of the board.

I love what Southwest's employees did on Boss's Day in 1994 because it shows the kind of connection Kelleher made with his people. They took out a full-page ad in *USA Today* and addressed the following message to Kelleher:

Thanks, Herb

For remembering every one of our names.

For supporting the Ronald McDonald House.

For helping load baggage on Thanksgiving.

For giving everyone a kiss (and we mean everyone).

For listening.

For running the only profitable major airline.

For singing at our holiday party.

For singing only once a year.

For letting us wear shorts and sneakers to work.

For golfing at The LUV Classic with only one club.

For outtalking Sam Donaldson.

For riding your Harley Davidson into Southwest Headquarters.

For being a friend, not just a boss.

Happy Boss's Day from Each One of Your 16,000 Employees.[5]

A display of affection like that occurs only when a leader has worked hard to connect with his people.

Don't ever underestimate the importance of building relational bridges between yourself and the people you lead. There's an old saying: To lead yourself, use your head; to lead others, use your heart. That's the nature of the Law of Connection. Always touch a person's heart before you ask him for a hand.

Applying
THE LAW OF CONNECTION
To Your Life

1. What does it really mean to "connect with yourself"? It means *knowing* and *liking* who you are. Start by measuring your level of self-awareness. Answer each of the following questions:

- How would I describe my personality?
- What is my greatest character strength?
- What is my greatest character weakness?
- What is my single greatest asset?
- What is my single greatest deficit?
- How well do I relate to others (1 to 10)?
- How well do I communicate with others (1 to 10)?
- How likable am I (1 to 10)?

Now ask three people who know you well to answer the same questions about you. Compare answers. If their answers are significantly different from yours, then you have a blind spot you need to rectify. Engage a mentor, growth and accountability partner, or counselor to help you become more self-aware and to help you value your strengths and deal positively with your weaknesses.

2. Learn to walk slowly through the crowd. When you are out among your employees or coworkers, make relationship building and connecting a priority. Before getting into work matters, make a connection. With people you don't yet know, that may take some time. With people you know well, still take a moment to connect relationally. It may cost you only

a few minutes a day, but it will pay huge dividends in the future. And it will make the workplace a more positive environment.

3. Good leaders are good communicators. On a scale of 1 to 10, how would you rate yourself as a public speaker? If you give yourself anything lower than an 8, you need to work on improving your skills. Read books on communication, take a class, or join Toastmasters. And sharpen your skills by practicing your teaching and communicating. If you don't have opportunities to do that on the job, then try volunteering.

11

❦

THE LAW OF
THE INNER CIRCLE

*A Leader's Potential Is Determined
by Those Closest to Him*

W hen we see any incredibly gifted person, it's always tempting to believe that talent alone made him successful. To think that is to buy into a lie. Nobody does anything great alone. Leaders do not succeed alone. A leader's potential is determined by those closest to him. What makes the difference is the leader's inner circle.

UNBELIEVABLE TALENT

Lance Armstrong is one of the most talented athletes on the planet. Because of his physical gifts, he has been called a freak of nature. His sport, cycling, is perhaps the most grueling. The Tour de France, which he has won an astounding seven times in a row, has been compared to running twenty marathons on twenty consecutive days. Racers cover approximately two thousand miles of often mountainous terrain in a three-week period. On peak race days, they consume as many as ten thousand calories to provide the energy they need.

Armstrong has become a legend as the conqueror of the Tour de France. Writer Michael Specter provides perspective on Armstrong's ability:

— 127 —

Three types of riders succeed in long stage races like the Tour de France: those who excel at climbing but are only adequate in time trials, in which a cyclist races alone against the clock; those who can win time trials but struggle in the mountains; and cyclists who are moderately good at both. Now there appears to be a fourth group: Armstrong. He has become the best climber in the world . . . And there is no cyclist better at time trials.[1]

Clearly, Armstrong is in a class that few others can approach. His determination is unquestionable. His training regimen is unmatched. His talent is extraordinary. Yet without a team, he would not have won a single Tour title.

UNBELIEVABLE TEAM

Cycling is truly a team sport, though it may not seem that way to the casual observer. During his Tour de France run, Armstrong had an incredible team. Anchoring the team were Chris Carmichael, his coach; and Johan Bruyneel, an ex-cyclist who functioned as the team's sports director and master tactician. Both men were indispensable, since Armstrong tended at first to follow his own less efficient training regimen and execute his own tactics, causing him to lose badly. But once those two inner circle members were in place, Armstrong began to maximize his gift.

Taking the team approach even further, Armstrong's sponsors and equipment suppliers—Trek, Nike, AMD, Bontrager, Shimano, and Oakley—were asked to work together as a group rather than merely contributing as individuals without knowing what the others were doing. It was revolutionary at the time and helped raise the entire team to a higher level. It is now standard practice in professional cycling.

And then, of course, there were the other cyclists who rode with him each year. In 2005, Armstrong's last year, they included José Azevedo of Portugal; Manuel Beltrán, Benjamin Noval, and José Luis Rubiera of Spain; Pavel Padrnos of the Czech Republic; Yaroslav Popovych of Ukraine; Paolo Savoldelli of Italy; and George Hincapie of the United States. "I wanted an experienced team for Lance's last Tour and that was the determining factor," explained Bruyneel.[2] Each person brought unique skills to the team.

"I think we have fielded our strongest team ever with this formation," said Armstrong. "It has many consistent elements from years past, like the Spanish armada for the climbs, strong guys like George, Pavel and Benjamin, the Giro winner in Savoldelli plus a guy like Popo (Popovych) with a very bright future. I look forward to leading this team and attempting to give the great folks at Discovery a yellow jersey."

"Lance is the first to say he would never have won the Tour de France without the help of his teammates," explains the Team Discovery Web site. "Every other rider sacrifices individual glory at the race in order to work for one rider, Lance, which says a lot considering what's at stake. Yet, over the years, Lance delivered every single time following the work of his team, so it goes hand in hand. If the team sacrificed itself and Lance didn't have what it took to come through in the end, we would have had to rethink the plan."[3]

Leaders have to deliver. There is no substitute for performance. But without a good team, they often don't get the opportunity. Their potential is determined by those closest to them. That is the Law of the Inner Circle.

WHY YOU AND I NEED A TEAM

In recent years, people in the business world have rediscovered the significance of teams. In the 1980s, the buzzword in business circles was management. Then in the 1990s, the emphasis was on leadership. Now in the twenty-first century, the emphasis is on team leadership. Why? Because nobody does everything well.

As I began teaching the laws of leadership years ago, I could tell that many people were daunted by the idea of 21 Laws. I understood their

> *"You can do what I cannot do. I can do what you cannot do. Together we can do great things."*
> —MOTHER TERESA

feelings. I am a great believer in making things as simple as possible. I've always contended that good communicators take something complicated and make it simple. I would have loved to compile fewer than 21 Laws of Leadership. But when I boil leadership down to its essence, I still see 21 things a leader must do well to lead effectively. However, at the same time I also recognize that *no single leader* can do all 21 things well. That's why every leader needs a team of people. As Mother Teresa observed, "You can do what I cannot do. I can do what you cannot do. Together we can do great things." That is the power of the Law of the Inner Circle.

> There are no Lone Ranger leaders. Think about it: if you're alone, you're not leading anybody, are you?

NO LEADER RIDES ALONE

Not everyone recognizes that those closest to you will make or break you. There are still leaders who hold up the Lone Ranger as their model for leadership. One of the best illustrations of how unrealistic that ideal of leadership really is can be found in *American Spirit* by Lawrence Miller:

> Problems are always solved in the same way. The Lone Ranger and his faithful Indian companion . . . come riding into town. The Lone Ranger, with his mask and mysterious identity, background, and lifestyle, never becomes intimate with those whom he will help. His power is partly in his mystique. Within ten minutes the Lone Ranger has understood the problem, identified who the bad guys are, and has set out to catch them. He quickly outwits the bad guys, draws his gun, and has them behind bars. And then there was always that wonderful scene at the end [where] the helpless victims are standing in front of their ranch or in the town square marveling at how wonderful it is now that they have been saved.[4]

What baloney! There are no Lone Ranger leaders. Think about it: if you're alone, you're not leading anybody, are you?

Leadership expert Warren Bennis was right when he maintained, "The leader finds greatness in the group, and he or she helps the members find it in themselves."[5] Think of any highly effective leader, and you will find someone who surrounded himself with a strong inner circle. My friend Joseph Fisher reminded me of that as he talked about the impact of evangelist Billy Graham. His success has come as the result of a fantastic inner circle: Ruth Bell Graham, Grady Wilson, Cliff Barrows, and George Beverly Shea. They made him better than he ever would have been alone. You can see it in business, ministry, sports, and even family relationships. Those closest to you determine your level of success.

WHO ARE YOU DRAWING INTO YOUR INNER CIRCLE?

Most people create an inner circle of people. However, they are usually not strategic in doing so. We naturally tend to surround ourselves with either people we like or people with whom we are comfortable. Few people give enough thought to how those closest to them impact their effectiveness or leadership potential. You see it all the time with certain athletes who tran-

Only if you reach your potential as a leader do your people have a chance to reach their potential.

sition to the professional ranks and entertainers who achieve success professionally. Some self-destruct and never reach their potential, and it can often be attributed to the kind of people they spend their time with.

To practice the Law of the Inner Circle, you must be intentional in your relationship building. You must give thought to the accomplishment of your mission and the success of the people who follow you. Only if you reach your potential as a leader do your people have a chance to reach their potential.

As you consider whether individuals should be in your inner circle, ask yourself the following questions. If you can answer yes to these questions, then they are excellent candidates for your inner circle:

1. DO THEY HAVE HIGH INFLUENCE WITH OTHERS?
One key to successful leadership is the ability to influence the people who

influence others. How do you do that? By drawing influencers into your inner circle. That was what I did with Jim at the church in Lancaster, Ohio, whom I wrote about in the Law of Connection. Jim was the single most influential person in the organization when I arrived. By building a relationship with Jim and taking him into my inner circle, I was doing two things. First, I was exerting my influence on him—sharing my values, vision, and philosophy of leadership with him. I wanted him to be a carrier of the vision to other people in the organization. Second, I was finding out what he thought. If he had questions or objections to what I wanted to do, I was able to find out about it immediately and work through it with him. And because he had so many years of experience with the people in the organization, he often helped me to navigate around potential landmines I knew nothing about.

2. Do They Bring a Complementary Gift to the Table?

Because of my leadership gifting, I naturally attract leaders. And I am also highly attracted to leaders. It's said of great baseball hitters that when they get together with other good hitters, all they talk about is hitting. It's similar with good leaders. When they get together, they share their experiences, ask each other questions, and test ideas. But one of the best things I have done in my leadership career is to bring a few key people into my inner circle who possess strengths in my areas of weakness.

One of those people is Linda Eggers, my assistant. I advise young executives that their first and most important hire should be their assistant. In Linda, I have an absolute gem! She has been working with me for twenty years. She has an incredible mind for details, she is tireless, and like "Radar" O'Reilly from *MASH*, she has the ability to anticipate what I need before I realize it. What's more, she now knows me so well that she can speak to others on my behalf, knowing how I would answer questions at least 90 percent of the time.

3. Do They Hold a Strategic Position in the Organization?

Some people belong in your inner circle because of their importance to the organization. If you and they are not working on the same page, the entire organization is in trouble. John Hull certainly fits that description in my life. The two organizations he leads for me, EQUIP and ISS, cannot function without his leadership. Some of the most significant and effective things I'm doing are being accomplished through EQUIP. The organization has already trained more than a million leaders around the globe and is gearing up to train even more.

If something were to happen at EQUIP that took it in the wrong direction, many things in my life would come to a grinding halt. That's why I have John, who is an outstanding leader, heading up the organization—and why he remains close to me in my inner circle.

4. Do They Add Value to Me and to the Organization?

I discussed in the Law of Addition how people add, subtract, multiply, or divide when it comes to others. The people in your inner circle must be adders or multipliers. They should have a proven track record as assets to the organization. There is a poem by Ella Wheeler Wilcox that my mother used to recite to me when I was growing up:

> There are two kinds of people on earth today,
> Just two kinds of people, no more, I say.
> Not the good and the bad, for 'tis well understood
> That the good are half-bad and the bad are half-good.
> No! The two kinds of people on earth I mean
> Are the people who lift and the people who lean.
> There are two kinds of people on earth to-day;
> Just two kinds of people, no more, I say.
> Not the sinner and saint, for it's well understood,
> The good are half bad, and the bad are half good . . .
> No; the two kinds of people on earth I mean,
> Are the people who lift, and the people who lean.

Look only for lifters for your inner circle.

Inner circle members should also add value to you personally. That's not selfish. If they have a negative effect, they will hinder your ability to lead well, and that can hurt your people and the organization.

Someone once told me, "It's lonely at the top, so you had better know why you're there." It's true that leaders carry heavy loads. When you're out front, you can be an easy target. That's why I say, "It's lonely at the top, so you'd better take someone with you." Who could be a better companion than someone who lifts you up, not as a yes-man but as a solid supporter and friend? Solomon of ancient Israel recognized this truth: "As iron sharpens iron, friends sharpen the minds of each other."[6] Seek for your inner circle people who help you improve.

> *It's lonely at the top, so you'd better take someone with you.*

5. DO THEY POSITIVELY IMPACT OTHER INNER CIRCLE MEMBERS?

I'm a big believer in team chemistry, and if your inner circle is going to work together and function as a team, then you need to take into account how members interact. First, you want them to have a good fit with one another. Just as members of a championship basketball team have complementary skills and compatible roles, you want each inner circle member to have a place in your life where he contributes without stepping on the others' toes.

Second, you want inner circle members to make one another better, to raise one another's game. Sometimes that comes because they encourage one another. Sometimes it happens when they help one another by sharing information and wisdom. And sometimes it comes from friendly competition. No matter how it happens, if they improve the ability of other team members, they also improve your leaders.

IDENTIFY . . . CULTIVATE . . . RECRUIT

There is one more question you need to ask about potential inner circle members. I did not list it as one of the five questions, because a yes in answer to the question does not automatically mean they should be in your inner circle. However, a no would definitely mean they should not. The question is this: do they display excellence, maturity, and good character in everything they do?

You will be able to answer that question only once you've gotten to know them fairly well, which means you will probably be selecting inner circle members from within your organization. In fact, in most cases you will also need to develop them before they are ready to take their place in that circle. As you look for people and work with them, take the advice of longtime executive and retired president, CEO, and chairman of Agilent Technologies, Ned Barnholt. He believes there are three kinds of people in an organization when it comes to leadership: (1) those who get it almost immediately and they're off and running with it; (2) those who are skeptical and not sure what to do with it; and (3) another third who start out negative and hope it will go away. "I used to spend most of my time with those who were the most negative," says Barnholt, "trying to convince them to change. Now I spend my time with the people in the first [group]. I'm investing in my best assets."

NEVER STOP IMPROVING YOUR INNER CIRCLE

I have to admit that I am blessed with an incredible inner circle, made up of family members, longtime employees, admired colleagues, and personal mentors. All of them add value to me and help me have an impact beyond what I can personally touch and do. I'm always on the lookout for people to come into this circle, because I've known since I was forty that you can go only so far on your own. Once you've reached your capacity in time and energy, the only way you can increase your impact is through others. Every person in my inner circle is a high performer and either extends my influence beyond my reach or helps me to grow and become a better leader.

Of course, no leader starts out with a strong inner circle. When leaders take on new positions, they often have to build their inner circle from scratch. That was the case for me in 1981 when I accepted the offer to lead Skyline Church in the San Diego, California, area. The church had a great history and nationally recognized reputation. It had been founded in the 1950s by Orval Butcher, a wonderful man, who was retiring after serving there for twenty-seven years. Dr. Butcher had touched the lives of thousands of people with his leadership. It was a good church, but it did have one problem. It had not grown in years.

One of the first things I did after taking the job was to meet with each staff member to assess individual abilities. Almost immediately I discovered why the church had flatlined. The staff members were good people, but they were not strong leaders. No matter what I did with them, they would never be able to take the organization to the place we needed to go. In a church of that size, the staff is the leader's inner circle. If the staff is strong, then the leader can make a huge impact. If the staff is weak, he can't. That is the Law of the Inner Circle.

> *A leader's potential is determined by the people closest to him.*

The task that lay ahead of me was clear. I needed to remove the weak leaders and bring in better ones. That was the only way I would be able to turn the situation around. Mentally, I divided the people into three groups according to their ability to lead and deliver results. The bottom third I dismissed right away and began replacing them with the best people I could find. Then I began working on the middle third and the top third. The organization immediately began growing. By the end of three years, all but two on the original staff had been replaced by better leaders. Because the inner circle had gone to a new level, the organization was able to go to a new level. Over the years, we tripled in size from 1,000 to more than 3,300 weekly attenders.

The growth and success we experienced at Skyline were due to the Law of the Inner Circle. When we had the right staff, our potential skyrocketed. And in 1995 when I left, other leaders from around the country sought to hire my key staff members for their organizations. They recognized the power of the Law of the Inner Circle and wanted to hire the very best they could find to boost their potential.

Lee Iacocca says that success comes not from what you know but from who you know and how you present yourself to each of those people. There is a lot of truth in that. If you want to increase your capacity and maximize your potential as a leader, your first step is always to become the best leader you can. The next is to surround yourself with the best leaders you can find. Never forget that a leader's potential is

> *Hire the best staff you can find, develop them as much as you can, and hand off everything you possibly can to them.*

determined by those closest to him. That's the Law of the Inner Circle. That's the only way you can reach the highest level possible.

Applying
THE LAW OF THE INNER CIRCLE
To Your Life

1. Do you know who your inner circle members are? They are the people you seek out for advice, turn to for support, and rely on to help you get things done. If you lead a small staff, all of those employees are also part of your inner circle.

List the names of your inner circle members. Next to each name write what that person contributes. If they do not have a clear role or function, then write what you believe they have the *potential* to contribute. Look for holes and duplications. Then begin looking for people to fill the holes and consider how you might eliminate redundancies. And be prepared to challenge current members with potential to rise to your expectations.

2. Great inner circles do not come together by accident. Effective leaders are continually developing current and future inner circle members. How do they do it?

- They spend extra time with them strategically to mentor them and to develop relationships.
- They give them extra responsibility and place higher expectations on them.
- They give them more credit when things go well and hold them accountable when they don't.

Examine your list of inner circle members to determine whether you are taking these steps with them. If not, make changes. In addition, be sure to use this development strategy with a pool of new potential inner circle members.

3. If you lead a larger staff, then not everyone who works for you will be part of your inner circle. When should you transition to a smaller inner circle, a sort of team within the team?

- When your immediate staff numbers more than seven
- When you can no longer directly lead everyone
- In the volunteer world, when others besides paid staff should be in the inner circle

If this describes your situation, then begin thinking in terms of creating a smaller inner circle group using the same development strategy listed above.

12

❦

THE LAW OF EMPOWERMENT

Only Secure Leaders Give Power to Others

N early everyone has heard of Henry Ford, the revolutionary automobile industry innovator and legend in American business history. In 1903, he cofounded the Ford Motor Company with the belief that the future of the automobile lay in putting it within the reach of the average American worker. Ford said,

> I will build a motorcar for the multitude. It will be large enough for the
> family but small enough for the individual to run and care for. It will be
> constructed of the best materials, by the best men to be hired, after the
> simplest designs that modern engineering can devise. But it will be so low
> in price that no man making a good salary will be unable to own one—
> and enjoy with his family the blessings of hours of pleasure in God's great
> open spaces.

Henry Ford carried out that vision with the Model T, and it changed the face of twentieth-century American life. By 1914, Ford was producing nearly 50 percent of all automobiles in the United States. The Ford Motor Company looked like an American success story.

A LESS-KNOWN CHAPTER OF THE STORY

However, all of Ford's story is not about positive achievement, and one reason is that he didn't embrace the Law of Empowerment. Henry Ford was so in love with his Model T that he never wanted to change or improve it—nor did he want anyone else to tinker with it. One day when a group of his designers surprised him by presenting him with the prototype of an improved model, Ford furiously ripped its doors off the hinges and proceeded to destroy the car with his bare hands.

For almost twenty years, the Ford Motor Company offered only one design, the Model T, which Henry Ford had personally developed. It wasn't until 1927 that he finally—grudgingly—agreed to offer a new car to the public. The company produced the Model A, but it was incredibly far behind its competitors in technical innovations. Despite its early head start and the incredible lead over its competitors, the Ford Motor Company's market share kept shrinking. By 1931, it was down to only 28 percent, a little more than half of what it produced seventeen years earlier.

Henry Ford was the antithesis of an empowering leader. He continually undermined his leaders and looked over the shoulders of his people. He even created a sociological department within Ford Motor Company to check up on his employees and direct their private lives. As time went by, he became more and more eccentric. He once went into his accounting office and tossed the company's books into the street, saying, "Just put all the money we take in in [sic] a big barrel and when a shipment of material comes in reach into the barrel and take out enough money to pay for it."

Perhaps Ford's most peculiar dealings were with his executives, especially his son Edsel. The younger Ford had worked at the company since he was a boy. As Henry became more eccentric, Edsel worked harder to keep the company going. If it weren't for Edsel, the Ford Motor Company probably would have gone out of business in the 1930s. Henry eventually gave Edsel the presidency of the company, but at the same time he undermined his son. Further, whenever a promising leader was rising up in the company, Henry tore him down. As a result, the company kept losing its best executives. The few who stayed did so because they figured that someday old Henry would die, and Edsel would finally take over and set things right. But that's not what happened. In 1943, Edsel died at age forty-nine.

ANOTHER HENRY FORD

Edsel's oldest son, the twenty-six-year-old Henry Ford II, quickly left the navy so that he could return to Dearborn, Michigan, and take over the company. At first, he faced opposition from his grandfather's entrenched followers. But within two years, he gathered the support of several key people, received the backing of the board of directors (his mother controlled 41 percent of Ford Motor Company's stock), and convinced his grandfather to step down so that he could become president in his place.

Young Henry was taking over a company that hadn't made a profit in fifteen years. At that time, it was losing one million dollars *a day*! The young president knew he was in over his head, so he set out to find leaders. Fortunately, the first group actually approached him. Colonel Charles "Tex" Thornton headed a team of ten men who had worked together at the War Department during World War II. Their contribution to Ford Motor Company was substantial. In the years to come, the group produced six company vice presidents and two presidents.

The second influx of leadership came with the entrance of Ernie Breech, an experienced General Motors executive and the former president of Bendix Aviation. Young Henry hired him to be Ford's executive vice president, a position second to Henry's, with the expectation that he would take command and turn the company around. He succeeded. Breech quickly brought in more than 150 outstanding executives from General Motors, and by 1949, Ford Motor Company was on a roll again. In that year, the company sold more than a million Fords, Mercurys, and Lincolns—the best sales since the Model A.

WHO'S THE BOSS?

If Henry Ford II had lived by the Law of Empowerment, the Ford Motor Company might have grown enough to eventually overtake General Motors and become the number one car company again. But only secure leaders are able to give power to others, and Henry felt threatened. The success of Tex Thornton, Ernie Breech, and Lewis Crusoe, a legendary GM executive whom Breech had brought into the company, made Henry worry about his own place at Ford. His position was based not on influence but on his name and his family's control of company stock.

> *"The best executive is the one who has sense enough to pick good men to do what he wants done, and self-restraint enough to keep from meddling with them while they do it."*
> —THEODORE ROOSEVELT

What was Henry's solution? He began pitting one top executive against another, first Thornton against Crusoe. Then after Thornton was fired, he turned Crusoe against Breech. Ford biographers Peter Collier and David Horowitz described the second Henry Ford's method this way:

Henry's instinct for survival manifested itself as craftiness combined with a kind of weakness. He had endowed Crusoe with the power to do virtually whatever he wished. By withdrawing his grace from Breech and bestowing it on his lieutenant, he had made antagonists of the two men most vital to Ford's success. While Henry had lost confidence in Breech, however, he had left him officially in charge because this increased his own maneuverability. And, as Crusoe's official superior, Breech could be useful if Henry wanted to keep Crusoe in check.[1]

This became a pattern in the leadership of Henry Ford II. Anytime an executive gained power and influence, Henry undercut the person's authority by moving him to a position with less clout, supporting the executive's subordinates, or publicly humiliating him. This maneuver continued all the days Henry II was at Ford. As one Ford president, Lee Iacocca, commented after leaving the company, "Henry Ford, as I would learn firsthand, had a nasty habit of getting rid of strong leaders."

Iacocca says that Henry Ford II once described his leadership philosophy to him, years before Iacocca himself became its target. Ford said, "If a guy works for you, don't let him get too comfortable. Don't let him get cozy or set in his ways. Always do the opposite of what he expects. Keep your people anxious and off-balance."[2]

WHAT DOES IT MEAN TO LEAD WELL?

Both Henry Fords failed to abide by the Law of Empowerment. Rather than identifying leaders; building them up; giving them resources, authority, and responsibility; and then turning them loose to achieve, they alternately encouraged and undermined their best people. Their insecurity made it impossible for them to give power to others. Ultimately, it undermined their personal leadership potential, created havoc in the lives of the people around them, and damaged their organization. If leaders want to be successful, they have to be willing to empower others. I like the way President Theodore Roosevelt stated it: "The best executive is the one who has sense enough to pick good men to do what he wants done, and the self-restraint enough to keep from meddling with them while they do it."

To lead others well, we must help them to reach their potential. That means being on their side, encouraging them, giving them power, and helping them to succeed. That's not traditionally what we're taught about leadership. What were the two leadership games we were taught as kids? King of the Hill and Follow the Leader. What was the object of King of the Hill? To knock other people down so that you can be the leader. And what's the point in Follow the Leader? You do things you *know* followers can't do to separate yourself from them and make yourself look more powerful. The problem with those games is that to win, you have to make all of the other people lose. The games are based on insecurity and are opposite of the way to raise up leaders.

When I travel to developing countries, I am made especially aware of how alien the idea of empowerment can be to emerging leaders. In cultures where you have to fight to make something of yourself, the assumption often is that you need to fight others to maintain your leadership. But that reflects a scarcity mind-set. The truth is that if you give some of your power away to others, there is still plenty to go around.

When I teach the Law of Empowerment in emerging countries, I usually ask a volunteer to come up so that I can show visually what happens when

> *Leading well is not about enriching yourself—it's about empowering others.*

a leader tries to keep others down instead of raising them up. I ask the volunteer to stand in front of me, and I put my hands on his shoulders. Then I begin pushing him down. The lower I want to push him, the more I have to bend down to do it. As I push him lower, I go lower. That's the same way it is in leadership: to keep others down, you have to go down with them. And when you do that, you lose any power to lift others up.

BARRIERS TO EMPOWERMENT

Leading well is not about enriching yourself—it's about empowering others. Leadership analysts Lynne McFarland, Larry Senn, and John Childress say that the "empowerment leadership model shifts away from 'position power' to 'people power,' within which all people are given leadership roles so they can contribute to their fullest capacity."[3] Only empowered people can reach their potential. When a leader can't or won't empower others, he creates barriers within the organization that followers cannot overcome. If the barriers remain long enough, then the people give up and stop trying, or they go away to another organization where they can maximize their potential.

When leaders fail to empower others, it is usually due to three main reasons:

THE #1 BARRIER TO EMPOWERMENT: DESIRE FOR JOB SECURITY
The number one enemy of empowerment is the fear of losing what we

have. Weak leaders worry that if they help subordinates, they themselves will become dispensable. But the truth is that the only way to make yourself *indispensable* is to make yourself *dispensable*. In other words, if you are able to continually empower others and help them develop so that they become capable of taking over your job, you will become so valuable to the organization that you become indispensable. That's a paradox of the Law of Empowerment.

What if I work myself out of a job by empowering others, you may ask, *and my superiors don't recognize my contribution?* That can happen in the short term. But if you keep raising up leaders and empowering them, you will develop a pattern of achievement, excellence, and leadership that will be recognized and rewarded. If the teams you lead always seem to succeed, people will figure out that you are leading them well.

> *The number one enemy of empowerment is the fear of losing what we have.*

THE #2 BARRIER TO EMPOWERMENT: RESISTANCE TO CHANGE

Nobel Prize–winning author John Steinbeck asserted, "It is the nature of man as he grows older to protest against change, particularly change for the better." By its very nature, empowerment brings constant change because it encourages people to grow and innovate. Change is the price of progress. That's not always easy to live with.

Most people don't like change. That's a fact. Yet one of the most important responsibilities of leaders is to continually improve their organizations. As a leader, you must train yourself to embrace change, to desire it, to make a way for it. Effective leaders are not only willing to change; they become change agents.

THE #3 BARRIER TO EMPOWERMENT: LACK OF SELF-WORTH

John Peers observed, "You can't lead a cavalry charge if you think you look funny on a horse." Self-conscious people are rarely good leaders. They focus on themselves, worrying how they look, what others think, whether they are liked. They can't give power to others because they feel that they have no power themselves. And you can't give what you don't have.

The best leaders have a strong sense of self-worth. They believe in themselves, their mission, and their people. As author Buck Rogers says, "To those who have confidence in themselves, change is a stimulus because they believe one person can make a difference and influence what goes on around them. These people are the doers and motivators." They are also the empowerers.

Only secure leaders are able to give themselves away. Mark Twain once remarked that great things happen when you don't care who gets the credit. But I believe you can take that a step further. I believe the greatest things happen *only* when you give others the credit. One-time vice presidential candidate Admiral James B. Stockdale declared, "Leadership must be based on goodwill . . . It means obvious and wholehearted commitment to helping followers . . . What we need for leaders are men of heart who are so

> "Great leaders gain authority by giving it away."
> —JAMES B. STOCKDALE

helpful that they, in effect, do away with the need of their jobs. But leaders like that are never out of a job, never out of followers. Strange as it sounds, great leaders gain authority by giving it away." If you aspire to be a great leader, you must live by the Law of Empowerment.

THE PRESIDENT OF EMPOWERMENT

One of the greatest leaders of the United States was known for his humility and willingness to give his power and authority to others: Abraham Lincoln. The depth of his security as a leader can be seen in the selection of his cabinet. Most presidents pick like-minded allies. But not Lincoln. At a time of turmoil for the country when factions were strong, Lincoln brought together a group of leaders who would bring strength through diversity and mutual challenge. One Lincoln biographer said this of his method:

For a President to select a political rival for a cabinet post was not unprecedented; but deliberately to surround himself with all of his disappointed antagonists seemed to be courting disaster. It was a mark of his sincere intentions that Lincoln wanted the advice of men as strong as himself or stronger. That he entertained no fear of being crushed or overridden by such men revealed either surpassing naïveté or a tranquil confidence in his powers of leadership.[4]

Lincoln's desire to unify the country was more important than his personal comfort. His strength and self-confidence allowed him to practice the Law of Empowerment and bring strong leaders into his circle.

FINDING STRONG LEADERS TO EMPOWER

Lincoln displayed the ability to empower others again and again. That played a major role in his relationships with his generals during the Civil War. In the beginning, he had trouble finding worthy recipients of his confidence. When the Southern states seceded, the finest generals in the land went south to serve the Confederacy. But Lincoln never lost hope, nor did he neglect to give his leaders power and freedom, even when that strategy had failed with previous generals.

For example, in June of 1863, Lincoln put the command of the Army of the Potomac into the hands of General George G. Meade. Lincoln hoped that he would do a better job than had preceding generals Ambrose E. Burnside and Joseph Hooker. Within hours of Meade's appointment, Lincoln sent a courier to him. The president's message, in part, said,

> Considering the circumstances, no one ever received a more important command; and I cannot doubt that you will fully justify the confidence which the government has reposed in you. You will not be hampered by any minute instructions from these headquarters. Your army is free to act as you may deem proper under the circumstances as they arise . . . All forces within the sphere of your operations will be held subject to your orders.[5]

As it turned out, Meade's first significant challenge came as he commanded the army at a small Pennsylvania town named Gettysburg. It was

> To push people down, you
> have to go down with them.

a test he passed with authority. In the end, though, Meade was not the general who would make full use of the power Lincoln offered. It took Ulysses S. Grant to turn the war around. But Meade stopped Lee's army when it counted, and he prevented the Confederate general from moving on Washington.

Lincoln's use of the Law of Empowerment was as consistent as Henry Ford's habit of breaking it. When his generals performed well, Lincoln gave them the credit; when they performed poorly, Lincoln took the blame. Lincoln expert Donald T. Phillips acknowledged, "Throughout the war Lincoln continued to accept public responsibility for battles lost or opportunities missed."[6] Lincoln was able to stand strongly during the war and continually give power to others because of his rock-solid security.

THE POWER OF EMPOWERMENT

You don't have to be a leader of Lincoln's caliber to empower others. The main ingredient for empowering others is a high belief in people. If you believe in others, they will believe in themselves.

When I receive an encouraging note from someone close to me, I tuck it away and save it. I cherish such things. Years ago, I received a note from Dan Reiland, the one person outside my family whom I have probably worked hardest to empower over the years. Dan was my executive pastor when I was at Skyline. Here is what Dan wrote:

John,

The ultimate in mentoring has come to pass. I am being asked to teach on the topic of empowerment! I can do this only because you first empowered me. The day is still crystal clear in my mind when you took a risk and chose me as your executive pastor. You trusted me with significant responsibility, the day to day leadership of the staff and ministries of your church. You released me with authority . . . You believed in me—perhaps more than I believed in myself. You demonstrated your faith and confidence in me in such a way that I could tap into your belief, and eventually it became my own . . .

I am so very grateful for your life-changing impact on my life. Saying thank you hardly touches it. "I love and appreciate you" is better. Perhaps the best way I can show my gratitude is to pass on the gift you have given me to other leaders in my life.

Dan

I am grateful to Dan for all he has done for me, and I believe he has returned to me much more than I have given to him. And I've genuinely enjoyed the time I've spent with Dan helping him grow.

The truth is that empowerment is powerful—not only for the person being developed but also for the mentor. Enlarging others makes you larger. Dan has made me better than I am, not just because he helped me achieve much more than I could have done on my own, but also

> *Enlarging others makes you larger.*

because the whole process made me a better leader. That is the impact of the Law of Empowerment. It is an impact you can experience as a leader as long as you are willing to believe in people and give your power away.

Applying
THE LAW OF EMPOWERMENT
To Your Life

1. How would you characterize yourself in the area of self-worth? Are you confident? Do you believe you have value? Do you operate from an assumption that you have positive things to offer other people and your organization? Are you willing to take risks?

If you rate yourself low in the area of security, you will have a hard time with the Law of Empowerment. You will need to take positive steps to add value to yourself or explore why your self-worth is so low.

2. Are you someone who believes in people? Make a list of the people who work for you. If there are too many to list, then write the names of those closest to you. Next rate each person's potential—not current ability—on a scale of 1 to 10.

If the numbers are low, then your belief in people is probably not very high. Until you change that, you will have difficulty empowering others. Begin dwelling on people's positive qualities and characteristics. Look for people's greatest strengths and envision how they could leverage those strengths to achieve significant things. Imagine what individuals could become if they made the most of their gifts and opportunities. Then help them to do so.

3. If your natural inclination is to build and hold on to your power, then you must experience a paradigm shift to become an empowering leader. Start by selecting your best people and setting them up for success. Train them, give them resources, and then help them set accomplishable goals that will help you and the organization. Then give them the responsibility

and authority to follow through. And if they at first fail, help them keep trying until they succeed. Once you experience the joy and organizational effectiveness of empowering others, you will have a hard time *not* giving your power away.

13

THE LAW OF THE PICTURE

People Do What People See

S everal years ago, filmmaker Steven Spielberg and actor Tom Hanks produced a series of television shows on HBO called *Band of Brothers*, based on the book of the same name by historian Stephen Ambrose. The ten episodes chronicled the story of Easy Company, a group of paratroopers from the 101st Airborne who fought during World War II. The men of Easy Company were as tough as soldiers get, and they fought heroically from the invasion of Normandy to the end of the war.

The story of Easy Company is a great study in leadership, for the various sergeants, lieutenants, and captains who commanded the men displayed many styles of leadership, both good and bad. When the leadership was good, it made the difference, not only in the way the soldiers performed but in the outcome of their battles and, ultimately, of the war.

THE WRONG PICTURE

From the very first episode of the television series, the contrasting leadership styles were on display. Herbert Sobel, Easy Company's commanding officer during its training, was shown to be a brutal and autocratic leader with a sadistic streak. He drove the men harder than the commander of any other company. He arbitrarily revoked passes and inflicted punishment. But judging from Ambrose's research, Sobel was even worse than he was depicted in the series.

Sobel drove the men mercilessly, which was fine, since he was preparing them for combat. But he didn't push himself the same way, being barely capable of passing the physical test required of paratroopers. Nor did he display the high level of competence he demanded from everyone else. Ambrose writes about an incident during training that was representative of Sobel's leadership:

> On one night exercise he [Sobel] decided to teach his men a lesson. He and Sergeant Evans went sneaking through the company position to steal rifles from sleeping men. The mission was successful; by daylight Sobel and Evans had nearly fifty rifles. With great fanfare, Evans called the company together and Sobel began to tell the men what miserable soldiers they were.[1]

What Sobel didn't realize was that the men he was berating weren't his own. He had wandered into the wrong camp and stolen the rifles belonging to Fox Company. Sobel didn't even realize his mistake until the commander of Fox Company came up with forty-five of his men.

The men who served under Sobel mocked him and undermined him. By the time Easy Company began preparations for the invasion of Normandy, many men were taking bets on which of them would shoot Sobel when they finally got into combat. Fortunately, Sobel was removed from his position as company commander and reassigned before they went into combat.

ANOTHER BAD PICTURE

Another officer's highly incompetent leadership was depicted in an episode called "The Breaking Point." It recounted the Battle of the Bulge when the soldiers were preparing to take the town of Foy from the Germans. By then, the men of Easy Company were experienced veterans, and they were facing one of the most difficult times of the war. They suffered from bitter cold and from merciless shelling by German artillery.

During that time, an Easy Company platoon was commanded by Lieutenant Dike, a leader with political connections but no previous combat experience. Dike's method of leadership was to avoid his men, refuse to make a decision, and disappear for long periods of time to "take a walk," including when he was needed most. Not one of the men respected him. And when Dike was finally required to lead his men into an assault on the town, he failed miserably and was relieved of command.

A DIFFERENT KIND OF PICTURE

Fortunately, most of Easy Company's leaders were excellent, and one in particular was awarded the Distinguished Service Cross and was considered by the men to be "the best combat leader in World War II."[2] That person was Dick Winters. He started out as a platoon leader in Easy Company during their training and was promoted to company commander after Normandy and then to battalion executive officer. He finished his military career with the rank of major.

Time after time, Winters helped his men to perform at the highest level. And he always led from in front, setting the example and taking the risks along with his men. Ambrose describes Winters's philosophy of leadership simply as "officers go first."[3] Whenever his troops needed to assault an enemy position, Winters was in front leading the charge.

One of the most remarkable incidents demonstrating Winters's way of leading by example occurred soon after D-Day on the road to Carentan, a town that Easy Company needed to take from the Germans. As the American paratroopers under his command approached the town, they became pinned down by German machine-gun fire. Huddled in ditches on either side of the road, they wouldn't move forward when ordered to. Yet if they didn't move, they would eventually be cut to pieces. Winters tried rallying them. He coaxed them. He kicked them. He ran from one ditch to the other as machine-gun bullets flew by. Finally, he jumped into the middle of the road, bullets glancing off the ground near him, and shouted at the men to get moving. Everyone got up and moved forward as one. And they helped to take the town.

More than thirty-five years later, Floyd Talbert, a sergeant at the time, wrote to Winters to comment about the incident: "I'll never forget seeing you in the middle of that road. You were my total inspiration. All my boys felt the same way."[4] In 2006, Winters summed up his approach to leadership, saying, "I may not have been the best combat commander, but I always strove to be. My men depended on me to carefully analyze every tactical situation, to maximize the resources that I had at my disposal, to think under pressure, and then to lead them by personal example."[5]

When Ambrose was asked what allowed Easy Company to distinguish itself during the war, to "rise above" its peers, Ambrose was clear in his response: "They weren't all that much better than other paratroopers, or the Rangers, or the Marines. They were one of many elite units in the war. But what made them special, even among those who were already self-selected and special, was their leadership . . . The great COs, platoon leaders, and sergeants—not all elite units had such luck in their leaders, and that's the difference."[6] Why did that make such a difference? Because people do what people see. That is the Law of the Picture. When the leaders show the way with the right actions, their followers copy them and succeed.

> *Great leaders always seem to embody two seemingly disparate qualities. They are both highly visionary and highly practical.*

MAKING THE PICTURE COME ALIVE

Great leaders always seem to embody two seemingly disparate qualities. They are both highly *visionary* and highly *practical.* Their vision enables them to see beyond the immediate. They can envision what's coming and what must be done. Leaders possess an understanding of how:

Mission provides *purpose*—answering the question, *Why?*
Vision provides a *picture*—answering the question, *What?*
Strategy provides a *plan*—answering the question, *How?*

As author Hans Finzel observed, "Leaders are paid to be dreamers. The higher you go in leadership, the more your work is about the future."

At the same time, leaders are practical enough to know that vision without action achieves nothing. They make themselves responsible for helping their followers to take action. That can be difficult because followers often cannot envision the future as the leader does. They can't picture what's best for the team. They lose track of the big picture. Why? Because vision has a tendency to leak.

Leaders are stewards of the vision. So what should they do to bridge the vision gap between them and their

> *The leader's effective modeling of the vision makes the picture come alive!*

followers? The temptation for many leaders is to merely communicate about the vision. Don't get me wrong: communication is certainly important. Good leaders must communicate the vision clearly, creatively, and continually. The leader's effective *communication* of the vision makes the picture clear. But that is not enough. The leader must also live the vision. The leader's effective *modeling* of the vision makes the picture come alive!

Good leaders are always conscious of the fact that they are setting the example and others are going to do what they do, for better or worse. In general, the better the leaders' actions, the better their people's.

That's not to say that leaders have all the answers. Anyone who has led anything knows that. The leaders who make the greatest impact are often those who lead well in the midst of uncertainty. Andy Stanley, an excellent leader and communicator, has addressed this issue. A few years ago at the Catalyst conference for leaders, he said,

Uncertainty is not an indication of poor leadership. Rather it indicates a need for leadership. The nature of leadership demands that there always be an element of uncertainty. The temptation is to think, *If I were a good leader, I would know exactly what to do.* Increased responsibility means dealing with more and more intangibles and therefore more complex uncertainty. Leaders can afford to be uncertain, but we cannot afford to be unclear. People will not follow fuzzy leadership.

When times are tough, uncertainty is high, and chaos threatens to overwhelm everyone, followers need a clear picture from their leaders the most. That's when they need a leader who embraces the Law of the Picture. The living picture they see in their leader produces energy, passion, and motivation to keep going.

MODELING INSIGHTS FOR LEADERS

If you desire to be the best leader you can become, you must not neglect the Law of the Picture. As you strive to improve as an example to your followers, remember these things:

1. FOLLOWERS ARE ALWAYS WATCHING WHAT YOU DO

If you are a parent, you have probably already realized that your children are always watching what you do. Say anything you want, but your children learn more from what they see than from anywhere else. As parents, Margaret and I realized this early. No matter what we taught our children, they insisted on behaving like us. How frustrating. Legendary UCLA basketball coach John Wooden quotes a poem that explains it perfectly:

No written word
　　nor spoken plea
Can teach our youth
　　what they should be

Nor all the books
　　on all the shelves

It's what the teachers
are themselves.[7]

Just as children watch their parents and emulate their behavior, so do employees watching their bosses. If the bosses come in late, then employees feel that they can, too. If the bosses cut corners, employees cut corners. People do what people see.

Followers may doubt what their leaders say, but they usually believe what they do. And they imitate it. Former U.S. Army general and secretary of state Colin Powell observed,

> *Followers may doubt what their leaders say, but they usually believe what they do.*

"You can issue all the memos and give all the motivational speeches you want, but if the rest of the people in your organization don't see you putting forth your very best effort every single day, they won't either."

Whitley David asserted, "A good supervisor is a catalyst, not a drill sergeant. He creates an atmosphere where intelligent people are willing to follow him. He doesn't command; he convinces." Nothing is more convincing than living out what you say you believe.

2. It's Easier to Teach What's Right Than to Do What's Right

Writer Mark Twain quipped, "To do what is right is wonderful. To teach what is right is even more wonderful—and much easier." Isn't that the truth? It's always easier to teach what's right than it is to do it. That's one of the reasons why many parents (and bosses) say, "Do as I say, not as I do."

One of my earliest challenges as a leader was to raise my living to the level of my teaching. I can still remember the day that I decided that I would not teach anything I did not try to live out. That was a tough decision, but as a young leader, I was learning to embrace the Law of the Picture. Author Norman Vincent Peale stated, "Nothing is more confusing than people who give good advice but set a bad example." I would say a related thought is also true: nothing is more *convincing* than people who give good advice and set a good example.

Recently, I received calls on the same day from two reporters—one from the *Chicago Tribune* and the other from *USA Today*—about teaching ethics in the business arena. Both asked similar questions. They wanted to know if ethics could be taught. My answer was yes.

"But many of the companies that teach ethics classes had ethics problems," one reporter pushed back.

"That's because ethics can be instilled in others only if it is taught *and modeled* for them," I replied. Too many leaders are like bad travel agents. They send people places they have never been. Instead, they should be more like tour guides, taking people places they have gone and sharing the wisdom of their own experiences.

> *"Leaders tell but never teach until they practice what they preach."*
> —FEATHERSTONE

John Wooden used to say to his players, "*Show* me what you can do; don't *tell* me what you can do." I believe followers have the same attitude toward their leaders. They want to *see* their leaders in action, doing their best, showing the way, and setting the example. Featherstone remarked, "Leaders tell but never teach until they practice what they preach." That is the Law of the Picture.

3. WE SHOULD WORK ON CHANGING OURSELVES BEFORE TRYING TO IMPROVE OTHERS

Leaders are responsible for the performance of their people. The buck stops with them. They accordingly monitor their people's progress, give them direction, and hold them accountable. And to improve the performance of the team, leaders must act as change agents. However, a great danger to good leadership is the temptation to try to change others without first making changes to yourself.

As a leader, the first person I need to lead is me. The first person that I should try to change is me. My standards of excellence should be higher for myself than those I set for others. To remain a credible leader, I must always work first, hardest, and longest on changing myself. This is neither easy nor natural, but it is essential. In all honesty, I am a lot like Lucy in the *Peanuts* comic strip who tells Charlie Brown that she wants to change the world. When an overwhelmed Charlie Brown asks where she would start, her response is, "I would start with you, Charlie Brown. I would start with you."

Not long ago, I was teaching on the idea of the 360-degree leader. That is, a leader exerts his influence not just down with those he leads but also up with his boss and across with his colleagues. During a Q&A session, an attendee asked, "Which is the most difficult—leading up, across, or down?"

"None of the above," I answered quickly. "Leading myself is the toughest."

To lead any way other than by example, we send a fuzzy picture of leadership to others. If we work on improving ourselves first and make that our primary mission, then others are more likely to follow.

4. THE MOST VALUABLE GIFT A LEADER CAN GIVE IS BEING A GOOD EXAMPLE

A survey conducted by Opinion Research Corporation for Ajilon Finance asked American workers to select the one trait that was most important for a person to lead them. Here are the results:

RANK	CHARACTERISTIC	PERCENTAGE
1	Leading by example	26%
2	Strong ethics or morals	19%
3	Knowledge of the business	17%
4	Fairness	14%
5	Overall intelligence and competence	13%
6	Recognition of employees	10%[8]

More than anything else, employees want leaders whose beliefs and actions line up. They want good models who lead from the front.

Leadership is more caught than taught. How does one "catch" leadership? By watching good leaders in action! The majority of leaders emerge because of the impact made on them by established leaders who modeled leadership and mentored them.

When I think about my leadership journey, I feel that I have been fortunate to have had excellent leadership models from whom I have "caught" various aspects of leadership:

- I caught perseverance by watching my father face and overcome adversity.
- I caught intensity by observing Bill Hybels's passionate leadership.
- I caught encouragement by looking at how Ken Blanchard valued people.
- I caught vision by seeing Bill Bright make his vision become reality.

I continue to learn from good models, and I strive to set the right example for the people who follow me—my children and grandchildren, the employees in my companies, and the people who attend my conferences and read my books. Living what I teach is the most important thing I do as a leader. As Nobel Peace Prize–winner Albert Schweitzer observed, "Example is leadership."

FOLLOWING THEIR LEADER'S EXAMPLE

A story that illustrates the Law of the Picture is that of King David of ancient Israel. Just about everyone has heard the story of David and Goliath. When the armies of the Philistines faced off against King Saul and the people of Israel, Goliath, a large, powerful professional warrior, laid out a challenge. He said he'd fight Israel's greatest champion in a winner-take-all battle. And who stepped forward to accept the challenge? Not Saul, the mighty king, or any of his seasoned veterans. It was David, a lowly shepherd boy, who stood to face him. Using a sling, he hurled a rock at Goliath and knocked him out. Then he cut Goliath's head off with the warrior's own sword.

We all identify with a story like that because we like to cheer for the underdog. But many people don't know the rest of the story. David grew up to be a warrior and eventually became king. Along the way, he raised up a group of warriors who were called his "mighty men." No fewer than five of them also became giant killers, just like their leader. The example set by David taught his followers how to become great warriors and even giant killers.

LEADERSHIP IN THE FACE OF TERROR

Leadership by example always has a powerful impact on followers. One of the leaders I admire is Rudy Giuliani, former mayor of New York City. During his career, first as an attorney working for the U.S. government and then later as an elected official, Giuliani led by example. He says in his book *Leadership* that he is very aware that what he does sets the tone for those who follow him.[9] "You cannot ask those who work for you to do something you're unwilling to do yourself," he states. "It is up to you to set a standard of behavior."[10]

Central to Giuliani's philosophy of leadership is the idea of accountability. Giuliani writes,

More than anyone else, leaders should welcome being held accountable. Nothing builds confidence in a leader more than a willingness to take responsibility for what happens during his watch. One might add that nothing builds a stronger case for holding employees to a high standard than a boss who holds himself to even higher ones. This is true in any organization.[11]

Accountability was the basis of one of Giuliani's regular practices: the morning meeting he convened with his top staff every day at eight o'clock. He had done it since 1981. It put him and his people on the same page every day. They had to give him answers—and he was forced to make quick decisions. Nobody could hide. Everyone was accountable.

Many people acknowledged Giuliani's ability as a mayor. Under his watch, crime in the city fell dramatically, New York returned to its former glory as a tourist destination, taxes decreased, and business thrived. But the event that really revealed Giuliani's leadership ability was, of course, 9/11. When the unthinkable occurred and the city was in chaos, the mayor was on the front lines, leading, keeping in close contact with state and federal leaders, and directing the various phases of city government.

And when the worst part of the crisis was behind them, Giuliani was also leading by example. Not only was he an advocate of his city, opening the theaters, encouraging people to live their lives as close to normal as possible, and asking visitors to come to New York—but he also grieved with those who had lost loved ones. He estimates that in the wake of the terrorist attacks, there were six to twenty funerals every day. He made sure to attend at least six every day and to be sure that a representative from city government was in attendance at every service.

Giuliani's example of leadership, strength, and resilience inspired the nation. In many ways, people all over the Unites States learned how to conduct themselves in a post-9/11 world by watching Rudolph Giuliani's modeling. He was not going to let terrorists determine the way he would live. And that's what good leaders always do: they set the example.

Giuliani sums up his leadership this way:

> All my life, I have been thinking about how to be a leader—whether it was when I was running the Corruption Unit of the U.S. Attorney's office in the Southern District of New York, then the Narcotics Unit, or turning around a bankrupt Kentucky coal company after being appointed as receiver, or watching Ronald Reagan, Judge MacMahon, and others. I realized later that much of what I was doing in studying these people so closely was preparing. Unconsciously, I was learning how to run things.[12]

In other words, he has simply done what he had seen his leaders do throughout his career. He has practiced the Law of the Picture.

Applying
THE LAW OF THE PICTURE
To Your Life

1. If you are already practicing the Law of Process, then you are currently working to sharpen your skills to increase your leadership ability. (If you're not, get started!) But there is more to leadership than just technical skills. Character is also vital to leadership, and that is communicated through the Law of the Picture. The primary example you set for your followers comes in the area of character, and that is the area you need to address first before trying to change others.

Give yourself a character audit. First, make a list of your core values, such as integrity, hard work, honesty, and so on. Then, think about your actions of the last month. What incidents, if any, stand out as inconsistent with those values? List as many things as you can recall. Don't dismiss anything too quickly, and don't rationalize any of them. These items will show you where you need to work on yourself. Work on changing not only your actions but also your attitude.

2. Ask a trusted colleague or friend to watch you for an extended period of time (at *least* a week) to compare what you teach with how you conduct yourself. Ask him or her to record any inconsistencies. Then plan to meet at the end of the observation period to review the results. At that meeting, you may ask questions for clarification, but you are not allowed to defend yourself. Plan to change either your actions or your philosophy to make them consistent with one another.

3. What are the three to five things you wish your people did better than they currently do now? List them. Now, grade *your performance* for

each. (You may want to ask someone else to grade you as well to make sure your perception of yourself is accurate.) If your self-scores are low, then you need to change your behavior. If your scores are high, then you need to make your example more visible to your people. Adjust accordingly.

14
❧

THE LAW OF BUY-IN

People Buy into the Leader, Then the Vision

In the fall of 1997, a few members of my staff and I had the opportunity to travel to India and teach four leadership conferences, something we've done many more times in the last decade. India is an amazing country, full of contradictions. It's a place of beauty, with warm and generous people. It has a strong emerging economy. Yet at the same time millions and millions of its inhabitants live in the worst poverty imaginable. It was there that I was reminded of the Law of Buy-In.

I'll never forget when our plane landed in Delhi. Exiting the airport, I felt as if we had been transported to another planet. There were crowds everywhere. People on bicycles, in cars, on camels and elephants. People on the streets, some sleeping right on the sidewalks. Animals roamed free, no matter where we were. And everything was in motion. As we drove along the main street toward our hotel, I also noticed something else. Banners. Wherever we looked, we could see banners celebrating India's fifty years of liberty, along with huge pictures of one man: Mahatma Gandhi.

OBSCURE BEGINNINGS

Today, people take for granted that Gandhi was a great leader. But the story of his leadership is a marvelous study in the Law of Buy-In. Mohandas K.

Gandhi, called Mahatma (which means "great soul"), was educated in London. After finishing his education in law, he traveled back to India and then to South Africa. There he worked for twenty years as a barrister and political activist. And in that time he developed as a leader, fighting for the rights of Indians and other minorities who were oppressed and discriminated against by South Africa's apartheid government.

By the time he returned to India in 1914, Gandhi was very well-known and highly respected among his countrymen. Over the next several years, as he led protests and strikes around the country, people rallied to him and looked to him more and more for leadership. In 1920—a mere six years after returning to India—he was elected president of the All India Home Rule League.

The most remarkable thing about Gandhi isn't that he became a leader in India, but that he was able to change the people's vision for obtaining

> *The leader finds the dream and then the people. The people find the leader and then the dream.*

freedom. Before he began leading them, the people used violence in an effort to achieve their goals. For years riots against the British establishment had been common. But Gandhi's vision for change in India was based on nonviolent civil disobedience. He once said, "Nonviolence is the greatest force at the disposal of mankind. It is mightier than the mightiest weapon of destruction devised by the ingenuity of man."

A NEW APPROACH

Gandhi challenged the people to meet oppression with peaceful disobedience and noncooperation. Even when the British military massacred more than one thousand people at Amritsar in 1919, Gandhi called the people to stand—without fighting back. Rallying everyone to his way of thinking wasn't easy. But because the people had come to buy into him as their leader, they embraced his vision. And then they followed him faithfully. He asked them not to fight, and eventually, they stopped fighting. When he called for everyone to burn foreign-made clothes and start wearing nothing but homespun material, millions of people started doing it. When he decided that a March to the Sea to protest the Salt Act would be their rallying point for civil disobedience against the British, the nation's leaders followed him the two hundred miles to the city of Dandi, where government representatives arrested them.

Their struggle for independence was slow and painful, but Gandhi's leadership was strong enough to deliver on the promise of his vision. In 1947, India gained home rule. Because the people had bought into Gandhi, they accepted his vision. And once they had embraced the vision, they were able to carry it out. That's how the Law of Buy-In works. The leader finds the dream and then the people. The people find the leader and then the dream.

DON'T PUT THE CART FIRST

When I teach leadership seminars, I field a lot of questions about vision. Invariably, someone will come up to me during a break, give me a brief description of an evolving vision, and ask me, "Do you think my people will buy into my vision?"

My response is always the same: "First tell me this. Do your people buy into you?"

You see, many people who approach the area of vision in leadership have it all backward. They believe that if the cause is good enough, people will automatically buy into it and follow. But that's not how leadership really works. People don't at first follow worthy causes. They follow worthy leaders who promote causes they can believe in. People buy into the leader first, then the leader's vision. Having an understanding of that changes your whole approach to leading people.

People don't at first follow worthy causes. They follow worthy leaders who promote causes they can believe in.

For the person who attends one of my conferences and asks whether his people will follow, the question really becomes, "Have I given my people

a

reasons to buy into me?" If the answer is yes, they will gladly buy that leader's vision. But if the leader has not built credibility with his people, it really doesn't matter how great the vision is.

During the dot-com boom, I read an article in *Business Week* that profiled entrepreneurs who partnered with venture capitalists in the computer industry. At that time, Silicon Valley in California was full of people who worked in the computer industry for a short time and then tried to start their own companies. Every day hundreds of them were buzzing around trying to find investors so that they could get their ideas and enterprises off the ground. Most never found backing. But whenever an entrepreneur succeeded once, she found it pretty easy to find money the next time around. Many times, the investors weren't even interested in finding out what the entrepreneur's vision was. If they'd bought into the person, then they readily accepted the ideas.

The writer of the article interviewed software entrepreneur Judith Estrin and her partner. At that time, they had founded two companies. She said that funding her first company took six months and countless presentations, even though she had a viable idea and believed in it 100 percent. But the start-up of her second company happened almost overnight. It took only two phone calls that lasted mere minutes for her to land five million dollars in backing. When the word got out that she was starting her second company, people were dying to give her even more money. She said, "We had venture capitalists calling us and begging us to take their money."[1]

> *Every message that people receive is filtered through the messenger who delivers it.*

Why had everything changed so drastically for her? Because of the Law of Buy-In. People had bought into her, so they were ready to buy into whatever vision she offered, sight unseen.

YOU ARE THE MESSAGE

Every message that people receive is filtered through the messenger who delivers it. If you consider the messenger to be credible, then you believe the message has value. That's one reason that actors and athletes are hired as promoters of products. People buy Nike shoes because they have bought into Michael Jordan, Tiger Woods, or Michael Vick, not necessarily because of the quality of the shoes.

The same is true when actors promote causes. Have the actors being employed suddenly become experts in the cause they're promoting? Usually

> *People want to go along with people they get along with.*

not. But that doesn't matter. People want to listen to them because they believe in them as people or because they have credibility as performers. Once people have bought into someone, they are willing to give the person's vision a chance. People want to go along with people they get along with.

IT'S NOT AN EITHER/OR PROPOSITION

You cannot separate leaders from the causes they promote. It cannot be done, no matter how hard you try. It's not an either/or proposition. The two always go together. Take a look at the following table. It shows how people react to leaders and their vision under different circumstances:

LEADER	+	VISION	=	RESULT
Don't buy in		Don't buy in		Get another leader
Don't buy in		Buy in		Get another leader
Buy in		Don't buy in		Get another vision
Buy in		Buy in		Get behind the leader

WHEN FOLLOWERS DON'T LIKE THE LEADER OR THE VISION . . . THEY LOOK FOR ANOTHER LEADER

The only time people will follow a leader they don't like with a vision they don't believe in is when the leader has some kind of leverage. That could be something as sinister as the threat of physical violence or as basic as the ability to withhold a paycheck. If the followers have a choice in the matter, they don't follow. And even if they don't have much of a choice, they start looking for another leader to follow. This is a no-win situation for everyone involved.

When Followers Don't Like the Leader but They Do Like the Vision . . . They Look for Another Leader

You may be surprised by this. Even though people may think a cause is good, if they don't like the leader, they will go out and find another one. That's one reason that coaches change teams so often in professional sports. The vision for any team always stays the same: everyone wants to win a championship. But the players don't always believe in their leader. And when they don't, what happens? The owners don't fire all of the players. They fire the leader and bring in someone they hope the players will buy into. The talent level of most professional coaches is similar. The effectiveness of their systems isn't much different. What often separate them are their leadership abilities and their level of credibility with players.

When Followers Like the Leader but Not the Vision . . . They Change the Vision

When followers don't agree with their leader's vision, they react in many ways. Sometimes they work to convince their leader to change the vision. Sometimes they abandon their point of view and adopt their leader's. Other times they find a compromise. But as long as they still buy into the leader, they rarely out-and-out reject him. They will keep following.

An excellent example occurred in Great Britain. Tony Blair had a long tenure in office as prime minister. He was a popular leader, elected to serve three times. Yet at the same time, the majority of people in Great Britain were against Blair's policy of involving the nation in the war with Iraq. Why did Blair remain in office so long? Because they had bought into him as a leader. As a result, they were willing to live with their philosophical difference with him.

THE LAW OF BUY-IN

WHEN FOLLOWERS LIKE THE LEADER AND THE VISION . . . THEY
GET BEHIND BOTH

When people believe in their leader and the vision, they will follow their leader no matter how bad conditions get or how much the odds are stacked against them. That's why the Indian people in Gandhi's day refused to fight back as soldiers mowed them down. That's what inspired the U.S. space program to fulfill John F. Kennedy's vision and put a man on the moon. That's the reason people continued to have hope and keep alive the dream of Martin Luther King Jr., even after he was gunned down. That's what continues to inspire followers to keep running the race, even when they feel they've hit the wall and given everything they've got.

As a leader, having a great vision and a worthy cause is not enough to get people to follow you. You have to become a better leader; you must get your people to buy into you. That is the price you have to pay if you want your vision to have a chance of becoming a reality. You cannot ignore the Law of Buy-In and remain successful as a leader.

BUYING TIME FOR PEOPLE TO BUY IN

If in the past you tried to get people to act on your vision but were unable to make it happen, you probably came up against the Law of Buy-In—maybe without even knowing it. I first recognized the importance of the Law of Buy-In in 1972 when I accepted my second leadership position. In the chapter on the Law of Navigation, I mentioned that after I had been at that church several years, I took them through a multimillion-dollar construction program in which we built a new auditorium. But when I first got there, that was not the direction that the people had wanted to go. The week before I arrived at my new church, more than 65 percent of the members had voted in favor of building a new community activity center.

Now, I had done some homework on that church, and I knew coming in that its future growth and success depended not on a new activity center but on a new auditorium. My vision for the years ahead was absolutely clear to me. But I couldn't walk in and say, "Forget the decision you just made and all the agonizing you did to make it. Follow me instead." I needed to buy some time to build my credibility with the people.

So I developed a strategy. I arranged for a committee to make a thorough study of all the issues involved with the activity center project. I told the members, "If we're going to invest this kind of time and money, we have to be sure about it. I must have information on every possible issue related to it." That seemed fair enough to everyone, and off the committee went to work.

For the next year, the group came back to me every month or so and reported on the information they gathered. And each time I'd praise their work and ask several questions that would prompt them to do more research.

BUY-IN IS NOT ABOUT THE LEADER

As the leader, I had the responsibility to make sure the organization didn't make an expensive mistake that would hurt it in the future. Delaying the decision helped me buy enough time for them to buy into me. Mean-

As a leader, your success is measured by your ability to actually take the people where they need to go. But you can do that only if the people first buy into you.

while, I worked hard to build my credibility with the people. I forged relationships with the leaders in the church. I answered everybody's questions so that they could understand me and how I thought as a leader. I shared my ideas, hopes, and dreams for the work we were doing. And I started to produce growth in the organization. That, more than anything else, gave the people confidence in me and my leadership ability.

After about six months, the people started to see that the church was changing and beginning to move in a new direction. In a year, the building committee decided that the activity center was not in the church's best interest, and they recommended that we not build it. In another year, the people reached consensus: the key to the future was the building of a new auditorium. And when the time came, 98 percent of the people voted yes on the issue, and off we went.

When I arrived at that church, I could have tried to push my vision and agenda on the people. That's probably what I would have done in my first leadership position because I was inexperienced and didn't understand that belief in the leader was as important as belief in the vision. But by then I had matured a little. I knew my vision was the right thing to do when I arrived in 1972, just as sure as I was two years later when we implemented it. But if I had tried to sell my vision instead of selling myself, I wouldn't have succeeded in helping those people get where they needed to go. And in the process I would have undermined my ability to lead them.

As a leader, you don't earn any points for failing in a noble cause. You don't get credit for being "right" as you bring the organization to a halt. Your success is measured by your ability to actually take the people where they need to go. But you can do that only if the people first buy into you as a leader. That's the reality of the Law of Buy-In.

Applying
THE LAW OF BUY-IN
To Your Life

1. Do you have a vision for your leadership and your organization? Why do you lead? What are you trying to accomplish? Write your thoughts in a vision statement. Is that vision worthy of your time and effort? Is it something you're willing to give a significant portion of your life to? (If not, rethink what you are doing and why.)

2. What is the level of buy-in for the people you lead? If your team is small, list all of its members. If it is large, list the key players who influence the team. Now rate each person's buy-in on a scale of 1 to 10. (A 1 means they won't even follow you in areas where they are required to according to their job description. A 10 means they would follow you into battle even in the face of death.) If your people don't buy into you, they will not help you execute your vision—even if they love it. They will find a new leader to lead them.

3. Think about ways you can earn credibility with individuals. There are many ways you can do that:

- By developing a good relationship with them
- By being honest and authentic and developing trust
- By holding yourself to high standards and setting a good example
- By giving them the tools to do their job better
- By helping them to achieve their personal goals
- By developing them as leaders

Develop a strategy with each person. If you make it your primary goal to add value to all of them, your credibility factor will rise rapidly.

15
❧

THE LAW OF VICTORY

Leaders Find a Way for the Team to Win

Have you ever thought about what separates the leaders who achieve victory from those who suffer defeat? What does it take to make a team a winner? It's hard to identify the quality that separates winners from losers. Every leadership situation is different. Every crisis has its own challenges. But I think that victorious leaders have one thing in common: they share an unwillingness to accept defeat. The alternative to winning is totally unacceptable to them. As a result, they figure out what must be done to achieve victory.

THIS WAS HIS FINEST HOUR

Crisis seems to bring out the best—and the worst—in leaders because at such times the pressure is intense and the stakes are high. That was certainly true during World War II when Adolf Hitler was threatening to crush Europe and remake it according to his vision. But against the power of Hitler and his Nazi hordes stood a leader determined to win, a practitioner of the Law of Victory: Winston Churchill, the British prime minister. He inspired the British people to resist Hitler and ultimately win the war.

Long before he became prime minister in 1940, Churchill spoke out against the Nazis. He seemed like the lone critic in 1932 when he warned,

> ❧
>
> *Victorious leaders possess an unwillingness to accept defeat. The alternative to winning is totally unacceptable to them.*

"Do not delude yourselves . . . Do not believe that all Germany is asking for is equal status . . . They are looking for weapons and when they have them believe me they will ask for the return of lost territories or colonies." As a leader, Churchill could see what was coming, and he was trying to prepare the people of England for what he saw as an inevitable fight.

In successive years, Churchill continued to speak out against the Nazis. And when Hitler annexed Austria in 1938, Churchill said to members of the House of Commons:

> For five years I have talked to the House on these matters—not with very great success. I have watched this famous island descending incontinently, fecklessly, the stairway which leads to a dark gulf . . . Now is the time at last to rouse the nation. Perhaps it is the last time it can be roused with a chance of preventing war, or with a chance of coming through with victory should our effort to prevent war fail.[1]

Unfortunately, Prime Minister Neville Chamberlain and the other leaders of Great Britain did not make a stand against Hitler. They were not prepared to do what it took to achieve victory. And more of Europe fell to the Nazis.

By mid-1940, most of Europe was under Germany's thumb. But then something happened that probably changed the course of history for the free world. The leadership of England fell to the sixty-five-year-old Winston Churchill, a courageous leader who had practiced the Law of Victory throughout his life. He refused to buckle under the Nazis' threats. For more than a year, Great Britain stood alone facing the threat of German invasion. When Hitler indicated that he wanted to make a deal with England,

Churchill defied him. When Germany began bombing England, the British stood strong. And all the while, Churchill looked for a way to gain victory.

CHURCHILL WOULD ACCEPT NOTHING LESS

Time after time, Churchill rallied the British people. It began with his first speech after becoming prime minister:

> We have before us an ordeal of the most grievous kind. We have before us many, many long months of struggle and of suffering. You ask, what is our policy? I can say: It is to wage war, by sea, land and air, with all our might and with all the strength that God can give us; to wage war against a monstrous tyranny, never surpassed in the dark, lamentable catalogue of human crime. That is our policy. You ask, what is our aim? I can answer in one word: Victory—victory at all costs, victory in spite of all terror, victory, however long and hard the road may be; for without victory, there is no survival.[2]

Meanwhile, Churchill did everything in his power to prevail. He deployed troops in the Mediterranean against Mussolini's forces. Although he hated communism, he allied himself with Stalin and the Soviets, sending them aid even when Great Britain's supplies were threatened and its survival hung in the balance. And he developed his personal relationship with another powerful leader: Franklin Roosevelt. Though the president of the United States was reluctant to enter the war, Churchill worked to build a relationship with him, hoping to change it from one of friendship and mutual

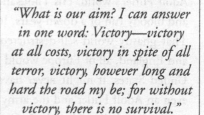

"What is our aim? I can answer in one word: Victory—victory at all costs, victory in spite of all terror, victory, however long and hard the road my be; for without victory, there is no survival."
—WINSTON CHURCHILL

respect to a full-fledged war alliance. In time his efforts paid off. On the day the Japanese bombed Pearl Harbor, ushering the United States into the war, Churchill is said to have remarked to himself, "So we have won after all."

ANOTHER LEADER DEDICATED TO VICTORY

When Churchill sought the aid of Franklin Roosevelt, he was enlisting a leader who had practiced the Law of Victory for decades. It was a hallmark of Roosevelt's entire life. He had found a way to achieve political victory while winning over polio. When he was elected president and became responsible for pulling the American people out of the Great Depression, it was just another impossible situation that he learned how to fight through. And fight he did. Through the 1930s, the country was slowly recovering due in large part to his leadership.

The stakes during the war were undoubtedly high. Pulitzer Prize–winning historian Arthur Schlesinger Jr. noted, "The Second World War found democracy fighting for its life. By 1941, there were only a dozen or so democratic states left on earth. But great leadership emerged in time to rally the democratic cause." The team of Roosevelt and Churchill provided that leadership like a one-two punch. Just as the prime minister had rallied England, the president brought together the American people and united them in a common cause as no one ever had before or has since.

To Churchill and Roosevelt, victory was the only option. If they had accepted anything less, the world would be a very different place today. Schlesinger stated, "Take a look at our present world. It is manifestly not Adolf Hitler's world. His Thousand-Year Reich turned out to have a brief and bloody run of a dozen years. It is manifestly not Joseph Stalin's world. That ghastly world self-destructed before our eyes."[3] Without Churchill and England, all of Europe would have fallen. Without Roosevelt and the United States, it might never have been reclaimed for freedom. But not even an Adolf Hitler and the army of the Third Reich could stand against two leaders dedicated to the Law of Victory.

GREAT LEADERS FIND A WAY TO WIN

When the pressure is on, great leaders are at their best. Whatever is inside them comes to the surface. In 1994, Nelson Mandela became president of

South Africa following that country's first full elections at the end of its apartheid government. It was a huge victory for the people of that country, and it was a long time coming.

The road to that victory was paved with twenty-seven years of Mandela's life spent in prison. Along the way, he did whatever it took to bring victory one step closer. He

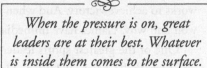

When the pressure is on, great leaders are at their best. Whatever is inside them comes to the surface.

joined the African National Congress, which became an outlawed organization. He staged peaceful protests. He went underground and traveled overseas to try to enlist support. When he needed to, he stood trial and accepted a prison sentence, with dignity and courage. And when the time was right, he negotiated changes in the government with F. W. de Klerk. Mandela describes himself as "an ordinary man who had become a leader because of extraordinary circumstances."[4] I say he is a leader made extraordinary because of the strength of his character and his dedication to victory for his people. Mandela found a way to win, and that's what leaders do for their people.

YOU CAN SEE IT EVERY DAY

The best leaders feel compelled to rise to a challenge and do everything in their power to achieve victory for their people. In their view . . .

  Leadership is responsible.
  Losing is unacceptable.
  Passion is unquenchable.
  Creativity is essential.
  Quitting is unthinkable.
  Commitment is unquestionable.
  Victory is inevitable.

With that mind-set, they embrace the vision and approach the challenges with the resolve to take their people to victory.

We can often see the Law of Victory in action at sporting events. In other areas of life, leaders do most of their work behind the scenes, and you never get to see it. But at a ball game, you can actually watch a leader as he works to achieve victory. And when the game ends, you know exactly who won and why. Games have immediate and measurable outcomes.

One of the greatest sports leaders when it came to the Law of Victory was basketball's Michael Jordan. He was an awesome athlete, but he was also an exceptional leader. He lived and breathed the Law of Victory every day that he played. When the game was on the line, Jordan found a way for the team to win. His biographer, Mitchell Krugel, says that Jordan's tenacity and passion for victory were evident in every part of his life. He even showed both in practice when his team, the Chicago Bulls, would scrimmage. Krugel explains:

> At Bulls' practices, the starters were known as the white team. The second five wore red. [Former Bulls' coach] Loughery had Jordan playing with the white team from his first day. With Jordan and [teammate] Woolridge, the white team easily rolled up leads of 8–1 or 7–4 in games to 11. The loser of these games always had to run extra wind sprints after practice. It was about that time of the scrimmage that Loughery would switch Jordan to the red team. And the red team would wind up winning more often than not.[5]

Jordan showed the same kind of tenacity every time he took the court. Early in his career, Jordan relied heavily on his personal talent and efforts to win games. But as he matured, he turned his attention more to being a leader and making the whole team play better. Jordan thinks that many people have overlooked that. He once said, "That's what everybody looks at when I miss a game. Can they win without me? . . . Why doesn't anybody ask why or what it is I contribute that makes a difference? I bet nobody would ever say they miss my leadership or my ability to make my teammates better." Yet that is exactly what he provides. Leaders always find a way for the team to win.

Finding a way to help their team win has been the mark of many outstanding basketball players of the past. A player such as Boston center Bill Russell measured his play by whether it helped the whole team play better. And the result was a remarkable eleven NBA titles. Lakers guard Magic Johnson, who was named NBA Most Valuable Player (MVP) three times and won five championships, was an outstanding scorer, but his greatest contribution was his ability to run the team and get the ball into the hands of his teammates. And Larry Bird, who made things happen for the Celtics in the 1980s, showed that he was a team leader not only as a player (he was named Rookie of the Year, became the MVP three times, and led his team to three NBA championships) but also as a coach. In his first year as head coach of the Indiana Pacers, he was named NBA Coach of the Year after leading his team to a 58–24 record, the best winning percentage in the franchise's history.

Good leaders find a way for their teams to win. That's the Law of Victory. Their particular sport is irrelevant. Michael Jordan, Magic Johnson, and Larry Bird did it in the NBA. John Elway and Joe Montana did it in the NFL. (Elway led his team to more fourth-quarter victories than any other quarterback in NFL history.) Pelé did it in soccer, winning an unprecedented three World Cups for Brazil. Leaders find a way for the team to succeed.

THREE COMPONENTS OF VICTORY

Whether it's a sports team, an army, a business, or a nonprofit organization, victory is possible as long as you have three components that contribute to a team's dedication to victory.

1. UNITY OF VISION
Teams succeed only when the players have a unified vision, no matter how much talent or potential there is. A team doesn't win the championship if its players are working from different agendas. That's true in professional sports. That's true in business. That's true in nonprofits.

I learned this lesson in high school when I was a junior on the varsity basketball team. We had a very talented group of kids, and many people had picked us to win the state championship. But we had a problem. The juniors and seniors on the team refused to work together. It got so bad that the coach eventually gave up trying to get us to play together and divided us into two different squads for our games: one comprised of seniors, the other comprised of juniors. In the end the team had miserable results. Why? We didn't share a common vision. People played for their fellow classmen, not the team.

2. DIVERSITY OF SKILLS

It almost goes without saying that a team needs diversity in skills. Can you imagine a whole hockey team of goalies? Or a football team of quarterbacks? How about a business where there are only salespeople or nothing but accountants? Or a nonprofit organization with just fund-raisers? Or only strategists? It doesn't make sense. Every organization requires diverse talents to succeed.

> *A team doesn't win the championship if its players are working from different agendas.*

Some leaders have blind spots in this area. In fact, I used to be one of them. I'm embarrassed to say there was a time in my life when I thought that if people would just be more like me, they would be successful. I'm wiser now and understand that every person has something to contribute. We're all like parts of the human body. For that body to do its best, it needs all of its parts, each doing its own job.

I recognize how each person on my team contributes using his or her unique skills, and I express my appreciation for them. The newer you are to leadership and the stronger your natural leadership ability, the more likely you will be to overlook the importance of others on the team. Don't fall into that trap.

3. A LEADER DEDICATED TO VICTORY AND RAISING PLAYERS TO THEIR POTENTIAL

It's true that having good players with diverse skills is important. As former Notre Dame head football coach Lou Holtz says, "You've got to have great athletes to win, I don't care who the coach is. You can't win without good athletes, but you can lose with them. This is where coaching makes the difference." In other words, you also require leadership to achieve victory.

Unity of vision doesn't happen spontaneously. The right players with the proper diversity of talent don't come together on their own. It takes a leader to make those things happen. It takes a leader to provide the motivation, empowerment, and direction required to win.

THE LAW OF VICTORY IS HIS BUSINESS

One of the most noteworthy success stories I've come across is that of Southwest Airlines and Herb Kelleher, whom I mentioned in the chapter on the Law of Connection. The company's story is an admirable example of the Law of Victory in action. Today Southwest looks like a powerhouse that has everything going for it. In the routes where it flies, it dominates the market. The company is on a steady growth curve, and its stock performs extremely well. It is the only U.S. airline that has earned a profit every year since 1973—even as other airlines have gone bankrupt and disappeared. It is the only airline that has thrived in the wake of 9/11.

"You've got to have great athletes to win, I don't care who the coach is. You can't win without good athletes, but you can lose with them. This is where coaching makes the difference."
—LOU HOLTZ

Employees love working there. Turnover is extremely low, and the company is considered to have the most productive workforce in the industry. And it's extremely popular with customers; Southwest gets consistently superior customer service ratings. It has maintained the fewest overall customer service complaints in the industry since 1987.[6]

Given Southwest's current position, you might think it has always been a powerhouse. That's not the case. In fact, it's a testament to the Law of Victory that the company even exists today. The airline was begun in 1967 by Rollin King, owner of a small commuter air service in Texas; John

Parker, a banker; and Herb Kelleher, an attorney. But it took them four years to get their first plane off the ground. As soon as the company incorporated, Braniff, Trans Texas, and Continental Airlines all tried to put it out of business. And they almost succeeded. One court battle followed another, and one man, more than any other, made the fight his own: Herb Kelleher. When their start-up capital was gone and they seemed to be defeated, the board wanted to give up. However, Kelleher said, "Let's go one more round with them. I will continue to represent the company in court, and I'll postpone any legal fees and pay every cent of the court costs out of my own pocket." Finally when their case made it to the Texas Supreme Court, the trio won, and they were at last able to put their planes in the air.

Once it got going, Southwest hired experienced airline leader Lamar Muse as its new CEO. He, in turn, hired the best executives available. And as other airlines kept trying to put them out of business, Kelleher and Muse kept fighting—in court and in the marketplace. When they had trouble filling their planes going to and from Houston, Southwest began flying into Houston's Hobby Airport, which was more accessible to commuters because of its proximity to downtown. When all the major carriers moved to the newly created Dallas–Fort Worth Airport, Southwest kept flying into convenient Love Field. When the airline had to sell one of its four planes to survive, the executives figured out a way for their remaining planes to be on the ground no longer than an amazingly short ten minutes between flights. That way Southwest could maintain routes and schedules. And when they couldn't figure out any other way to fill their planes, they pioneered peak and off-peak pricing, giving leisure travelers a huge break in the cost of fares.

Through it all, Kelleher kept fighting and helped keep Southwest alive. In 1978, seven years after he helped put the company's first small fleet of planes into the air, he became chairman of the company. In 1982, he was made president and CEO. Today he serves as executive chairman of the board. He and his colleagues continue to fight and find ways for the company to win. And look at the success:

SOUTHWEST AIRLINES YESTERDAY AND TODAY

	1971[7]	2006[8]
Size of fleet	4	468
Employees at year-end	195	30,000+
Customers carried	108,000	88.4 million
Cities served	3	51
Average trips flown daily	17	3,100+
Stockholders' equity	$3.3 million	$6.68 billion[9]
Total assets	$22 million	$14.2 billion

Southwest's President Colleen Barrett sums it up: "The warrior mentality, the very fight to survive is truly what created our culture."[10] What Kelleher, Barrett, and the rest of the Southwest leadership team have is not just a will to survive but a will to win. Leaders who practice the Law of Victory believe that anything less than success is unacceptable. And they have no Plan B. That is why they keep fighting. And it's why they continue to win!

What is your level of expectation when it comes to succeeding for your organization? How dedicated are you to winning your "game"? Are you going to have the Law of Victory in your corner as you fight? Or when

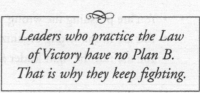

Leaders who practice the Law of Victory have no Plan B. That is why they keep fighting.

times get difficult, are you going to throw in the towel? Your answer to that question may determine whether you succeed or fail as a leader and whether your team wins or loses.

Applying
THE LAW OF VICTORY
To Your Life

1. The first step in practicing the Law of Victory is taking responsibility for the success of the team, department, or organization you lead. It must become personal. Your commitment must be higher than that of your team members. Your passion should be high. Your dedication must be unquestioned.

Do you currently demonstrate that kind of commitment? If not, you need to examine yourself to determine if it is in you. If you search yourself and are unable to convince yourself to bring that kind of commitment, then one of three things is probably true:

- You are pursuing the wrong vision.
- You are in the wrong organization.
- You are not the right leader for the job.

You will have to make adjustments accordingly.

2. If you are dedicated to leading your team to victory, you will be able to achieve it only if you have the right people on the team. Think about all the skills necessary to achieve your goals. Write them down. Now compare that list with the names of the people on your team. If there are functions or tasks for which no one on the team is suited, you need to add members to the team or train the ones you have.

3. The other crucial component for leading your team to victory is unity of vision. Do a little informal research to find out what's important to your team members. Ask them what they want to achieve personally.

And ask them to describe the purpose or mission of the team, department, or organization. If you get a diversity of answers, you need to work on communicating a single vision clearly, creatively, and continually until everyone is on the same page. You should also work with each team member to show how personal goals can align with the team's overall goals.

16

THE LAW OF THE BIG MO

Momentum Is a Leader's Best Friend

I f you've got all the passion, tools, and people you need to fulfill a great vision, yet you can't seem to get your organization moving and going in the right direction, you're dead in the water as a leader. If you can't get things going, you will not succeed. What do you need in such circumstances? You need to look to the Law of the Big Mo and harness the power of the leader's best friend: momentum.

STARTING FROM SCRATCH

If ever there was a person with talent and vision, it was Ed Catmull. As a boy, Catmull had grown up wanting to become an animator and filmmaker. But when he went to college, he had a realization: he wasn't good enough. He promptly changed his focus to physics and computer science, earning a bachelor's degree in each during the next four years. After working for Boeing for a few years, he decided on graduate school and enrolled in a new field within computer science—computer graphics. There he discovered that he could draw with the aid of a computer. It rekindled his dream to make movies. Even before he earned his PhD in 1974, Catmull was developing innovative software and looking for opportunities to make computer-generated movies.

In 1979, filmmaker George Lucas hired Catmull to run the computer graphics division of Lucasfilm Ltd. For the next seven years Catmull hired some of the best technicians in the country and attracted other talent, such as John Lasseter, who had once worked at Disney. Catmull's group broke new ground technologically and produced some incredible work, such as the "Genesis" sequence in *Star Trek II: The Wrath of Khan*. However, the division was very expensive to keep running. Catmull tried to convince Lucas to let him try to make computer-generated feature films, but the technology was still in its early stages and too expensive. Instead, Lucas decided to sell the division. In 1986 Steve Jobs bought it, paying five million dollars for it and putting an additional five million dollars into the company. He named it Pixar.

BABY STEPS

While it was struggling to become profitable, Pixar began making short films to demonstrate the power of its technology. The first was called *Luxo Jr.* It shows two animated desk lamps interacting as a parent and child would. Typically in those days after showing any kind of film demonstrating computer animation, filmmakers were asked a bunch of technical questions by industry experts who watched the film—about the algorithms they wrote or the software they used. Catmull and Lasseter knew they had made a significant step forward when one of the first questions asked was whether the "parent" lamp was the mother or the father. That's when they knew they had connected with their audience and succeeded in telling a story, not just showing off new technology. Lasseter says,

> We had absolutely no money, no computers, no people, no time to do the fancy flying camera moves that you were seeing and all the glitzy tracing and all that stuff—we just had no time. We just locked the camera down and had no background, but it made the audience focus on what was important in the film—the story and the characters. So for the first time, this film was entertaining people because it was made with computer animation.[1]

Luxo Jr. was so good that it was nominated for an Academy Award. But Catmull and his team were still a long way from achieving his dream of creating a full-length feature film. The company's greatest challenge at that time was merely surviving. Pixar continued to develop technology. The company also gained recognition and received awards, including its first Oscar in 1989. To help make ends meet, the team started to make computer-animated commercials. (You may remember a commercial with a Listerine bottle boxing. That was Pixar's work.) But it was difficult for Pixar to gain significant momentum. The firm was moving forward, but only very slowly.

FINALLY, SOME CREDIBILITY

Then in 1991, because of the credibility Pixar had earned, it got a significant break. The leaders thought the company was ready to take its next big step—creating a one-hour television special. Lasseter approached Disney, his former employer, to pitch the idea. The response amazed him. Disney offered Pixar a contract to create three full-length feature movies using computer animation. Disney would fund and distribute the projects; Pixar would create them and receive a percentage of the profits.

Pixar finally had an opportunity to fulfill Catmull's vision, but the company was still far from realizing it. The company got to work on what would become *Toy Story*, but the team had trouble with the characters and story. Disney pushed Lasseter to make the characters more edgy, but they were becoming unlikable. After two years of work, Disney's chief of animation told them, "Guys, no matter how much you try to fix it, it just isn't working."[2] Lasseter begged Disney not to pull the plug and to give them one more chance to work things out. "We called all hands on deck, stayed up all night, and redid the whole first act of *Toy Story* within two weeks," Lasseter recalls. "When we showed it to Disney, they were stunned."[3]

The work on *Toy Story* moved forward. It would take Pixar four years to make the movie. Meanwhile, other studios were using the technology developed by Catmull and his team and were producing movies like *Jurassic*

Park and *Terminator 2.* "It was kind of frustrating for us," says Catmull, "because we were busy making this movie for Disney, and everybody was taking credit for these other films. But we were the ones who wrote the software for them!"[4]

Though the rest of the world wasn't seeing it yet, Pixar was starting to develop momentum. That became obvious to everyone when *Toy Story* opened in November 1995. When the contract with Disney was signed four years earlier, Pixar CEO Steve Jobs estimated that if the first movie was "a modest hit—say $75 million at the box office—we'll both break even. If it gets $100 million, we'll both make money. But if it's a real blockbuster and earns $200 million or so at the box office, we'll make good money and Disney will make a lot of money."[5] Few people would have predicted that it would make $192 million domestically and $362 million worldwide.[6]

From that time, Pixar's momentum has been strong and, if anything, has continued to grow. The organization has won seventeen Oscars and been awarded forty-two patents.[7] And since *Toy Story* came out, the company has produced hit after hit: *A Bug's Life, Toy Story 2, Monsters Inc., Finding Nemo, The Incredibles,* and *Cars.* Worldwide those movies have earned more than $3.67 billion![8]

TURNABOUT

Ironically, while Pixar was gaining momentum, Disney, the company who helped it create its breakthrough, was losing momentum. Disney's animation division had fallen on hard times. Its last significant animated movie was *Lilo & Stitch* in 2002. And it had produced three highly expensive bombs, *Atlantis, Treasure Planet,* and *Home on the Range.* How could Disney possibly regain some momentum? Bob Iger, who became Disney's president and CEO in October 2005, knew how. He purchased Pixar! Now the people Disney once helped were helping Disney. Catmull became Disney's president of feature animation, and Lasseter was made chief creative officer. "Disney has had two major heydays," says Catmull. "We're going to make a third."[9]

And what about Pixar? It will continue to function as before under the care of Catmull and Lasseter. When you've got great momentum, you don't want to do anything to get in its way. After all, momentum is a leader's best friend!

TRUTHS ABOUT MOMENTUM

Why do I say that momentum really is a leader's best friend? Because many times it's the only thing that makes the difference between losing and winning. When you have no momentum, even the simplest tasks seem impossible. Small problems look like insurmountable obstacles. Morale becomes low. The future appears dark. An organization with no momentum is like a train at a dead stop. It's hard to get going, and even small wooden blocks on the track can keep it from going anywhere.

On the other hand, when you have momentum on your side, the future looks bright, obstacles appear small, and troubles seem inconsequential.

> *Why is momentum a leader's best friend? Many times momentum is the only thing that makes the difference between losing and winning.*

An organization with momentum is like a train that's moving at sixty miles per hour. You could build a steel-reinforced concrete wall across the tracks, and the train would plow right through it.

If you want your organization, department, or team to succeed, you must learn the Law of Momentum and make the most of it in your organization. Here are some things about momentum that you need to know:

1. MOMENTUM IS THE GREAT EXAGGERATOR

The Law of the Big Mo at work is easily seen in sports because the swings in momentum occur in the space of a few hours right before your eyes. When a team gets on a roll, every play seems to work. Every shot seems to score. The team seems to do no wrong. The opposite is also true. When a team is in a slump, no matter how hard you work or how many solutions you try, nothing seems to work. Momentum is like a magnifying glass; it makes things look bigger than they really are. That's why I call it the great exaggerator. And it's one reason that leaders work so hard to control momentum.

> *Momentum is like a magnifying glass; it makes things look bigger than they really are.*

Because momentum has such a great impact, leaders try to control it. That's why in basketball games, for instance, when the opposing team is scoring a lot of unanswered points and starts to develop momentum, a good coach will call a time-out. Why? He's trying to stop the other team's momentum before it becomes too strong. If he doesn't, his team will likely lose the game.

When was the last time you heard of a team on the cusp of winning a championship complain about injuries? Or second-guess the team's ability? Or totally rethink strategy? It doesn't happen. Is that because no one is injured and everything is perfect? No. It's because success is exaggerated by momentum. When you have momentum, you don't worry about small problems, and many larger ones seem to work themselves out.

2. MOMENTUM MAKES LEADERS LOOK BETTER THAN THEY ARE

When leaders have momentum on their side, people think they're geniuses. They look past shortcomings. They forget about the mistakes the leaders have made. Momentum changes everyone's perspective of leaders. People like associating themselves with winners.

Young leaders often get less credit than they deserve. I often encourage young leaders just not to lose heart. When leaders are new in their careers, they don't have any momentum yet, and others often don't give them any credit. Experienced leaders think the younger ones don't know anything. One of the reasons John Lasseter was pushed out of Disney was that he had a lot of ideas, and the executives at Disney, who had been second-tier animators under the best filmmakers, wanted him to pay his dues. Lasseter recalls one executive telling him, "Shut up and do your work for the next twenty years, and then maybe we'll listen to you." He knew he was better than that.

Once a leader creates some success for his organization and develops career momentum, then people give him more credit than he deserves. Why? Because of the Law of the Big Mo. Momentum exaggerates a leader's success and makes him look better than he really is. It may not seem fair, but that's just the way it works.

For many years I have tried to add value to people. After writing fifty books and hundreds of lessons on leadership and success, I have gained a lot of momentum. Everything I do to add value to people seems to be compounding in a positive way. Often I say that when I started my career, I wasn't as bad as people thought. Today, I'm not as good as people give me credit for. Why the difference? Momentum!

3. Momentum Helps Followers Perform Better Than They Are

When leadership is strong and there is momentum in an organization, people are motivated and inspired to perform at higher levels. They become effective beyond their hopes and expectations. If you remember the 1980 U.S. Olympic hockey team, you know what I'm talking about. The team was good, but not good enough to win the gold medal. Yet that's what the Americans did. Why? Because leading up to the championship game, they won game after game against

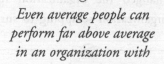

Even average people can perform far above average in an organization with great momentum.

very tough teams. They gained so much momentum that they performed beyond everyone's expectations. And after they beat the Russians, nothing could stop them from coming home with the gold medal.

The same kind of thing is true in business and volunteer organizations. When an organization has great momentum, all participants are more successful than they would be otherwise. I'll tell you how you know that's true. If you see leaders (especially mid-level ones) who had great success in an organization with momentum leave that organization and suddenly their performance becomes merely average, you know the Law of the Big Mo was at work. Even average people can perform far above average in an organization with great momentum.

4. Momentum Is Easier to Steer Than to Start

Have you ever been waterskiing? If you have, you know that it's harder to get up on the water than it is to steer once you're up there. Think about the first time you skied. Before you got up, the boat was dragging you along, and you probably thought your arms were going to give way as the water flooded against your chest and into your face. For a moment, you might have believed you couldn't hold on to the tow rope any longer. But then the force of the water drove your skis onto the surface, and off you went. At that point, you were able to make a turn with only a subtle shift of weight from one foot to another. That's the way the momentum of leadership works. Getting started is a struggle, but once you're moving forward, you can really start to do some amazing things.

5. Momentum Is the Most Powerful Change Agent

The story of Pixar is a classic example of the power of momentum. It changed the organization from an underfunded and understaffed organization scrapping to survive into an entertainment powerhouse. During the early days before it had momentum, the company considered becoming a provider of hardware to medical companies so it could store and access MRIs via computer. If that had happened, the organization would have lost its most talented and productive people. Instead, it transformed into an organization that is teaching Disney, the father of animated movies, how to regain its former glory.

> It takes a leader to create momentum.

Given enough momentum, nearly any kind of change is possible in an organization. People like to get on a winning bandwagon. Followers trust leaders with a proven track record. They accept changes from people who have led them to victory before. Momentum puts victory within reach.

6. MOMENTUM IS THE LEADER'S RESPONSIBILITY

It takes a leader to create momentum. Followers can catch it. Good managers are able to use it to their advantage once it has begun. Everyone can enjoy the benefits it brings. But *creating* momentum requires someone who has vision, can assemble a good team, and motivates others. If the leader is looking for someone to motivate him, then the organization is in trouble. If the leader is waiting for the organization to develop momentum on its own, then the organization is in trouble. It is the leader's responsibility to initiate momentum and keep it going. U.S. President Harry Truman once said, "If you can't stand the heat, get out of the kitchen." But for leaders, that statement should be changed to, "If you can't *make* some heat, get out of the kitchen."

7. MOMENTUM BEGINS INSIDE THE LEADER

Momentum begins within the individual leader. It starts with vision, passion, and enthusiasm. It starts with energy. Inspirational writer Eleanor Doan observed, "You cannot kindle a fire in any other heart until it is burning within your own."

If you don't believe in the vision and enthusiastically pursue it, doing all that you can to bring it to fruition, then you won't start making the small gains required to get the ball rolling. However, if you model enthusiasm to

> *"You cannot kindle a fire in any other heart until it is burning within your own."*
> —ELEANOR DOAN

your people day in and day out, you attract like-minded people to your team, department, or organization and motivate them to achieve. You will begin to see forward progress. Once you do, you will begin to generate momentum. And if you're wise, you'll value it for what it is: the leader's best friend. Once you have it, you can do almost anything. That's the power of the Big Mo.

MOVING THE IMMOVABLE

Of all the leaders I meet, the ones who become the most frustrated are those who try to make progress and develop momentum in bureaucratic organizations. In those organizations, people are often marking time. They've given up, and they either don't want change or don't believe it's possible.

Several years ago I saw a movie called *Stand and Deliver* that illustrates the hopelessness many people feel in an organization without momentum. Maybe you've seen it, too. It's about a real-life teacher named Jaime Escalante who worked at Garfield High School in East Los Angeles, California.

Teaching, motivating, and leading were in Jaime Escalante's blood, even from the time of his youth in his native Bolivia. He quickly became known as his city's finest teacher. When he was in his thirties, Escalante and his family immigrated to the United States. He worked several years in a restaurant and then at Russell Electronics. Though he could have pursued a promising career at Russell, he went back to school and earned a second bachelor's degree so that he could teach in the United States. Escalante's burning desire was to make a difference in people's lives.

At age forty-three, he was hired by Garfield High School to teach computer science. But when he arrived at Garfield on the first day of class, he found that there was no funding for computers. And because his degree was in mathematics, he would be teaching basic math. Disappointed, he went in search of his first class, hoping that his dream of making a difference wasn't slipping through his fingers.

FIGHTING A TIDAL WAVE OF NEGATIVE MOMENTUM

The change from computers to math turned out to be the least of Escalante's problems. The school, which had been empty and quiet during his summertime interview, was now in chaos. Discipline was nonexistent. Fights seemed to break out continually. Trash and graffiti were everywhere. Students—and even outsiders from the neighborhood—roamed all over the campus throughout the day. Gang activity was rampant. It was a teacher's worst nightmare.

Almost daily he thought of quitting. But his passion for teaching and his dedication to improving the lives of his students wouldn't allow him to give up. Yet at the same time Escalante was enough of a leader to know that the students were doomed if the school didn't change. They were all sliding backward fast, and they needed something to move them forward.

When a new principal was brought in, things began to change for the better. But Escalante wanted to take it further. He believed that the way to improve the school was to challenge the school's best and brightest with a calculus class that would prepare them for an AP class earning them college credit. A few AP tests were already being given on campus in Spanish. Occasionally, an individual student would attempt a test in physics or history. But the problem was that the school didn't have a leader with vision to take up the cause. That's where Escalante came into play.

SMALL BEGINNINGS

In the fall of 1978, Escalante organized the first calculus class. Rounding up every possible candidate who might be able to handle the course from Garfield's 3,500 students, he was able to find only fourteen students. In the first few classes, he laid out the work it would take for them to prepare for the AP calculus test at the end of the year. By the end of the second week of school, he had lost seven students. Even the ones who stayed were not well prepared for calculus. And by late spring, he was down to only five students. All of them took the AP test in May, but only two passed.

Escalante was disappointed, but he refused to give up, especially since he had made progress. He knew that if he could help his students experience a few wins, build their confidence, and give them hope, he could move them forward. He was determined to do whatever it took. To motivate them, he'd give them extra homework or challenge one of the school's athletes to a handball match. (Escalante never lost!) If they needed encouragement, he'd take them out to McDonald's as a reward. If they got lazy, he'd inspire, amaze, amuse, and even intimidate them. And all along the way, he modeled hard work, dedication to excellence, and what he called *ganas*—desire.

> *Leaders always find a way to make things happen.*

IT STARTS WITH A LITTLE PROGRESS

The next fall, Escalante put together another calculus class, this time with nine students. At the end of the year, eight took the test and six passed. He was making progress. Word of his success spread. Students heard that Escalante's protégés were earning college credit, and in the fall of 1980, his calculus class numbered fifteen. When they all took the test at the end of the year, fourteen students passed. The steps forward weren't huge, but Escalante could see that the program was building momentum.

The next group of students, numbering eighteen, was the subject of the movie *Stand and Deliver*. Like their predecessors, they worked very hard to learn calculus, many coming to school at 7:00 a.m. every day—a full hour and a half before school started. And often they stayed until 5:00, 6:00, or 7:00 p.m. And though Educational Testing Service (ETS) questioned the validity of the first test the students took and they had to take it a second time, 100 percent of them passed.

After that, the math program exploded. In 1983, the number of students passing the AP calculus exam almost doubled, from 18 to 31. The next year it doubled again, the number reaching 63. And it continued growing. In 1987, 129 students took the test, with 85 of them receiving college credit. Garfield High School in East Los Angeles, once considered the sinkhole of the district, produced 27 percent of all passing AP calculus test scores by Mexican-Americans in the entire United States.

THE MOMENTUM EXPLOSION

The benefits of the Law of the Big Mo were felt by all of Garfield High School's students. The school started offering classes to prepare students for other AP exams. In time, Garfield held regular AP classes in Spanish, calculus, history, European history, biology, physics, French, government, and computer science.

In 1987, nine years after Escalante spearheaded the program, Garfield students took more than 325 AP examinations. Most incredibly, Garfield had a waiting list of more than four hundred students from areas outside its boundaries wanting to enroll. The school that was once the laughing-stock of the district and that had almost lost its accreditation had become one of the top three inner-city schools in the entire nation![10] That's the power of the Law of the Big Mo.

1. Momentum begins inside the leader and spreads from there. Have you taken responsibility for the momentum in the area of which you are the leader? Are you passionate about the vision? Do you display enthusiasm at all times? Do you work to motivate others even when you don't feel like it? You must model the attitude and work ethic that you would like to see in others. That often requires what I call *character leadership*.

2. Motivation is a key factor in developing momentum. The first step toward building motivation is removing demotivating elements within the organization. What in your area of responsibility is causing people to lose their passion and enthusiasm? How can you go about removing or at least minimizing those factors? Once you have done that, you can then take the next step, which is to identify and put into play specific elements that will motivate your followers.

3. To encourage momentum, you need to help your people celebrate their accomplishments. Make it a regular practice to honor people who "move the ball forward." You want to continually praise effort but *reward* accomplishments. The more you reward success, the more people will strive for it.

17

THE LAW OF PRIORITIES

*Leaders Understand That Activity
Is Not Necessarily Accomplishment*

L eaders never advance to a point where they no longer need to priori-
tize. It's something that good leaders keep doing, whether they're
leading a billion-dollar corporation, running a small business, pastoring a
church, coaching a team, or leading a small group. I think good leaders
intuitively know that to be true. However, not every leader practices the
discipline of prioritizing. Why? I believe there are a few reasons.

First, when we are busy, we naturally believe that we are achieving. But
busyness does not equal productivity. Activity is not necessarily accomplishment. Second, prioritizing requires leaders to continually think ahead, to
know what's important, to know what's next, to see how everything relates
to the overall vision. That's hard work. Third, prioritizing causes us to do
things that are at the least uncomfortable and sometimes downright painful.

TIME TO RETHINK PRIORITIES

I know the pain of reprioritizing from personal experience. In 1996, I was
living in San Diego, which is one of my favorite places on the planet. San
Diego is a gorgeous city, with one of the best climates in the world. If you
live in San Diego, you can be on the beach in minutes or on the ski slopes

in hours. The city has culture, professional sporting teams, and fine restaurants. It's a place where you can play golf year-round. Why would I ever want to leave a place like that? I expected to live there the rest of my life. It was very comfortable. But leadership has nothing to do with comfort and everything to do with progress.

Back then I spent a lot of time on airplanes. Living in San Diego, I spent entire days traveling to airline hubs like Dallas, Chicago, and Atlanta just to make connections. Most of my speaking and consulting work was east of the Mississippi River, and the travel was taking a toll. I knew in my gut that I needed to make changes. So I asked Linda, my assistant, to figure out exactly how

> *"A leader is the one who climbs the tallest tree, surveys the entire situation, and yells, 'Wrong jungle!'"*
> —STEPHEN COVEY

much time I was spending traveling. What I learned shocked me. In the previous year, I had spent the equivalent of twenty-seven full days traveling back and forth—just between San Diego and Dallas to make flight connections. It made me realize that I needed to sit down and reevaluate my priorities.

If I was going to live consistently with the priorities I had established for myself, I was going to have to move myself and my companies to one of the hub cities. Author Stephen Covey says, "A leader is the one who climbs the tallest tree, surveys the entire situation, and yells, 'Wrong jungle!'" I felt a little like that when I realized what we were about to do.

After a lot of research, we settled on Atlanta. It was a major airline hub. From there I would be able to reach 80 percent of the people in the United States within two hours by plane. And the area is beautiful, offering excellent cultural, recreational, and entertainment opportunities to my employees. I knew people could live well there. It would not be an easy move, but it was a necessary one.

It's been ten years since we made the move. You may ask, "Was it worth it?" My answer is an emphatic yes. Atlanta is a business-friendly area. The cost of living is very reasonable compared to other large cities. And most important for me and for the consultants who work for my company, travel has become so much easier. Most of the time I can travel, speak, and return home the same day. As a result, my productivity has skyrocketed. Can you imagine getting twenty-seven days of your life back every year? In the ten years since the move, I've gained 270 days. A normal work year for most people is 250 days. It's like I've had an extra year added to the most productive time of my life! And there's nothing like being at home with my wife at the end of a day of traveling instead of being in a hotel room.

THE THREE Rs

Leaders can't afford to just think inside the box. Sometimes they need to reinvent the box—or blow it up. Executive and author Max Depree says, "The first responsibility of a leader is to define reality." That requires the Law of Priorities. When you're the leader, everything is on the table.

Every year I spend about two weeks in December reevaluating my priorities. I review the previous year's schedule. I look at my upcoming commitments. I evaluate my family life. I think about my goals. I look at the big picture of what I'm doing to make sure the way I'm living lines up with my values and priorities.

One of the guiding principles I use during this process is the Pareto Principle. I've often taught it to people at leadership conferences over the years, and I also explain it in depth in my book *Developing the Leader Within You*. The idea is this: if you focus your attention on the activities that rank in the top 20 percent in terms of importance, you will have an 80 percent return on your effort. For example, if you have ten employees, you should

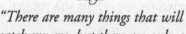

"There are many things that will catch my eye, but there are only a few things that will catch my heart."
—TIM REDMOND

give 80 percent of your time and attention to the best two. If you have one hundred customers, the top twenty will provide you with 80 percent of your business, so focus on them. If your to-do list has ten items on it, the two most important ones will give you an 80 percent return on your time. If you haven't already observed this phenomenon, test it and you'll see that it really plays out that way. One year as I went through this process, I realized that I had to totally refocus and restructure one of my organizations.

The other guidelines I use whenever I evaluate my priorities are the three Rs. No, not reading, writing, and 'rithmetic. My three Rs are *requirement*, *return*, and *reward*. I believe that to be effective, leaders must order their lives according to these three questions:

1. WHAT IS REQUIRED?

We're all accountable to somebody for the work we do—an employer, a board of directors, stockholders, the government, and so on. We also have responsibility for the important people in our lives, such as spouse, children, and parents. For that reason, any list of priorities must begin with what is required of us.

The question I ask myself is, *What must I do that nobody can or should do for me?* As I have gotten older, that list has gotten shorter and shorter. If I'm doing something that's not necessary, I should eliminate it. If I'm doing something that's necessary but not required of me personally, I need to delegate it.

2. WHAT GIVES THE GREATEST RETURN?

As a leader, you should spend most of your time working in your areas of greatest strength. Marcus Buckingham and Donald O. Clifton have done extensive research on this subject, which you can read about in their book *Now, Discover Your Strengths*. People are more productive and more content when their work is within their natural gifting and strengths. Ideally, leaders should get out of their comfort zone but stay in their strength zone.

> *Leaders should get out of their comfort zone but stay in their strength zone.*

What's the practical application for this? Here's my rule of thumb. If something I'm doing can be done 80 percent as well by someone else, I delegate it. If you have a responsibility that someone else could do according to that standard—or that could *potentially* meet that standard—then develop and train a person to handle it. Just because you *can* do something does not mean that you *should* do it. Remember, leaders understand that activity is not necessarily accomplishment. That's the Law of Priorities.

3. WHAT BRINGS THE GREATEST REWARD?
This final question relates to personal satisfaction. Tim Redmond, president of Redmond Leadership Institute, observed, "There are many things that will catch my eye, but there are only a few things that will catch my heart."

Life is too short not to do some things you love. I love teaching leadership. I love writing and speaking. I love spending time with my wife, children, and grandchildren. I love playing golf. No matter what else I do, I will make time for those things. They are the fire lighters in my life. They energize me and keep me passionate. And passion provides the fuel in a person's life to keep him going.

REORDERING PRIORITIES

A few years ago when I went through this process of reprioritizing, I revisited the way I was spending my time. Back when I wrote the first edition of this book, I determined to spend my work time according to the following guideline:

AREA	TIME ALLOTTED
1. Leadership	19 percent
2. Communicating	38 percent
3. Creating	31 percent
4. Networking	12 percent

These four areas represent my greatest strengths. They are the most rewarding aspects of my career. And for many years my responsibilities to my companies were aligned with them. However, as I was recently reviewing these areas, I realized that I was not maintaining the balance I desired. I was spending too much time in hands-on leadership at one of my companies, and it was taking away from higher priorities. Once again, I had to recognize that activity is not necessarily accomplishment. I knew I was in for another difficult business decision. If I was going to continue to be effective in fulfilling my vision, I would have to change and work according to the Law of Priorities. I made the decision to sell one of my companies. It wasn't easy, but it was the right thing for me to do.

REFOCUSING ON A WORLDWIDE SCALE

It is the responsibility of leaders to make tough decisions based on priorities. That can sometimes make them unpopular. Back in 1981 when Jack Welch became chairman and CEO of General Electric, it was a good company. It had a ninety-year history, the company stock traded at $4 per share, and the company was worth about $12 billion, eleventh best on the stock market. It was a huge, diverse company that included 350 strategic businesses. But Welch believed the company could become better. What was his strategy? He used the Law of Priorities.

Within a few months of taking over the company, he began what he called *the hardware revolution*. It changed the entire profile and focus of the company. Welch said,

> To the hundreds of businesses and product lines that made up the company we applied a single criterion: can they be number 1 or number 2 at whatever they do in the world marketplace? Of the 348 businesses or product lines that could not, we closed some and divested others. Their sale brought in almost $10 billion. We invested $18 billion in the ones that remained and further strengthened them with $17 billion worth of acquisitions.
>
> What remained [in 1989], aside from a few relatively small supporting operations, are fourteen world-class businesses . . . all well positioned for the '90s . . . each one either first or second in the world market in which it participates.[1]

I know Welch is out of favor in some circles, and recently, his methods have been criticized. But his leadership was right for his time and situation. He reprioritized GE, and his strong leadership and focus paid incredible dividends. During his tenure, GE's stock experienced a two-to-one split four times. And it traded at more than $80 per share when he retired. The company was ranked as the nation's most admired company, according to *Fortune*, and it continues to be one of the most valuable companies in the world. That came about because of Welch's ability to use the Law of Priorities in his leadership. He never mistook activity for accomplishment. He knew that the greatest success comes only when you focus your people on what really matters.

PRIORITIES WERE THE NAME OF HIS GAME

Examine the lives of all effective leaders, and you will see them putting priorities into action. Every time Norman Schwarzkopf assumed a new command, he didn't just rely on his leadership intuition; he also reexamined the unit's priorities. Lance Armstrong was able to win seven Tour de France championships because his priorities guided his training regimen. When explorer Roald Amundsen succeeded in taking his team to the South Pole and back, it was due, in part, to his ability to set right priorities.

Successful leaders live according to the Law of Priorities. They recognize that activity is not necessarily accomplishment. But the best leaders seem to be able to get the Law of Priorities to work for them by satisfying multiple priorities with each activity. This actually enables them to increase their focus while reducing their number of actions.

A leader who was a master at that was one of my idols: John Wooden, the former head basketball coach of the UCLA Bruins. He is called the Wizard of Westwood because the amazing feats he accomplished in the world of college sports were so incredible that they seemed to be magical.

Evidence of Wooden's ability to make the Law of Priorities work for him could be seen in the way he approached basketball practice. Wooden claimed that he learned some of his methods from watching Frank Leahy, the great former Notre Dame head football coach. He said, "I often went to his [Leahy's] practices and observed how he broke them up into periods. Then I would go home and analyze why he did things certain ways. As a player, I realized there was a great deal of time wasted. Leahy's concepts reinforced my ideas and helped in the ultimate development of what I do now."

EVERYTHING HAD A PURPOSE BASED ON PRIORITIES

People who have served in the military say that they often have to hurry up and wait. That seems to be true in sports, too. Coaches ask their players to work their hearts out one minute and then to stand around doing nothing the next. But that's not the way Wooden worked. He orchestrated every moment of practice and planned each activity with specific purposes in mind. He employed economy of motion. Here's how he worked:

Every year, Wooden determined a list of overall priorities for the team, based on observations from the previous season. Those items might include objectives such as "Build confidence in Drollinger and Irgovich," or "Use three on two continuity drill at least three times a week." Usually, he had about a dozen or so items that he wanted to work on throughout the season. But Wooden also reviewed his agenda for his teams every day. Each morning, he and an assistant meticulously planned the day's practice. They usually spent two hours strategizing for a practice that might not even last that long. He drew ideas from notes jotted on three-by-five cards that he always carried with him. He planned every drill, minute by minute, and recorded the information in a notebook prior to practice. Wooden once boasted that if you asked what his team was doing on a specific date at three o'clock in 1963, he could tell you precisely what drill his team was running. Like all good leaders, Wooden did the work of thinking ahead for his team.

Wooden always maintained his focus, and he found ways for his players to do the same thing. His special talent was for addressing several priority areas at once. For example, to help players work on their free throws—something that many of them found tedious—Wooden instituted a free-throw shooting policy during scrimmages that would encourage them to concentrate and improve instead of just marking the time. The sooner a sidelined player made a set number of free throws, the sooner he could get back into action. And Wooden continually changed the number of shots required of the guards, forwards, and centers so that team members rotated in and out at different rates. That way everyone, regardless of position or starting status, got experience playing together, a critical priority for Wooden's development of total teamwork.

The most remarkable aspect about John Wooden—and the most telling about his ability to focus on his priorities—is that he never scouted opposing teams. Instead, he focused on getting his players to reach *their* potential. And he addressed those things through practice and personal interaction with the players. It was never his goal to win championships or even to beat the other team. His desire was to get each person to play to his potential and to put the best possible team on the floor. And of course, Wooden's results were incredible. In more than forty years of coaching, he had only *one* losing season—his first. And he led his UCLA teams to four undefeated seasons and a record ten NCAA championships.[2] No other college team has ever come close. Wooden was a great leader. He just might be the finest person to coach in any sport. Why? Because every day he lived by the Law of Priorities. We should strive to do the same.

Applying
THE LAW OF PRIORITIES
To Your Life

1. Are you prepared to really shake up your life and get out of your comfort zone in order to live and work according to your priorities? Is there something in your life that is working so poorly that you intuitively know it will require a major revision in how you do things? What is that something? Describe *how* it is not working. Describe *why* it is not working. Can you think outside the box (or create a new box) to solve the issue and realign your priorities? Ignoring a major alignment problem in your priorities is like lining up a golf shot incorrectly. The farther you hit the ball, the more off course it will be; the longer you live out of alignment, the greater the chance you will miss achieving your vision.

2. If you have never done so before, take the time to write out your answers to the three R questions (Be sure to include family and other responsibilities, not just career.):

What is *required* of me?
What gives the greatest *return*?
What brings the greatest *reward*?

Once you have answered those three questions, create a list of the things you are doing that don't fit solidly into one of the three Rs. You need to delegate or eliminate these things.

3. Successful people live according to the Law of Priorities. Successful leaders help their organization, department, or team live according to the Law of Priorities. As the leader, have you taken responsibility for prioritizing

and thinking ahead for your area of responsibility? Have you carved out specific time on a regular basis to revisit priorities for that area? If not, you need to start doing so immediately. As a leader, it's not enough for you to be successful. You need to help your people be successful.

18

THE LAW OF SACRIFICE

A Leader Must Give Up to Go Up

W hy does an individual step forward to lead other people? For every person the answer is different. A few do it to survive. Some do it to make money. Many desire to build a business or organization. Others do it because they want to change the world. That was the reason for Martin Luther King Jr.

SEEDS OF GREATNESS

King's leadership ability began to emerge when he was in college. He had always been a good student. In high school, he skipped ninth grade. And when he took a college entrance exam as a junior, his scores were high enough that he decided to skip his senior year and enroll in Morehouse College in Atlanta. At age eighteen he received his ministerial license. At nineteen he was ordained and received his bachelor's degree in sociology.

King continued his education at Crozer Seminary in Pennsylvania. While he was there, two significant things happened. He heard a message about the life and teachings of Mahatma Gandhi, which forever marked him and put in motion his serious study of the Indian leader. He also emerged as a leader among his peers and was elected president of the senior class. From there, he studied for his PhD at Boston University. It was also during this time that he married Coretta Scott.

SEEDS OF SACRIFICE

King accepted his first pastorate in Montgomery, Alabama, at the Dexter Avenue Baptist Church in 1954 and settled into family life when his first child was born the next year in November. But that peace didn't last long. Less than a month later, Rosa Parks refused to relinquish her seat on a bus to a white passenger and was arrested. Local African American leaders arranged a one-day boycott of the transit system to protest her arrest and the city's segregation policy. When it was successful, they decided to create the Montgomery Improvement Association (MIA) to continue the boycott. Already recognized as a leader in the community, King was unanimously elected president of the newly formed organization.

For the next year, King led African American community leaders in a boycott with the goal of changing the system. The MIA negotiated with city leaders and demanded courteous treatment of African Americans by bus operators, first-come, first-served seating for all bus riders, and employment of African American bus drivers. While the boycott was on, community leaders organized carpools, raised funds to support the boycott financially, rallied and mobilized the community with sermons, and coordinated legal challenges with the NAACP. Finally in November 1956, the U.S. Supreme Court struck down the laws allowing segregated seating on buses.[1] King and the other leaders were successful. Their world was beginning to change.

The Montgomery bus boycott was a major step in the American civil rights movement, and it's easy to see what was gained as a result of it. But King also began paying a personal cost for it. Soon after the boycott began, King was arrested for a minor traffic violation. A bomb was thrown onto his porch. And he was indicted on a charge of being party to a conspiracy to hinder and prevent the operation of business without "just or legal cause."[2] King was emerging as a leader, but he was paying a price for it.

THE LAW OF SACRIFICE

THE PRICE KEEPS GETTING HIGHER

Each time King climbed higher and moved forward in leadership for the cause of civil rights, the greater the price he paid for it. His wife, Coretta Scott King, remarked in *My Life with Martin Luther King, Jr.*, "Day and night our phone would ring, and someone would pour out a string of obscene epithets . . . Frequently the calls ended with a threat to kill us if we didn't get out of town. But in spite of all the danger, the chaos of our private lives, I felt inspired, almost elated."

King did some great things as a leader. He met with presidents. He delivered rousing speeches that are considered some of the most outstanding examples of oration in American history. He led 250,000 people in a peaceful march on Washington DC. He received the Nobel Peace Prize. And he did create change in this country. But the Law of Sacrifice demands that the greater the leader, the more he must give up. During that same period, King was arrested many times and jailed on many occasions. He was stoned, stabbed, and physically attacked. His house was bombed. Yet his vision—and his influence—continued to increase. Ultimately, he sacrificed everything he had. But what he gave up he parted with willingly. In his last speech, delivered the night before he was assassinated in Memphis, he said,

> I don't know what will happen to me now. We've got some difficult days ahead. But it doesn't matter to me now. Because I've been to the mountaintop. I won't mind. Like anybody else, I would like to live a long life. Longevity has its place. But I'm not concerned about that now. I just want to do God's will. And He's allowed me to go up to the mountain. And I've looked over and I've seen the Promised Land. I may not get there with you, but I want you to know tonight that we, as a people, will get to the Promised Land. So I'm happy tonight . . . I'm not fearing any man. "Mine eyes have seen the glory of the coming of the Lord."[3]

The next day he paid the ultimate price of sacrifice.

King's impact was profound. He influenced millions of people to peacefully stand up against a system and society that fought to exclude them. The United States has changed for the better because of his leadership.

SACRIFICE IS THE HEART OF LEADERSHIP

There is a common misperception among people who aren't leaders that leadership is all about the position, perks, and power that come from rising in an organization. Many people today want to climb up the corporate

> *The heart of good leadership is sacrifice.*

ladder because they believe that freedom, power, and wealth are the prizes waiting at the top. The life of a leader can look glamorous to people on the outside. But the reality is that leadership requires sacrifice. A leader must give up to go up. In recent years, we've observed more than our share of leaders who used and abused their organizations for their personal benefit—and the resulting corporate scandals that came because of their greed and selfishness. The heart of good leadership is sacrifice.

If you desire to become the best leader you can be, then you need to be willing to make sacrifices in order to lead well. If that is your desire, then here are some things you need to know about the Law of Sacrifice:

1. THERE IS NO SUCCESS WITHOUT SACRIFICE

Every person who has achieved any success in life has made sacrifices to do so. Many working people dedicate four or more years and pay thousands of dollars to attend college to get the tools they'll need before embarking on their career. Athletes sacrifice countless hours in the gym and on the practice field preparing themselves to perform at a high level. Parents give up much of their free time and sacrifice their resources in order to do a good job raising their children. Philosopher-poet Ralph Waldo Emerson observed, "For everything you have missed, you have gained something else; and for everything you gain, you lose something." Life is a series of trades, one thing for another.

Leaders must give up to go up. That's true of every leader regardless of profession. Talk to leaders, and you will find that they have made repeated sacrifices. Effective leaders sacrifice much that is good in order to dedicate themselves to what is best. That's the way the Law of Sacrifice works.

2. LEADERS ARE OFTEN ASKED TO GIVE UP MORE THAN OTHERS

The heart of leadership is putting others ahead of yourself. It's doing what is best for the team. For that reason, I believe that leaders have to give up their rights. As Gerald Brooks, leadership speaker and pastor, says, "When you become a leader, you lose the right to think about yourself." Visually, it looks like this:

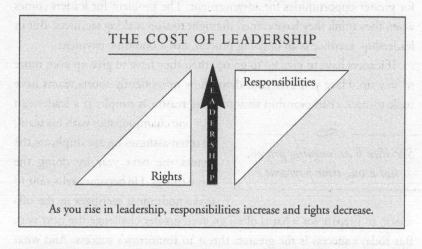

THE COST OF LEADERSHIP

Responsibilities

Rights

As you rise in leadership, responsibilities increase and rights decrease.

When you have no responsibilities, you can do pretty much anything you want. Once you take on responsibility, you start to experience limitations in what you can do. The more responsibility you accept, the fewer options you have.

Digital chairman and chief executive Robert Palmer said in an interview, "In my model of management, there's very little wiggle room. If you want a management job, then you have to accept the responsibility and accountability that goes with it."[4] He is really talking about the cost of leadership. Leaders must be willing to give up more than the people they lead.

For every person, the nature of the sacrifice may be different. Everyone who leads gives up other opportunities. Some people have to give up beloved hobbies. Many give up aspects of their personal lives. Some, like King, give their actual lives. The circumstances are different from person to person, but the principle doesn't change. Leadership means sacrifice.

3. You Must Keep Giving Up to Stay Up

Most people are willing to acknowledge that sacrifices are necessary early in a leadership career in order to make progress. They'll take an undesirable territory to make a name for themselves. They'll move their family to a less desirable city to accept a better position. They'll take a temporary cut in pay for greater opportunities for advancement. The problem for leaders comes when they think they have earned the right to stop making sacrifices. But in leadership, sacrifice is an ongoing process, not a one-time payment.

If leaders have to give up to go up, then they have to give up even more to stay up. Have you ever considered how infrequently sports teams have back-to-back championship seasons? The reason is simple: if a leader can win one championship with his team, he often assumes he can duplicate the results the next year by doing the same things. He becomes reluctant to make additional sacrifices in the off-

> *Sacrifice is an ongoing process, not a one-time payment.*

season to prepare for what is often an even greater challenge the next year. But today's success is the greatest threat to tomorrow's success. And what gets a team to the top isn't what keeps it there. The only way to stay up is to give up even more. Leadership success requires continual change, constant improvement, and ongoing sacrifice.

When I look back at my career, I recognize that there has always been a cost involved in moving forward. That's been true for me monetarily with every career change except one. When I accepted my first job, our family income decreased because my position paid less than my wife, Margaret, was making as a schoolteacher—she had to give up that job for us to relocate for my new position. Years later when I accepted a director's job at headquarters in Marion, Indiana, I once again took a pay cut. In 1981 I left that headquarters job to take my third pastoral position, which I accepted without even knowing what the salary would be. (It was lower.) When the board members who offered the job said they were surprised that I took it without knowing what it paid, I said, "If I do the job well, I believe the salary will take care of itself." And in 1995 when I finally left church lead-

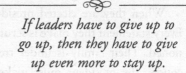

If leaders have to give up to go up, then they have to give up even more to stay up.

ership after a twenty-six-year career to teach and resource people full-time, I gave up a salary altogether. Why would I do that? Because I knew it would enable me to have greater influence and fulfill a larger vision. Anytime the step is right, a leader shouldn't hesitate to make a sacrifice.

4. THE HIGHER THE LEVEL OF LEADERSHIP, THE GREATER THE SACRIFICE

Have you ever been part of an auction? It's an exciting experience. An item comes up for a bid, and everyone in the room gets excited. When the bidding opens, lots of people jump in and take part. But as the price goes higher and higher, what happens? There are fewer and fewer bidders. When the price is low, everybody bids. In the end, only one person is willing to pay the high price that the item actually costs. It's the same in leadership: the higher you go, the more it's going to cost you. And it doesn't matter what kind of leadership career you pick. You will have to make sacrifices. You will have to give up to go up.

What's the highest level a person can go in leadership? In the United States, it's to the presidency. Some people say the president is the most powerful leader in the world. More than any other single person, his words and actions make an impact, not just on the people in the United States but around the globe.

Think about what people must give up to reach the office of president. First, they must learn to lead. Then they have to pay a lot of dues—usually years or even decades in lower leadership positions. Some, like Ulysses S.

Grant and Dwight D. Eisenhower, spend an entire career in military service before seeking elected office. Once they have paid their dues and they decide to run for the presidency, every aspect of their prior life goes under the microscope. Nothing is off-limits. It's the end of their personal privacy.

When they are elected president, their time is no longer their own. Every statement they make is scrutinized. Every decision they make is questioned. Their family is under tremendous pressure. And as a matter of course, the president must make decisions that mean life or death for others. Even after they leave office, retired presidents will spend the rest of their lives in the company of Secret Service agents who protect them from bodily harm. That is a price not many people are willing to pay.

STANDING ON OTHERS' SHOULDERS

There can be no success without sacrifice. Anytime you see success, you can be sure someone made sacrifices to make it possible. And as a leader, if you sacrifice, even if you don't witness the success, you can be sure that someone in the future will benefit from what you've given.

That was certainly true for Martin Luther King Jr. He did not live to see most of the benefits of his sacrifices, but many others have. One such person was an African American girl born in segregated Birmingham, Alabama, in 1954. A precocious child, she followed the news of the day, including civil rights struggles. A neighbor recalls that she was "always interested in politics because as a little girl she used to call me and say things like, 'Did you see what Bull Connor [a racist city commissioner] did today?' She was just a little girl and she did that all the time. I would have to read the newspaper thoroughly because I wouldn't know what she was going to talk about."[5]

Though she had an interest in current events, her passion was music. Perhaps her attraction to music was inevitable. Her mother and grandmother played piano. She began taking piano lessons from her grandmother at age three and was recognized as a prodigy. Music consumed her growing up years. Even her given name was inspired by music. Her parents named her Condoleezza, from the musical notation *con dolcezza*, which means "with sweetness."

Condoleezza Rice is a product of generations of sacrifice. Her grandfather, John Wesley Rice Jr., the son of slaves, was determined to get an education and, according to Condoleezza Rice, "saved up his cotton for tuition" and attended Stillman College in Tuscaloosa, Alabama. After graduating, he became a Presbyterian minister. That was no small accomplishment for a black man in the South in the 1920s. He set the course for the family, whose members were determined to become the best that they could be at whatever they did.

Granddaddy Rice passed his love for education down to his son, also named John, who in turn passed it down to Condoleezza. Her mother's side of the family was equally industrious and focused on education. Coit Blacker, a Stanford professor and friend of Rice, commented, "I don't know too many American families, period, who can claim that not only are their parents college-educated, but their grandparents are college-educated and all their cousins and aunts and uncles are college-educated."[6]

SACRIFICING TO BE THE BEST

Rice received a broad education at school and at home. She read extensively. She studied French. She took ballet classes. She learned the intricacies of football and basketball from her father, who, besides being a pastor, was a high school guidance counselor and part-time coach. And during the summers when the family went to Denver so that her parents could take graduate courses, she practiced figure skating. But her heart was set on music. While other children were out playing, she was studying and practicing piano.

Her schedule was often grueling. After the family moved to Denver when she was thirteen, she worked harder and made more sacrifices. She was highly disciplined. To be able to compete in both figure skating and piano competitions, she would get up at 4:30 in the morning to fit everything in. One of her teachers commented, "There was a core of her that revealed she knew what she wanted and was willing to make the sacrifices. I think in her mind they were not sacrifices, but things to do that were necessary to keep with her goals."[7] And her parents supported her fully and were willing to make sacrifices for her success as well. To assist her in her goals as a pianist, they took out a $13,000 loan (in 1969) to buy her a used Steinway grand piano.

Rice graduated early from high school and went to the University of Denver with the intention of earning a degree in music and becoming a professional concert pianist. It was something she had made sacrifices her entire life to do. But after her sophomore year, she attended the Aspen Music Festival and came to a realization. As hard as she had worked, she might not make it to the top. She observed, "I met eleven-year-olds who could play from sight what had taken me all year to learn and I thought I'm maybe going to end up playing piano bar or playing at Nordstrom, but I'm not going to end up playing Carnegie Hall."[8]

GIVING UP TO GO UP

Rice knew that if she was going to reach her personal potential, it would not be in music. So she made a sacrifice few people in her position would be willing to make. She dropped her music major. Her identity had been entirely wrapped up in music, but she was willing to strike out in a new direction. She began searching for a new field.

She found it in international politics. She was drawn like a magnet to the Russian culture and the Soviet government. For the next two years, she immersed herself in her courses, did extensive outside reading, and learned the Russian language. She had found her niche, and she was still willing to pay the price to go to the highest level. After graduating with her bachelor's degree, she went on to Notre Dame to get a master's degree. She then returned to the University of Denver and earned a PhD at age twenty-six. When she received an offer for a fellowship at Stanford, she jumped on it. A few months later, she was recruited to become a member of the university's faculty. She had arrived.

Most people would be happy if the rest of the story played out something like this: publish a few articles, then a book or two; earn tenure; and eventually settle into a comfortable life in the academic community. Not Rice. True, she did carve out a place for herself at Stanford; it was an environment she loved. She enjoyed the intellectual stimulation. She was a talented teacher who found teaching and counseling students highly rewarding. She even became an avid fan of the university's sports teams. She thrived and received one award after another. She spent a year at the Pentagon in an advisory position with the Joint Chiefs of Staff. She called it a reality check—practical experience that informed her teaching and writing. She was quickly made an associate professor. Rice biographer Antonia Felix writes,

> Condi found her passions in Soviet studies and teaching, and her life at Stanford was rich on many levels. She juggled classes, advising, research, writing, playing the piano, weight training, exercising, dating, and gluing herself to the television for twelve-hour football-watching marathons.[9]

Rice was living an ideal life. She was making the most of her talents, she had great influence, and she was helping to shape the next generation of leaders and thinkers. But then in 1989, the White House called. She was invited to accept a position on the National Security Council as the director of Soviet and East European affairs. She took a leave of absence from Stanford, and it turned out to be a wonderful decision. She was President George H. W. Bush's primary advisor on the Soviet Union as that government disintegrated. And she helped in creating policy for the unification of Germany. It made her one of the world's experts on the subject.

She returned to Stanford after two years in Washington. "It wasn't an easy decision," Rice remarked. "I felt that it's hard to keep an academic career intact if you don't come back in about two years . . . But I think of myself as an academic first. That means that you want to keep some coherence and integrity in your career."[10]

Back at Stanford, she possessed even greater clout. In two years she was made a full professor—at age thirty-eight. A month later, she was asked to become provost, a position that had never been held by an African American, by a woman, or by anyone so young. All her predecessors had been at least twenty years older when they took the position, and for good reason. The provost is not only the chief academic officer of the university but is also responsible for its $1.5 billion budget. And Rice was being asked to handle a budget with a $20 million deficit. Though it meant maintaining a grueling schedule and giving up more of her personal life, she accepted the challenge. And she succeeded, turning the budget around and creating a $14.5 million reserve—all while continuing to teach as a political science professor.

AT THE TOP

As the second in command at one of the world's premier universities, Rice had it made. She had proven herself as an executive. She was already sitting on many corporate boards. And she was in position to become president of any university in the nation. So some people might have been surprised when she stepped down as provost and began tutoring George W. Bush, then governor of Texas, on foreign policy. But it was a sacrifice she was willing to make—one that led to her becoming national security advisor and eventually U.S. secretary of state.

As I write this, Rice continues to serve in that role. What once looked like a sacrifice has made her more influential than ever. When she completes her term, she could return to teaching with great prestige—there isn't a university in the world that wouldn't want to have her on its political science faculty. She could become president of one of the top universities. She could run for the Senate. She could even run for the presidency of the United States. She has been consistently willing to give up to go up, and I have no doubt that she will make whatever sacrifices are necessary to take the next step. That's what happens when a leader understands and lives by the Law of Sacrifice.

✒

Applying
THE LAW OF SACRIFICE
To Your Life

---

1. To become a more influential leader, are you willing to make sacrifices? Are you willing to give up your rights for the sake of the people you lead? Give it some thought. Then create two lists: (1) the things you are willing to give up in order to go up, and (2) the things you are *not* willing to sacrifice to advance. Be sure to consider which list will contain items such as your health, marriage, relationships with children, finances, and so on.

2. Living by the Law of Sacrifice usually means being willing to trade something of value that you possess to gain something more valuable that you don't. King gave up many personal freedoms to gain freedoms for others. Rice gave up prestige and influence at Stanford to gain influence and impact around the world. In order to make such sacrificial trades, an individual must have something of value to trade. What do you have to offer? And what are you currently willing to trade your time, energy, and resources for that may give you greater personal worth?

3. One of the most harmful mind-sets of leaders is what I call *destination disease*—the idea that they can sacrifice for a season and then "arrive." Leaders who think this way stop sacrificing and stop gaining higher ground in leadership.

In what areas might you be in danger of having destination disease? Write them down. Then for each, create a statement of ongoing growth that will be an antidote to such thinking. For example, if you have the mind-set that you are finished learning once you graduate from school, you may need to write, "I will make it my practice to learn and grow in one significant area every year."

19

THE LAW OF TIMING

When to Lead Is As Important As
What to Do and Where to Go

I f ever there was an example of the importance of timing as it relates to leadership, it came in New Orleans in late August and early September of 2005.

New Orleans is an unusual city. Like Venice, Italy, it is surrounded by water. To the north lies Lake Pontchartrain. To the south flows the mighty Mississippi River. To the east and west are low-lying swamplands. Canals crisscross the city. You cannot drive into or out of New Orleans without crossing a major bridge. That may not seem like a big deal—until you consider that most of the city lies below sea level. New Orleans is shaped like a bowl. On average, the city is six feet below sea level. In the lowest areas, it's nine feet below sea level. And the land in New Orleans sinks a little more every year. For decades citizens have worried about the potential damage that a direct hit from a powerful hurricane could do to the city.

DISASTER ON THE HORIZON

On Wednesday, August 24, 2005, nobody in New Orleans could have known that the newly formed tropical storm, named Katrina, would be the big one—the hurricane the city had feared would someday come. It wasn't until Friday that the National Hurricane Center predicted that the storm would reach landfall on Monday somewhere near Buras, Louisiana, about sixty miles southeast of New Orleans. The hurricane was already looking like a bad one. The next morning, Saturday, August 27, the leaders of many of Louisiana's parishes around New Orleans ordered mandatory evacuations: St. Charles, Plaquemines, parts of Jefferson, and even St. Tammany, which is situated on higher ground north of New Orleans.

But what about New Orleans? Why didn't Mayor Ray Nagin, the leader of the city, order a mandatory evacuation at the same time? Many people say New Orleanians are fatalistic and they can't be made to move any faster than they want to go. Others say that Nagin, a businessman before he was elected, was worried about the legal and financial implications of an evacuation. I say he and others in government didn't understand the Law of Timing. When to lead is as important as what to do and where to go.

The time to move people out of New Orleans was when the other parish leaders announced their mandatory evacuations. Nagin waited. On Saturday evening he finally announced a *voluntary* evacuation of New Orleans—only after Max Mayfield, the director of the National Hurricane Center, called Nagin on Saturday night did the mayor become concerned enough to act. "Max scared the crap out of me," Nagin is reported to have said after the call.[1]

TOO LITTLE TOO LATE

The next morning at nine o'clock, Nagin finally ordered a *mandatory* evacuation—fewer than twenty-four hours before the hurricane would make landfall. It was much too late for many citizens of New Orleans. And how did he plan to help those people who couldn't make it out of town on such short notice? He advised them to get to the Superdome, the city's shelter of last resort, however they could. But he made no real provisions for them. In a press conference Nagin advised:

> If you can't leave the city and you have to come to the Superdome, come
> with enough food, [non]perishable items to last for three to five days.

Come with blankets, with pillows. No weapons, no alcohol, no drugs. You know, this is like the governor said, you're going on a camping trip. If you don't know what that's like, just bring enough stuff for you to be able to sleep and be comfortable. It's not going to be the best environment, but at least you will be safe.[2]

The results of Nagin's leadership played out in the national coverage of Katrina and its aftermath. Water was flowing into parts of the city by nine o'clock Monday morning. Conditions for the people at the Superdome were dreadful. Other people who couldn't get out of town flocked to the Convention Center. Many citizens were stranded on rooftops. How did Nagin respond? He complained to the media at press conferences.

ANOTHER CHANCE

If someone was going to step in and lead, it would have to occur somewhere other than the local level. Most people began looking to the federal government for leadership, but they violated the Law of Timing, too. Not until Wednesday, August 31, did Director of Homeland Security Michael Chertoff release a memo declaring Katrina an "Incident of National Significance"—a key designation needed to trigger swift federal coordination.[3] President Bush didn't meet with his cabinet until the following day to determine how to launch the White House Task Force on Hurricane Katrina Response. Meanwhile, the people stranded in New Orleans waited for help. On Thursday, September 1, the Red Cross requested permission to take water, food, and supplies to the people who were stranded in the city, but their request was denied by the Louisiana office of Homeland Security. They were asked to wait another day.[4] Finally, on Sunday, September 4—six days after New Orleans flooded—the evacuation of the Superdome was finally complete.

The way Katrina was handled shows leadership timing at its worst. It was botched at every level. Even the local animal shelter did better than the mayor. Two days prior to Katrina's arrival, it evacuated hundreds of animals to Houston, Texas.[5] In the end, more than 1,836 people died as a result of the hurricane; 1,577 of those people were from Louisiana.[6] Eighty percent of the deaths in Louisiana occurred in Orleans and St. Bernard parishes, with the overwhelming majority occurring in New Orleans.[7] If the leaders had paid greater attention not only to *what* they did but also to *when* they did it, many more lives would have been saved.

TIMING IS EVERYTHING

Good leaders recognize that *when* to lead is as important as what to do and where to go. Timing is often the difference between success and failure in an endeavor.

Every time a leader makes a move, there are really only four outcomes:

1. THE WRONG ACTION AT THE WRONG TIME LEADS TO DISASTER

A leader who takes the wrong action at the wrong time is sure to suffer negative repercussions. That was certainly the case in New Orleans as Katrina approached. Nagin's poor leadership set in motion a series of wrong actions at the wrong time. He waited until it was too late to call for a mandatory evacuation. He sent faxes to local churches, hoping they would help with evacuating people, but by the time he did so, the people who would have received the faxes were already long gone. He picked a poor location for the shelter of last resort, neglected to supply it properly, and failed to provide adequate transportation for people to get there. One wrong action after another led to disaster.

Obviously, the stakes for every leadership decision are not as high as they were for Mayor Nagin. But every leadership situation requires that leaders heed the Law of Timing. If you lead a department or a small team and you take the wrong action at the wrong time, your people will suffer. And so will your leadership.

2. THE RIGHT ACTION AT THE WRONG TIME BRINGS RESISTANCE

When it comes to good leadership, having a vision for the direction of the organization or team and knowing how to get there aren't enough. If you take the right action but do it at the wrong time, you may still be unsuccessful because the people you lead can become resistant.

Good leadership timing requires many things:

- **Understanding**—leaders must have a firm grasp on the situation.
- **Maturity**—if leaders' motives aren't right, their timing will be off.
- **Confidence**—people follow leaders who know what must be done.
- **Decisiveness**—wishy-washy leaders create wishy-washy followers.
- **Experience**—if leaders don't possess experience, then they need to gain wisdom from others who do possess it.
- **Intuition**—timing often depends on intangibles, such as momentum and morale.
- **Preparation**—if the conditions aren't right, leaders must create those conditions.

I've had my share of blunders in the area of timing. One in particular that stands out was my attempt to introduce a small group program at Skyline, my church in San Diego. It was the right thing to do at the church, but it failed miserably. Why? The timing was wrong. We were trying to do this back in the early 1980s, and there weren't many leaders with experience in this area, so we were playing it by ear. But most important, the church

> *If a leader repeatedly shows poor judgment, even in little things, people start to think that having him as the leader is the real mistake.*

wasn't prepared for it. We didn't understand that the success or failure of a small group launch depended on how many leaders had been developed to support it.

For a few years we tried to make it work with the system we had introduced, but ultimately, it failed. It wasn't until six years later that we got it to work—after shutting down the original system, training leaders, and starting over again. The second time around it was very successful.

3. THE WRONG ACTION AT THE RIGHT TIME IS A MISTAKE

People who are naturally entrepreneurial often possess a strong sense of timing. They intuitively know when it's time to make a move—to seize an opportunity. They sometimes make mistakes in their actions at those key moments. My brother, Larry, who is an excellent businessman, has coached me in this area. Larry says that the greatest mistake made by entrepreneurs and other people in business is knowing when to cut their losses or when to increase their investment to maximize their gains. Their mistakes come from taking the wrong action at the right time.

Once again, I have experience in this area. Because I'm known primarily as a communicator, for years people tried to talk me into doing a radio program. For a long time I resisted the idea. In the mid-1990s, however, I could see there was a need for a growth-oriented program for people of faith. So we decided to create a program called *Growing Today*. The problem was the format. Most programs of that type are supported by donations, but I believe in free-market economics. I wanted the program to support itself by selling products, the way any other commercial program would. What a mistake. The show never broke even. It was the right time but the wrong idea. The Law of Timing had spoken again.

4. THE RIGHT ACTION AT THE RIGHT TIME RESULTS IN SUCCESS

When the right leader and the right timing come together, incredible things happen. An organization achieves its goals, reaps incredible rewards, and gains momentum. Success almost becomes inevitable. If you look at the history of nearly any organization, you will find a pivotal moment when the right leader took the right action at the right time, and it transformed the organization. Winston Churchill, whose greatness in leadership depended on the Law of Timing, described the impact that leaders can make—and the satisfaction they can experience—when they take the right action at the right time. He said, "There comes a special moment in everyone's life, a

> When the right leader and the right timing come together, incredible things happen.

moment for which that person was born. That special opportunity, when he seizes it, will fulfill his mission—a mission for which he is uniquely qualified. In that moment, he finds greatness. It is his finest hour." Every leader desires to experience that moment.

THE CRUCIBLE OF WAR DISPLAYS
THE LAW OF TIMING

When the stakes are high, the consequences of the Law of Timing are dramatic and immediate. That is certainly true in war. In any major battle, the critical importance of timing becomes evident. The Battle of Gettysburg during the American Civil War is a prime example.

When Confederate General Robert E. Lee took the Army of Northern Virginia into Pennsylvania in late June of 1863, he had three goals: (1) draw the Union army out of Virginia, (2) resupply his troops using Pennsylvania's resources, and (3) bring the fighting to the heart of enemy territory, thereby prodding the Union army into hasty and unwanted action. It was the third year of the war, and both the Union and the Confederacy were growing weary of the conflict. Lee hoped his actions would bring an end to the conflict. Several days prior to the battle, Lee told General Trimble,

> Our army is in good spirits, not overfatigued, and can be concentrated on any one point in twenty-four hours or less. I have not yet heard that the enemy have crossed the Potomac, and am waiting to hear from General Stuart. When they hear where we are, they will make forced marches . . . They will come up . . . broken down from hunger and hard marching, strung out on a long line and much demoralized, when they come into Pennsylvania. I shall throw an overwhelming force on their advance, crush it, follow up the success, drive one corps back on another, and by successive repulses and surprises, before they can concentrate, create a panic and virtually destroy the army.[8]

Lee was trying to seize the opportunity for overwhelming victory. He didn't know until the morning of July 1 that the Union army had already moved north. By then some of its forces were already engaging Confederate troops on the Chambersburg Road west of Gettysburg. That development disrupted Lee's strategy and ruined his timing. Lee's first instinct was to hold back and wait for his army's full strength to assemble before forcing a major engagement. But always conscious of the importance of timing, he recognized when his troops had a sudden advantage. As Lee watched from a nearby ridge, he saw that Federal troops were being routed and retreating. There was still a chance to take action that could lead to victory.

Confederate forces could attack and seize the high ground of Cemetery Hill, defended only by a few Union infantry reserves and artillery. If they could capture and control that position, Lee reasoned, they would control the whole area. It would be the key to a Confederate victory and possibly bring an end to the war.

In position to take that hill was Confederate General R. S. Ewell. It was still early in the day, and if Ewell moved forward, he could take it. But instead of pressing his advantage when the time was ripe and engaging the enemy, Ewell simply watched. He let the opportunity slip away, and the Confederates didn't take Cemetery Hill. By the next morning, Union troops had reinforced their previous positions, and the South's chance was gone. The Northern and Southern armies fought for two more days, but in the end, Lee's forces suffered defeat, having lost about 33,000 of his 76,300 men to injury or death.[9] Their only choice was to retreat and make their way back to Virginia.

ANOTHER OPPORTUNITY LOST

After the South's defeat, Lee expected the Union forces under the leadership of General Meade to immediately pursue a counterattack and utterly destroy his reeling army. That was also the expectation of Abraham Lincoln after he received the news of the Union's victory at Gettysburg. Anxious to make the most of the Law of Timing, Lincoln sent a communication from

Washington DC, to Meade via General Halleck on July 7, 1863. In it, Halleck said,

> I have received from the President the following note, which I respectfully communicate.
>
> "We have certain information that Vicksburg surrendered to General Grant on the 4th of July. Now, if General Meade can complete his work so gloriously prosecuted thus far by the literal or substantial destruction of Lee's army, the rebellion will be over."[10]

Lincoln recognized that the timing was right. The Union army could crush what was left of the Confederate forces and could end the war. But just as the Southern forces did not seize the moment for victory when it was available to them, neither did their Northern counterparts. Meade took his time following up his victory at Gettysburg, and he didn't pursue Lee aggressively enough. He was content to let the Confederates run, stating that his goal was to "drive from our soil every vestige of the presence of the invader." When Lincoln heard that, his response was, "My God, is that all?" Lincoln knew he was seeing the Union's chance slip away. And he was right. What remained of the Army of Northern Virginia crossed over the Potomac, escaping destruction, and the war continued for almost two more years. And hundreds of thousands more troops died. Lincoln later said that Meade's efforts had reminded him of "an old woman trying to shoo her geese across a creek."[11] Leaders from both sides had known what to do to achieve victory, but they failed to follow through at the critical moment.

Reading a situation and knowing what to do are not enough to make you succeed in leadership. If you want your organization, department, or team to move forward, you must pay attention to timing. Only the right action *at the right time* will bring success. Anything else exacts a high price. No leader can escape the Law of Timing.

Applying
THE LAW OF TIMING
To Your Life

1. It has been said that managers do things right while leaders do the right things. The Law of Timing says that leaders do more than that: they do the right things at the right time. In your approach to leadership, does timing play an important part in your strategy? Do you think about the appropriateness of the timing as much as you do the rightness of the action? Review the major actions you've initiated in the recent past, and discern how much attention you've given to timing.

2. Spend some time analyzing recent failed initiatives for your organization, department, or team to determine whether they were caused by the wrong action or the wrong timing. (These initiatives can be yours or others'.) To help you, answer the following questions:

- What was the goal of the initiative?
- Who was the individual responsible for leading it?
- What factors were taken into account while the strategy was planned?
- Whose experience did the strategy draw upon?
- What was the condition or temperature of the organization at the time of the launch?
- What were the market or industry conditions?
- What "leverage" was available and being used to aid in the initiative?
- What factors were clearly working against it?
- Might the initiative have been more successful had it been launched either earlier or later?
- Why did the initiative ultimately fail?

3. As you prepare to engage in future plans, use the list of factors from the chapter to prepare for the timing of your actions:

- **Understanding**: Do you have a firm grasp on the situation?
- **Maturity**: Are your motives right?
- **Confidence**: Do you believe in what you are doing?
- **Decisiveness**: Can you initiate action with confidence and win people's trust?
- **Experience**: Have you drawn upon wisdom from others to inform your strategy?
- **Intuition**: Have you taken into account intangibles such as momentum and morale?
- **Preparation**: Have you done everything you must to set up your team for success?

Remember, only the right action at the right time will bring success to your team, department, or organization.

20

❦

THE LAW OF
EXPLOSIVE GROWTH

To Add Growth, Lead Followers—
To Multiply, Lead Leaders

I haven't always felt the way I do now about leadership. My belief in the power of leadership and my passion for training leaders have developed over the course of my professional life. When I started in my career, I thought personal growth was the key to being able to make an impact. My father had been very strategic in my development as I was growing up. He actually paid me to read books that he knew would help me and sent me to conferences when I was a teenager. Those experiences provided a great foundation for me. And after I began working, I discovered the Law of Process. That prompted me to take a proactive approach to my personal growth.

As a result, when people asked me to help them be more successful, I focused on teaching personal growth. It wasn't until I was forty years old that I began to understand the Law of the Inner Circle and the importance of developing a team. That's when my ability to grow an organization and reach greater goals began to increase. But it wasn't until I began to focus on developing leaders that my leadership *really* took off. I had discovered the Law of Explosive Growth: to add growth, lead followers—to multiply, lead leaders.

HELPING OTHERS TO LEAD

In 1990, I traveled to a country in South America with my wife, Margaret, to teach leadership in a national conference. One of the great joys of my life is teaching leadership to people of influence who desire to make a difference. I was really looking forward to this conference because it was an opportunity to add value to people outside my regular sphere of influence. But it didn't turn out the way I expected.

Everything started well. The people were very gracious, and I was able to connect with them despite the language and cultural barriers. But it wasn't long before I could tell that the attendees and I were not on the same page. When I started to teach about leadership, I could tell my comments were not connecting with them. They didn't engage, and what I was trying to communicate didn't seem to make an impact.

My read on the situation was confirmed after my first session with them. As I spoke with individuals, they didn't want to talk about leadership issues. They didn't ask questions about growing their organizations or fulfilling a vision. They sought advice about personal issues, problems, and conflicts with other people. I felt that I was back doing personal counseling similar to what I did at the beginning of my career. For the next three days, I grew more and more frustrated. The people I spoke to didn't understand leadership, and they had no desire to learn anything about it. For someone like me who believes that everything rises and falls on leadership, it drove me crazy!

This wasn't the first time I had experienced such frustration. I noticed that whenever I traveled to developing countries, I faced similar situations. I suspect that in nations where there is no strong business infrastructure and where government doesn't allow the citizens much freedom, it is difficult for leaders to develop.

On the flight home, I talked to Margaret about all my frustrations. I finally summed it up, saying, "I don't want to do this anymore. I traveled thousands of miles just to counsel people on petty conflicts. If they would just turn their attention to becoming leaders, it would change their lives."

After listening patiently, Margaret replied, "Maybe you're the one who's supposed to do something about this."

THE NEXT STEP

Margaret's exhortation to do something about the leadership problems I had seen overseas stirred something within me. For the next several years, I reflected on the issue and thought about possible solutions. Finally in 1996, I decided what I would do. I brought together a group of leaders to help me create a nonprofit organization to develop leaders in government, education, and the religious community. I named it EQUIP—encouraging qualities undeveloped in people.

For the next five years, EQUIP made modest progress in its goals. But in the months after the terrorist attacks of September 11, 2001, we went through a difficult period in which we had to lay off half the staff. But we took that as an opportunity to reexamine our priorities. We narrowed our focus and developed a new goal—one so large and daunting it looked almost impossible. We would try to develop *one million leaders* around the globe by 2008. How could a small nonprofit organization hope to accomplish such a feat? By using the Law of Explosive Growth!

THE STRATEGY

EQUIP's strategy, which came to be called the Million Leader Mandate, was to develop 40,000 leaders in countries around the world. Those leaders would attend a training session every six months in a city near them for three years. The only thing that would be asked of them in return was that they commit to personally develop twenty-five leaders in their own city, town, or village. EQUIP would provide the training materials for the 40,000 leaders it trained, and it would provide materials for the twenty-five leaders each of them would be developing.

EQUIP already employed some excellent leaders, including John Hull, president and CEO; Doug Carter, senior vice president; and Tim Elmore, vice president of leadership development. They assembled a top-notch team and began creating the training materials. Then they formed strategic alliances with organizations overseas. These organizations would help EQUIP figure out the cities in which to do the training, identify country and city coordinators to run the training sessions, and identify and recruit the 40,000 leaders to be trained.

The final step was to recruit excellent leaders who would be willing to volunteer their time to do the training in these cities around the world. Two trainers would travel to a city twice a year for three years, paying their own way and donating funds to help underwrite the materials the attendees would need. They would train the 40,000 who would in turn train twenty-five each. If the strategy succeeded, we would develop one million leaders. It was an ambitious plan. The question was, would it work? I'll give you the answer to that question later in this chapter.

MOVING FORWARD WITH LEADERS' MATH

Leaders are naturally impatient. At least, all of the leaders I know are. Leaders want to move fast. They want to see the vision fulfilled. They delight in progress. Good leaders quickly assess where an organization is, project where it needs to go, and have strong ideas about how to get it there. The problem is that most of the time the people and the organization lag behind the leader. For that reason, leaders always feel a tension between where they and their people *are* and where they *ought to be*. I have experienced this tension my entire life. In every organization I've ever been a part of, I had a strong sense of where it should go. I even felt that way as a kid. (I wasn't always *right* about where we should go, but I always thought I *knew*!)

> Becoming a leader who develops leaders requires an entirely different focus and attitude from simply attracting and leading followers. It takes a different mind-set.

How do you relieve that tension between where the organization is and where you want it to be? The answer can be found in the Law of Explosive Growth:

If you develop yourself, you can experience personal success.
If you develop a team, your organization can experience growth.
If you develop leaders, your organization can achieve explosive growth.

You can grow by leading followers. But if you want to maximize your leadership and help your organization reach its potential, you need to develop leaders. There is no other way to experience explosive growth.

A DIFFERENT FOCUS

Becoming a leader who develops leaders requires an entirely different focus and attitude from simply attracting and leading followers. It takes a different mind-set. Consider some of the differences between leaders who attract followers and leaders who develop leaders:

Leaders Who Attract Followers . . . Need to Be Needed
Leaders Who Develop Leaders . . . Want to Be Succeeded
Excitement comes from becoming a leader. When you speak, people listen. When you want to get something done, you can enlist other people to help you. Having followers can make you feel needed and important. However, that is a pretty shallow reason to pursue leadership. Good leaders lead for the sake of their followers and for what they can leave behind after their time of leadership is completed.

Leaders Who Attract Followers . . . Develop the Bottom 20 Percent
Leaders Who Develop Leaders . . . Develop the Top 20 Percent
When you're leading a group of people, who typically asks for the most time and attention? The weakest ones in the group. If you allow them to, they will consume 80 percent or more of your time. However, proactive leaders who practice the Law of Explosive Growth don't allow that bottom 20 percent to

take all their time. They seek out the *best* 20 percent—the people with the greatest leadership potential—and they invest their time developing them. They know that if they develop the best, the best will help with the rest.

Leaders Who Attract Followers . . . Focus on Weaknesses
Leaders Who Develop Leaders . . . Focus on Strengths
A necessity of working with the bottom 20 percent is that you must continually deal with their weaknesses. Unsuccessful people usually need help with the basics. Problems in those areas keep them from achieving consistent performance on a regular basis. However, when you work with your best people, you can build on their strengths.

Leaders Who Attract Followers . . . Treat Everyone the Same
Leaders Who Develop Leaders . . . Treat Individuals Differently
There is a myth in some leadership circles that promotes the idea of treating everyone the same for the sake of "fairness." What a mistake. As Mick Delaney says, "Any business or industry that pays equal rewards to its goof-offs and its eager beavers sooner or later will find itself with more goof-offs than eager beavers." Leaders who develop leaders give rewards, resources, and responsibility based on results. The greater the impact of leaders, the greater the opportunities they receive.

Leaders Who Attract Followers . . . Spend Time with Others
Leaders Who Develop Leaders . . . Invest Time in Others
Leaders who attract only followers and never develop them don't increase the value of those they lead. However, when leaders take time to develop the leaders they attract, they are making a valuable investment in them. Every moment they spend helps to increase their ability and influence. And that pays dividends to them and the organization.

Leaders Who Attract Followers . . . Grow by Addition
Leaders Who Develop Leaders . . . Grow by Multiplication
Leaders who attract followers grow their organization only one person at a

time. When you attract one follower, you impact one person. And you receive the value and power of one person. However, leaders who develop leaders multiply their organization's growth, because for every leader they develop, they also receive the value of all of that leader's followers.

Add ten followers to your organization, and you have the power of ten people. Add ten leaders to your organization, and you have the power of ten leaders times all of the followers and leaders they influence. That's what I call leader's math. It's the difference between addition and multiplication. It's like growing your organization by teams instead of by individuals.

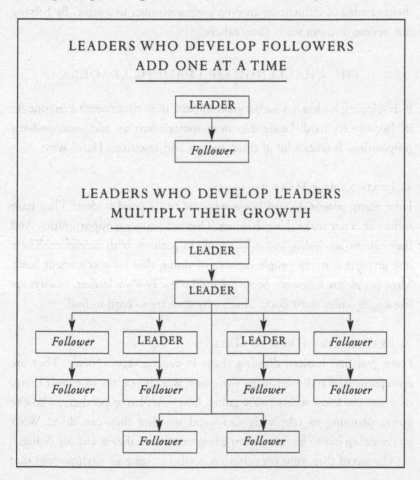

LEADERS WHO DEVELOP FOLLOWERS
ADD ONE AT A TIME

LEADER

Follower

LEADERS WHO DEVELOP LEADERS
MULTIPLY THEIR GROWTH

LEADER

LEADER

Follower · LEADER · LEADER · *Follower*

Follower · *Follower* · *Follower* · *Follower*

Follower · *Follower*

Leaders Who Attract Followers . . . Impact Only People They Touch
Leaders Who Develop Leaders . . . Impact People Beyond Their Reach
Leaders who attract followers but never develop leaders get tired. Why? Because they themselves must deal with every person under their authority. Being able to impact only the people you can touch personally is very limiting. In contrast, leaders who develop leaders impact people far beyond their personal reach. The better the leaders they develop, the greater the quality and quantity of followers and the greater the reach. Every time you develop leaders and help them increase their leadership ability, you make them capable of influencing an even greater number of people. By helping one person, you can reach many others.

THE CHALLENGE OF LEADING LEADERS

If developing leaders has such a great impact, then why doesn't everyone do it? Because it's hard! Leadership development isn't an add-water-and-stir proposition. It takes a lot of time, energy, and resources. Here's why:

1. Leaders Are Hard to Find
How many people do you know who are really good leaders? They have influence. They make things happen. They see and seize opportunities. And they can attract, enlist, and rally people to perform with excellence. There just aren't that many people capable of doing that on a consistent basis. Most people are followers. Some are producers. Few are leaders. Leaders are like eagles—they don't flock. That's why they are so hard to find.

2. Leaders Are Hard to Gather
Once you find leaders, drawing them in can be very difficult. They are entrepreneurial and want to go their own way. If you try to recruit them, they want to know where you're going, how you plan to get there, who else you're planning to take with you—and whether they can drive! What you're doing has to be more compelling than what they're already doing.

On top of that, your organization needs to create an environment that is attractive to them. That is often not the case. Most organizations desire stability. Leaders want excitement. Most organizations desire structure. Leaders want flexibility. Most organizations place a high value on following rules. Leaders want to think outside the box. If you want to gather leaders, you must create a place where they can thrive.

3. LEADERS ARE HARD TO KEEP

As hard as it is to find and gather good leaders, it's even more difficult to keep them. The only way to lead leaders is to become a better leader yourself. If you keep growing and stay ahead of the people you lead, then you will be able to keep adding value to the leaders who follow you. Your goals must be to keep developing them so that they can realize their potential. Only a leader can do that for another leader, because it takes a leader to raise up another leader.

One year in my leadership conferences, I took an informal poll to find out what prompted the attendees to become leaders. The results were as follows:

Natural gifting	10 percent
Result of crisis	5 percent
Influence of another leader	85 percent

Only one leader in ten is able to blossom without the help of another leader. The rest need the help of other leaders who are ahead of them in the journey. If you keep adding value to the leaders you lead, then they will be willing to stay with you. Do that long enough, and they may never want to leave.

THE LAUNCH OF THE MILLION LEADER MANDATE (MLM)

Convinced that developing leaders was the key to reaching our goal of training a million leaders, EQUIP launched the MLM initiative in 2002 in several cities in India, Indonesia, and the Philippines. We had chosen those areas because we had the best contacts there and had experienced success there in previous years. The response was overwhelming. Hundreds of hungry leaders traveled to each site to engage in the two-day training. Some attendees spent as many as five days *walking* to get to the event! And at the end of the training when we asked attendees to commit to developing twenty-five leaders over the next three years using the materials we would give them, more than 90 percent of the attendees signed on.

With the first success under our belt, we moved forward. The next year we began training leaders in other parts of Asia and the Middle East. In 2004, we started training in Africa; in 2005, Europe; and in 2006, South America. On every continent the strategy was the same:

1. Connect with key influential leaders in organizations already working with people locally and enlist their assistance.
2. Ask those key leaders to identify the cities in their country in which to do the training and to host the training events.
3. Rely on those key leaders to recruit leaders to attend the training.
4. Recruit leaders in the United States willing to travel overseas to train leaders and support the effort financially.
5. Receive a commitment from local attendees to find and train leaders for three years while we trained them.

In some cities, we had very modest success, with a few dozen leaders attending the training. In other cities, people came by the hundreds. Many leaders were able to commit to developing twenty-five leaders. Some could commit to training only five or ten. But others were training 100, 200, or 250 in their towns and cities!

As I mentioned, we wanted to reach our goal of training one million leaders by 2008. At times, it was a struggle. In some countries we had a difficult time gaining credibility. In others it took us a long time to make connections with leaders. But to our great surprise and delight, in the spring of 2006 we reached our goal—two years ahead of schedule! Now what seemed to be an impossible goal seems modest. In 2007, we trained our second million. And we launched an initiative to develop five million leaders in five years. My hope and prayer are that before I'm finished, EQUIP and its partners will train fifty million leaders around the globe. That's explosive growth.

Now that I'm sixty I've found that leadership development compounds. The more you invest in people and the longer you do it, the greater the growth and the higher the return. And though I may not be as fast as I once was or as energetic, I am now in a compounding stage of life. The thirty-five years of investments I've made in other people are starting to pay incredible dividends.

I don't know where you are in your journey of leadership development. You may already be a highly developed leader. Or you may just be getting started. No matter where you are, I know one thing: you will be able to reach your potential and help your

> *Leadership development compounds. The more you invest in people and the longer you do it, the greater the growth and the higher the return.*

organization reach its loftiest goals only if you begin developing leaders instead of merely attracting followers. Leaders who develop leaders experience an incredible multiplication effect in their organizations that can be achieved in no other way—not by increasing resources, reducing costs, increasing profit margins, improving systems, implementing quality procedures, or doing anything else. The only way to experience an explosive level of growth is to do the math—leader's math. That's the incredible power of the Law of Explosive Growth.

Applying
THE LAW OF EXPLOSIVE GROWTH
To Your Life

1. In which stage of the leadership development process do you currently find yourself?

Stage 1: Developing yourself
Stage 2: Developing your team
Stage 3: Developing leaders

To validate your answer, cite specific actions you have taken to develop yourself, to develop a team, and to help specific individuals improve their leadership ability. If you haven't begun to develop leaders, try to identify reasons why. Are you someone who needs to be needed, focuses on the bottom 20 percent, tries to treat everyone the same, or isn't strategic about investing in others? If you aren't developing leaders, identify what steps you must take to get started.

2. What are you currently doing to find and gather leaders? Are there places you go, events you attend, and networks you plug into to look for potential leaders? If not, start looking for some. If so, then what do you do to connect with leaders and recruit them for your organization, department, or team?

3. What are you doing to gather and hold leaders? Are you becoming a better leader so that leaders will want to follow you? Are you trying to create an environment where leaders can thrive and succeed? Are you giving leaders freedom to lead and be innovative? Are you clearing away red tape? Are you providing them with resources and greater responsibilities? Are you praising risk and rewarding success?

21

THE LAW OF LEGACY

A Leader's Lasting Value Is Measured by Succession

What do you want people to say at your funeral? That may seem like an odd question, but it may be the most important thing you can ask yourself as a leader. Most people never consider it. And that's not good, because if they don't, their lives and leadership can take a direction different from that of their greatest potential impact. If you want your leadership to really have meaning, you need to take into account the Law of Legacy. Why? Because a leader's lasting value is measured by succession.

STRIVING FOR MEANING

Eleanor Roosevelt commented, "Life is like a parachute jump; you've got to get it right the first time." I've always been conscious of the fact that our time here on earth is limited and we need to make the most of it. Life is not a dress rehearsal. My father impressed that upon me when I was a teenager. As a result, I've always had drive and desired to be the best I could be at whatever I did. But I have to admit, my goals and desires have changed quite a bit over the years, and that has affected the direction of my leadership.

Clare Boothe Luce, the writer, politician, and ambassador, popularized the idea of the "life sentence"—a statement summarizing the goal and purpose of one's life. When I started in my career in the late 1960s, my life sentence could have been expressed as, "I want to be a great pastor." Several years later as I worked and realized my shortcomings as a speaker, my sentence changed to be, "I want to be a great communicator." For more than a decade, improving my speaking skills became a major focus. However, when I reached my early thirties, I realized that if all I ever did was speak, my impact would always be limited. There are only so many days in a year and so many people who will come to an event to hear you. I wanted to reach more people than that. That's when I decided, "I want to be a great writer."

It took me three years to write my first book; it's a small volume of only 128 pages. Each chapter is only three or four pages long. Someone at a conference once complimented me, saying how smart she thought it was to create a book with such short chapters. Smart had nothing to do with it. I just didn't have very much to say! I've written many books since then, and I'm grateful that my writing has afforded me the opportunity to communicate with more people. But when I reached my forties, my focus changed again. That's when I decided, "I want to become a great leader." I wanted to build and lead organizations that could make a difference.

CHANGE IN PERSPECTIVE

I've discovered that at each stage of my life, I've grown and my world has gotten bigger. As a result, my "life sentence" has changed. When I was in my late fifties, I thought about all of the previous statements I had embraced, and I realized that they all had a common denominator: adding

value to others. That was really my desire. I wanted to be an effective pastor, communicator, writer, and leader so that I could help people. Now that I've turned sixty, I have finally settled on the life sentence that I believe will

> *My life sentence is, "I want to add value to leaders who will multiply value to others."*

serve me the rest of my days. When they hold my funeral, I hope I will have lived a life that prompts people to know why I was here and they won't

THE LAW OF LEGACY

have to guess at it. My life sentence is, "I want to add value to leaders who will multiply value to others."

Why is it so important to pay attention to your "life sentence"? Because your life sentence not only sets the direction for your life but it also deter-

> *Most people simply accept their lives—they don't lead them.*

mines the legacy you will leave. It took me a long time to figure that out. My hope is that you can learn the lesson more quickly than I did. Success doesn't count for much if you leave nothing behind. The best way to do that is through a leadership legacy.

DEVELOPING YOUR LEADERSHIP LEGACY

If you desire to make an impact as a leader on a future generation, then I suggest that you become highly intentional about your legacy. I believe that every person leaves some kind of legacy. For some it's positive. For others it's negative. But here's what I know: we have a choice about what legacy we will leave, and we must work and be intentional to leave the legacy we want. Here's how:

1. KNOW THE LEGACY YOU WANT TO LEAVE

Most people simply accept their lives—they don't lead them. I believe that people need to be proactive about how they live, and I believe that is especially true for leaders. Grenville Kleiser, in his classic personal development book, *Training for Power and Leadership*, wrote,

> Your life is like a book. The title page is your name, the preface your intro-
> duction to the world. The pages are a daily record of your efforts, trials,
> pleasures, discouragements, and achievements. Day by day your thoughts
> and acts are being inscribed in your book of life. Hour by hour, the record
> is being made that must stand for all time. Once the word *finis* must be
> written, let it then be said of your book that it is a record of noble purpose,
> generous service, and work well-done.[1]

—259—

Someday people will summarize your life in a single sentence. My advice: pick it now!

2. LIVE THE LEGACY YOU WANT TO LEAVE

I believe that to have any credibility as a leader, you must live what you say you believe. (I've touched on that in the Law of Solid Ground and the Law of the Picture.) Because my legacy involves adding value by influencing leaders, I have focused most of my attention on leaders, and I have become highly intentional in my efforts to lead them.

I believe there are seven major areas of influence in society: religion, economics, government, family, media, education, and sports. In the early years of my career, I had influence in just one of those seven areas. I am constantly striving to reach and gain credibility in more of the others. I try to do that by building bridges, relating to people on a heart-to-heart level, and seeking to give more than I receive.

> Someday people will summarize your life in a single sentence. My advice: pick it now!

If you want to create a legacy, you need to live it first. You must become what you desire to see in others.

3. CHOOSE WHO WILL CARRY ON YOUR LEGACY

I don't know what you want to accomplish in life, but I can tell you this: a legacy lives on in people, not things. Max Depree, author of *Leadership Is an Art*, declared, "Succession is one of the key responsibilities of leadership." Yet the Law of Legacy is something that few leaders seem to practice. Too often leaders put their energy into organizations, buildings, systems, or other lifeless objects. But only people live on after we are gone. Everything else is temporary.

There is often a natural progression to how leaders develop in the area of legacy, starting with the desire to achieve:

- Achievement comes when they do big things by themselves.
- Success comes when they empower followers to do big things for them.

- Significance comes when they develop leaders to do great things with them.
- Legacy comes when they put leaders in position to do great things without them.

It's like my friend Chris Musgrove says, "Success is not measured by what you're leaving to, but by what you are leaving behind."

Truett Cathy, the founder of the Chick-fil-A restaurant chain, says, "Somebody told me, 'Truett, the determination of how good a fellow you are is the conduct of your grandchildren.' I said, 'Oh, don't tell me that. I thought I did pretty good on my three children; now I've got to see how my twelve grandchildren turn out.'"[2] Why would someone say you need to look at a person's grandchildren? Because it's a good indication of how the people to whom you have chosen to invest your legacy will carry on without you. For that reason, you must choose wisely.

A legacy is created only when a person puts his organization into the position to do great things without him.

4. MAKE SURE YOU PASS THE BATON

Tom Mullins, an excellent leader and former coach who sits on EQUIP's board, tells me that the most important part of a relay race is the place that's called *the exchange zone*. That's where the runners must pass the baton to their teammates. You can have the fastest runners in the world—each one a record setter—but if they blow the exchange, they lose the race. The same is true when it comes to the Law of Legacy. No matter how well you lead or how good your successor is, if you don't make sure you pass the baton, you will not leave the legacy you desire.

Tom knows this so well that for the last several years, he has been working on his succession plan. He began grooming his son, Todd, who is also an excellent leader, to take the baton and lead in his place. As time has gone by, Todd has taken on more and more responsibility. Tom tells me that his greatest joy now comes from seeing Todd and other leaders step up and do an even better job of leading than he did.

Just about anybody can make an organization look good for a moment— by launching a flashy new program or product, drawing crowds to a big event, or slashing the budget to boost the bottom line. But leaders who leave a legacy take a different approach. They take the long view. Author, educator, and theologian Elton Trueblood wrote, "We have made at least a start in discovering the meaning in human life when we plant shade trees under which we know full well we will never

> "We have made at least a start in discovering the meaning in human life when we plant shade trees under which we know full well we will never sit."
> —ELTON TRUEBLOOD

sit." The best leaders lead today with tomorrow in mind by making sure they invest in leaders who will carry their legacy forward. Why? Because a leader's lasting value is measured by succession. That is the Law of Legacy.

A LEGACY OF SUCCESSION

In the fall of 1997 on a trip to India with some colleagues, we decided to visit the headquarters of a great leader of the twentieth century: Mother Teresa. Her headquarters, which the local people call the Mother House, is a plain concrete block building located in Kolkata. As I stood outside the doors, I thought that no one could tell by looking at it that this modest place had been the home base of such an effective leader.

We walked through a foyer and into a central patio that was open to the sky. Our intention was to visit Mother Teresa's tomb, which is located in the facility's dining room. But when we got there, we found out that the room was in use and we would not be allowed to go in until the ceremony was over.

We could see a group of about forty to fifty nuns seated, all dressed in the familiar habit that Mother Teresa had worn.

"What's going on in there?" I asked a nun passing by.

She smiled. "Today we are taking forty-five new members into our order," she said and then hurried away into another part of the building.

Since we were already running late and soon had to catch a plane, we couldn't stay. We looked around briefly and then left. As I walked out of the compound, through an alley, and among the throngs of people, I thought, *Mother Teresa would have been proud.* She was gone, but her legacy was continuing. She had made an impact on the world, and she had developed leaders who were carrying on her vision. And all appearances indicate that they will continue influencing people for generations to come. Mother Teresa's life is a vivid example of the Law of Legacy.

FEW LEADERS PASS IT ON

Last year when I was watching the Academy Awards ceremony on television, something struck me. One segment of the program showed brief images of the people in the movie industry who had died the previous year—from writers and directors to actors and technicians. Many images were greeted with polite applause while a few received tremendous ovations. Undoubtedly, those individuals were at the top of their profession. Some were perhaps the best at their craft who ever lived. But after a few seconds on screen and a bit of applause, they were forgotten. Everyone in the audience was focused on the next set of nominees for the Oscar.

> *"A life isn't significant except for its impact on other lives."*
> —Jackie Robinson

Life is fleeting. When all is said and done, your ability as a leader will not be judged by what you achieved personally. You can make a blockbuster film, but it will be forgotten in a few generations. You can write a prize-winning novel, but it will be forgotten in a few centuries. You can create a masterpiece of art, but in a millennium or two, no one will remember that you created it.

No, our ability as leaders will not be measured by the buildings we built, the institutions we established, or what our team accomplished during our tenure. You and I will be judged by how well the people we invested in carried on after we are gone. As baseball great Jackie Robinson observed, "A life isn't significant except for its impact on other lives." In the end, we will be judged according to the Law of Legacy. A leader's lasting value is measured by succession. May you and I live and lead according to that standard.

Applying
THE LAW OF LEGACY
To Your Life

1. What do you want your legacy to be? If you are early in your leadership journey, I wouldn't expect you to have the definitive answer to that question yet. However, I still think there is value in your considering what you want your life to stand for.

Take some time to consider the big picture concerning why you lead. This will not be a quick process. The idea of legacy is closely related to a person's sense of purpose in life. Why are you here? What gifts and skills do you possess that relate to your highest potential as a human being? What unique opportunities do you possess based on your personal circumstances and what's happening in the world around you? Who might you be able to impact and what might you be able to accomplish as a leader in your lifetime?

2. Based on your ideas you developed concerning the legacy you want to leave, what must you change in the way you conduct yourself so that you live that legacy? Write them out. Your list may include behavioral changes, character development, education, working methods, relationship building style, and so on. Only by changing the way you live will you be able to create the legacy you want to leave.

3. In whom will you invest to carry on your legacy? Ideally, you should pick people with greater potential than your own who will be able to "stand on your shoulders" and do more than you did. Begin investing in them today.

CONCLUSION

Everything Rises and Falls on Leadership

Well, there you have them—the 21 Irrefutable Laws of Leadership. Learn them, take them to heart, and apply them to your life. If you follow them, people will follow you. I've been teaching leadership for more than thirty years now, and during those years I've told the people I've trained something that I'm now going to say to you: everything rises and falls on leadership. Some people don't believe me when I say that, but it's true. The more you try to do in life, the more you will find that leadership makes the difference. Any endeavor you can undertake that involves other people will live or die depending on the leadership. As you work to build your organization, remember this:

- Personnel determine the potential of the organization.
- Relationships determine the morale of the organization.
- Structure determines the size of the organization.
- Vision determines the direction of the organization.
- Leadership determines the success of the organization.

Now that you know the laws and understand them, share them with your team. And take time to evaluate yourself regarding each of the laws using the evaluation tool on the following pages. As I mentioned at the beginning of this book, nobody does all the laws well. That's why you need to build a team.

I wish you great leadership success. Pursue your dreams. Strive for excellence. Become the person you were created to be. And accomplish all that you were put on this earth to do. Leadership will help you to do that. Learn to lead—not just for yourself but for the people who follow you. And as you reach the highest levels, don't forget to take others with you to be the leaders of tomorrow.

APPENDIX A:
21 LAWS LEADERSHIP EVALUATION

Read each statement below and score yourself for each, using the following scale:

0 Never
1 Rarely
2 Occasionally
3 Always

1. THE LAW OF THE LID
Leadership Ability Determines a Person's Level of Effectiveness

_____ a) When faced with a challenge, my first thought is, *Who can I enlist to help?* not *What can I do?*

_____ b) When my team, department, or organization fails to achieve an objective, my first assumption is that it's some kind of leadership issue.

_____ c) I believe that developing my leadership skills will increase my effectiveness dramatically.

_____ TOTAL

2. THE LAW OF INFLUENCE
The True Measure of Leadership Is Influence—Nothing More, Nothing Less

_____ a) I rely on influence rather than on my position or title to get others to follow me or do what I want.

_____ b) During discussions or brainstorming settings, people turn to me and ask for my advice.

_____ c) I rely on my relationships with others rather than organizational systems and procedures to get things done.

_____ TOTAL

3. THE LAW OF PROCESS
Leadership Develops Daily, Not in a Day

_____ a) I have a concrete, specific plan for personal growth that I engage in weekly.

_____ b) I have found experts and mentors for key areas of my life with whom I engage on a regular basis.

_____ c) To promote my professional growth, I have read at least six books (or taken at least one worthwhile class or listened to twelve or more audio lessons) per year for the last three years.

_____ TOTAL

4. THE LAW OF NAVIGATION
Anyone Can Steer the Ship, but It Takes a Leader to Chart the Course

_____ a) I spot problems, obstacles, and trends that will impact the outcome of initiatives the organization puts into place.

_____ b) I can clearly see a pathway for the implementation of a vision, including not only the process but also the people and resources needed.

_____ c) I am called upon to plan initiatives for the organization.

_____ TOTAL

APPENDIX A

5. THE LAW OF ADDITION
Leaders Add Value by Serving Others

_____ a) Rather than being annoyed when team members have issues preventing them from doing their jobs effectively, I see the issues as an opportunity to serve and help those people.

_____ b) I look for ways to make things better for the people I lead.

_____ c) I find great personal satisfaction in helping other people become more successful.

_____ TOTAL

6. THE LAW OF SOLID GROUND
Trust Is the Foundation of Leadership

_____ a) The people I lead confide in me regarding sensitive issues.

_____ b) When I tell someone in the organization that I will do something, he can count on me to follow through.

_____ c) I avoid undermining others or talking behind their backs.

_____ TOTAL

7. THE LAW OF RESPECT
People Naturally Follow Leaders Stronger Than Themselves

_____ a) People are naturally drawn to me and often want to do things with me just to spend time with me.

_____ b) I go out of my way to show respect and loyalty to the people I lead.

_____ c) I make courageous decisions and take personal risks that could benefit my followers even if there is no benefit to me.

_____ TOTAL

8. THE LAW OF INTUITION
Leaders Evaluate Everything with a Leadership Bias

____ a) I can easily gauge morale, whether in a room full of people, on a team, or in an organization.

____ b) I often take the right action as a leader even if I cannot explain why.

____ c) I can read situations and sense trends without having to gather hard evidence.

____ TOTAL

9. THE LAW OF MAGNETISM
Who You Are Is Who You Attract

____ a) I am satisfied with the caliber of people who report to me.

____ b) I expect the people I attract to be similar to me in values, skills, and leadership ability.

____ c) I recognize that no personnel process can improve the quality of people I recruit compared to improving myself.

____ TOTAL

10. THE LAW OF CONNECTION
Leaders Touch a Heart Before They Ask for a Hand

____ a) When I am new to a leadership situation, one of the first things I try to do is to develop a personal connection with the individuals involved.

____ b) I know the stories, hopes, and dreams of the people I lead.

____ c) I avoid asking people to help accomplish the vision until we have built a relationship that goes beyond the nuts and bolts of our work together.

____ TOTAL

11. THE LAW OF THE INNER CIRCLE
A Leader's Potential Is Determined by Those Closest to Him

_____ a) I am strategic and highly selective about which people are closest to me personally and professionally.

_____ b) I regularly rely on some key people in my life to help accomplish my goals.

_____ c) I believe that 50 percent or more of the credit for my accomplishments goes to the people on my team.

_____ TOTAL

12. THE LAW OF EMPOWERMENT
Only Secure Leaders Give Power to Others

_____ a) I embrace change easily and become dissatisfied with the *status quo*.

_____ b) I believe that no matter how talented the people who work for me are, my position is secure.

_____ c) It is my regular practice to give people I lead the authority to make decisions and take risks.

_____ TOTAL

13. THE LAW OF THE PICTURE
People Do What People See

_____ a) If I observe an undesirable action or quality in team members, I check for it in myself first before addressing it with them.

_____ b) I am continually working to try to make my actions and words consistent with one another.

_____ c) I do what I should rather than what I want because I am conscious that I am setting an example for others.

_____ TOTAL

14. THE LAW OF BUY-IN
People Buy into the Leader, Then the Vision

_____ a) I recognize that a lack of credibility can be as harmful to an organization as a lack of vision.

_____ b) I wait until I see that most of the people on the team have confidence in me before asking for a commitment to the vision.

_____ c) Even when my ideas are not very good, my people tend to side with me.

_____ TOTAL

15. THE LAW OF VICTORY
Leaders Find a Way for the Team to Win

_____ a) When I lead a team, I feel ultimate responsibility for whether it achieves its goals.

_____ b) If members of my team are not unified in their efforts to achieve the vision, I take action to get them on the same page.

_____ c) I make personal sacrifices to help ensure victory for my team, department, or organization.

_____ TOTAL

16. THE LAW OF THE BIG MO
Momentum Is a Leader's Best Friend

_____ a) I am enthusiastic and maintain a positive attitude every day for the sake of my team members.

_____ b) Whenever I make a major leadership decision, I consider how that decision will impact momentum in my team, department, or organization.

_____ c) I initiate specific actions with the purpose of generating momentum when introducing something new or controversial.

_____ TOTAL

17. THE LAW OF PRIORITIES
Leaders Understand That Activity Is Not Necessarily Accomplishment

_____ a) I avoid tasks that are not required by my leadership, don't have a tangible return, or don't reward me personally.

_____ b) I set aside time daily, monthly, and yearly to plan my upcoming schedule and activities based on my priorities.

_____ c) I delegate any task for which a team member can be at least 80 percent as effective as I could be.

_____ TOTAL

18. THE LAW OF SACRIFICE
A Leader Must Give Up to Go Up

_____ a) I know making trade-offs is a natural part of leadership growth, and I make sacrifices to become a better leader as long as they don't violate my values.

_____ b) I expect to give more than my followers do in order to accomplish the vision.

_____ c) I will give up my rights in order to reach my potential as a leader.

_____ TOTAL

19. THE LAW OF TIMING
When to Lead Is As Important As What to Do and Where to Go

_____ a) I expend as much effort figuring out the timing for an initiative as I do figuring out the strategy.

_____ b) I will launch something using a less-than-ideal strategy because I know the timing is right.

_____ c) I can sense whether or not people are ready for an idea.

_____ TOTAL

Appendix A

20. The Law of Explosive Growth
To Add Growth, Lead Followers—To Multiply, Lead Leaders

_____ a) I believe that I can grow my organization more rapidly by developing leaders than by any other method.

_____ b) I spend a significant amount of time every week investing in the development of the top 20 percent of my leaders.

_____ c) I would rather see leaders I develop succeed out on their own than keep them with me so that I can keep mentoring them.

_____ TOTAL

21. The Law of Legacy
A Leader's Lasting Value Is Measured by Succession

_____ a) I possess a strong sense of why I am in my job and why I am leading.

_____ b) In each position I've held, I have identified people who can carry on after me, and I have invested in them.

_____ c) One of my strongest motivations is to leave any team I lead better than I found it.

_____ TOTAL

Now that you have completed the evaluation, examine each law and note your strengths and weaknesses. Use the following guidelines to help you proceed.

8–9 This law is in your strength zone. Make the most of this skill and mentor others in this area.

5–7 Target this law for growth. You have potential to make it a strength.

0–4 This is a weakness. Hire staff with this strength or partner with others in this area.

APPENDIX B:
21 LAWS GROWTH GUIDE

For many years I have written books to add value to people. Now that you and your team have completed the leadership evaluation, I encourage you to use the following resources to enable you to lead yourself and others more efficiently.

1. THE LAW OF THE LID
Leadership Ability Determines a Person's Level of Effectiveness

> *The 21 Indispensable Qualities of a Leader*
> *The Right to Lead*
> *The 360-Degree Leader*—Value #2: "Leaders Are Needed at Every
>   Level of the Organization" and Value #4: "Good Leaders in the
>   Middle Make Better Leaders at the Top"

2. THE LAW OF INFLUENCE
The True Measure of Leadership Is Influence—Nothing More, Nothing Less

> *Developing the Leader Within You*—Chapter 1: "The Definition of
>   Leadership: Influence"

— 277 —

The 360-Degree Leader—Section I: "The Myths of Leading from the Middle of an Organization" and Section II: "The Challenges 360-Degree Leaders Face"
Winning with People

3. THE LAW OF PROCESS
Leadership Develops Daily, Not in a Day

Today Matters
Your Road Map for Success—Chapter 5: "What Should I Pack in My Suitcase?"
The 360-Degree Leader—Lead-Up Principle #9: "Be Better Tomorrow Than You Are Today"
Leadership Promises for Every Day
The 21 Most Powerful Minutes in a Leader's Day

4. THE LAW OF NAVIGATION
Anyone Can Steer the Ship, but It Takes a Leader to Chart the Course

Developing the Leader Within You—Chapter 5: "The Quickest Way to Gain Leadership: Problem-Solving"
Thinking for a Change—Skill 2: "Unleash the Potential of Focused Thinking"; Skill 4: "Recognize the Importance of Realistic Thinking"; Skill 5: "Release the Power of Strategic Thinking"
Becoming a Person of Influence—Chapter 7: "Navigates for Other People"

5. THE LAW OF ADDITION
Leaders Add Value by Serving Others

Today Matters—Chapter 12: "Today's Generosity Gives Me Significance"
Thinking for a Change—Skill 10: "Experience the Satisfaction of Unselfish Thinking"
Becoming a Person of Influence—Chapter 2: "Nurtures Other People"

The 360-Degree Leader—Lead-Up Principle #2: "Lighten Your
Leader's Load"; Lead-Up Principle #3: "Be Willing to Do What
Others Won't"; Lead-Across Principle #3: "Be a Friend";
Lead-Across Principle #3: "Let the Best Idea Win"
Your Road Map for Success—Chapter 8: "Is It a Family Trip?" and
Chapter 9: "Who Else Should I Take with Me?"

6. THE LAW OF SOLID GROUND
Trust Is the Foundation of Leadership

Developing the Leader Within You—Chapter 3: "The Most Important
Ingredient of Leadership: Integrity"
Becoming a Person of Influence—Chapter 1: "Integrity with People"
The 360-Degree Leader—Lead-Up Principle #1: "Lead Yourself
Exceptionally Well"
Ethics 101

7. THE LAW OF RESPECT
People Naturally Follow Leaders Stronger Than Themselves

Thinking for a Change—Skill 6: "Feel the Energy of Possibility
Thinking"
Your Road Map for Success—Chapter 4: "How Do I Get There
from Here?"
Winning with People
The 360-Degree Leader

8. THE LAW OF INTUITION
Leaders Evaluate Everything with a Leadership Bias

Thinking for a Change—Skill 8: "Question the Acceptance of Popular
Thinking"and Skill 11: "Enjoy the Return of Bottom-Line Thinking"
The 360-Degree Leader
Leadership Gold (coming March 2008)

9. THE LAW OF MAGNETISM

Who You Are Is Who You Attract

> *Today Matters*—Chapter 13: "Today's Values Give Me Direction"
> *The 360-Degree Leader*—Lead-Across Principle #4: "Avoid Office Politics"
> *Talent Is Never Enough*
> *The Choice Is Yours*

10. THE LAW OF CONNECTION

Leaders Touch a Heart Before They Ask for a Hand

> *25 Ways to Win with People*
> *The 360-Degree Leader*—Lead-Up Principle #5: "Invest in Relational Chemistry"; Lead-Across Principle #1: "Understand, Practice, and Complete the Leadership Loop"; Lead-Down Principle #1: "Walk Slowly Through the Halls"; Lead-Down Principle #2: "See Everyone as a '10'"
> *Becoming a Person of Influence*—Chapter 8: "Connects with People"
> *Winning with People*

11. THE LAW OF THE INNER CIRCLE

A Leader's Potential Is Determined by Those Closest to Him

> *The 17 Indisputable Laws of Teamwork*
> *The 17 Essential Qualities of a Team Player*
> *Teamwork Makes the Dream Work*
> *The 360-Degree Leader*—Lead-Down Principle #4: "Place People in Their Strength Zones" and Lead-Down Principle #7: "Reward for Results"

12. THE LAW OF EMPOWERMENT

Only Secure Leaders Give Power to Others

> *Failing Forward*

The 360-Degree Leader—Lead-Across Principle #7: "Don't Pretend You're Perfect"

Winning with People—Section 1: "Are We Prepared for Relationships?"

Becoming a Person of Influence—Chapter 9: "Empowers People"

Thinking for a Change—Skill 9: "Encourage the Participation of Shared Thinking"

Your Road Map for Success—Chapter 6: "How Do I Handle the Detours?"

The Difference Maker

13. THE LAW OF THE PICTURE
People Do What People See

The 360-Degree Leader—Lead-Down Principle #5: "Model the Behavior You Desire"

Developing the Leader Within You—Chapter 6: "The Extra Plus in Leadership: Attitude" and Chapter 9: "The Price Tag of Leadership: Self-Discipline"

Your Road Map for Success—Chapter 1: "The Journey Is More Fun if You Know Where You're Going" and Chapter 2: "How Far Can I Go?"

14. THE LAW OF BUY-IN
People Buy into the Leader, Then the Vision

Developing the Leader Within You—Chapter 8: "The Indispensable Quality of Leadership: Vision"

Your Road Map for Success—Chapter 3: "How Do I Get There from Here?"

25 Ways to Win with People

Winning with People

15. THE LAW OF VICTORY
Leaders Find a Way for the Team to Win

The 360-Degree Leader—Lead-Up Principle #8: "Become a Go-To Player"
Thinking for a Change—Skill 1: "Acquire the Wisdom of Big-Picture Thinking" and Skill 3: "Discover the Joy of Creative Thinking"
The Difference Maker

16. THE LAW OF THE BIG MO
Momentum Is a Leader's Best Friend

Developing the Leader Within You—Chapter 4: "The Ultimate Test of Leadership: Creating Positive Change"
The 360-Degree Leader—Lead-Up Principle #4: "Do More Than Manage—Lead!" and Lead-Up Principle #8: "Become a Go-To Player"

17. THE LAW OF PRIORITIES
Leaders Understand That Activity Is Not Necessarily Accomplishment

Developing the Leader Within You—Chapter 2: "The Key to Leadership: Priorities"
Today Matters—Chapter 4: "Today's Priorities Give Me Focus"
Thinking for a Change—Chapter 5: "Unleash the Potential of Focused Thinking"
The 360-Degree Leader—Lead-Up Principle #1: "Lead Yourself Exceptionally Well"

18. THE LAW OF SACRIFICE
A Leader Must Give Up to Go Up

Developing the Leader Within You—Chapter 3: "The Most Important Ingredient of Leadership: Integrity"
Your Road Map for Success—Chapter 7: "Are We There Yet?"

Today Matters—Chapter 8: "Today's Commitment Gives Me Tenacity"

Ethics 101—Chapter 5: "Five Factors That Can 'Tarnish' the Golden Rule"

19. THE LAW OF TIMING
When to Lead Is As Important As What to Do and Where to Go

The 360-Degree Leader—Lead-Up Principle #6: "Be Prepared Every Time You Take Your Leader's Time" and Lead-Up Principle #7: "Know When to Push and When to Back Off"

Thinking for a Change—Chapter 3: "Master the Process of Intentional Thinking" and Skill 10: "Embrace the Lessons of Reflective Thinking"

20. THE LAW OF EXPLOSIVE GROWTH
To Add Growth, Lead Followers—To Multiply, Lead Leaders

Developing the Leader Within You—Chapter 10: "The Most Important Lesson of Leadership: Staff Development"

Developing the Leaders Around You

Your Road Map for Success—Chapter 10: "What Should We Do Along the Way?"

Becoming a Person of Influence—Chapter 10: "Reproduces Other Influencers"

The 360-Degree Leader—Lead-Down Principle #3: "Develop Each Team Member as a Person"; Special Section: "Create an Environment That Unleashes 360-Degree Leaders"; Section VI: "The Value of 360-Degree Leaders"

21. THE LAW OF LEGACY
A Leader's Lasting Value Is Measured by Succession

The Journey from Success to Significance

Appendix B

Becoming a Person of Influence—Chapter 6: "Enlarges People"
The 360-Degree Leader—Lead-Down Principle #6: "Transfer the Vision"
Dare to Dream . . . Then Do It

NOTES

1. THE LAW OF THE LID

1. McDonald's Canada, "FAQs," http://www.mcdonalds.ca/en/aboutus/faq.aspx (accessed August 8, 2006).

2. THE LAW OF INFLUENCE

1. Peggy Noonan, *Time*, September 15, 1997.
2. Thomas A. Stewart, "Brain Power: Who Owns It . . . How They Profit from It," *Fortune*, March 17, 1997, 105–6.
3. Paul F. Boller Jr., *Presidential Anecdotes* (New York: Penguin Books, 1981), 129.

3. THE LAW OF PROCESS

1. Sharon E. Epperson, "Death and the Maven," *Time*, December 18, 1995.
2. James K. Glassman, "An Old Lady's Lesson: Patience Usually Pays," *Washington Post*, December 17, 1995, H01.
3. "The Champ," *Reader's Digest*, January 1972, 109.
4. Milton Meltzer, *Theodore Roosevelt and His America* (New York: Franklin Watts, 1994).

4. THE LAW OF NAVIGATION

1. *Forbes*.
2. John C. Maxwell, *Thinking for a Change: 11 Ways Highly Successful People Approach Life and Work* (New York: Warner Books, 2003), 177–80.
3. Jim Collins, *Good to Great: Why Some Companies Make the Leap . . . and Others Don't* (New York: Harper Business, 2001), 86.

5. THE LAW OF ADDITION

1. Julie Schmit, "Costo Wins Loyalty with Bulky Margins," *USA Today*, September 24, 2004, http://www.keepmedia.com/pubs/USATODAY/2004/09/24/586747?extID=10032&oliID=213 (accessed August 24, 2006).

2. Alan B. Goldberg and Bill Ritter, "Costco CEO Finds Pro-Worker Means Profitability," ABC News, August 2, 2006, http://abcnews.go.com/2020/Business/story?id=1362779 (accessed August 16, 2006).
3. Barbara Mackoff and Gary Wenet, *The Inner Work of Leaders: Leadership as a Habit of Mind* (New York: AMACOM, 2001), 5.
4. Steven Greenhouse, "How Costco Became the Anti-Wal-Mart," *New York Times*, July 17, 2005, http://select.nytimes.com/search/restricted/article (accessed August 22, 2006).
5. Goldberg and Ritter, "Costco CEO Finds Pro-Worker Means Profitability."
6. Greenhouse, "How Costco Became the Anti-Wal-Mart."
7. Matthew 25:31–40 (The Message).
8. Dan Cathy, Exchange [conference], November 2, 2005.

6. THE LAW OF SOLID GROUND

1. Robert Shaw, "Tough Trust," *Leader to Leader*, Winter 1997, 46–54.
2. Russell Duncan, *Blue-Eyed Child of Fortune* (Athens: University of Georgia Press, 1992), 52–54.
3. Robert S. McNamara with Brian VanDeMark, *In Retrospect: The Tragedy and Lessons of Vietnam* (New York: Times Books, 1995).

7. THE LAW OF RESPECT

1. M. W. Taylor, *Harriet Tubman* (New York: Chelsea House Publishers, 1991).
2. Careers By the People, "Principal," http://www.careersbythepeople.com/index/do/bio/ (accessed August 31, 2006).
3. NCAA, http://www.ncaa.org/stats/m_basketball/coaching/d1_500_coaching_records.pdf (accessed August 31, 2006).
4. Alexander Wolff, "Tales Out of School," *Sports Illustrated*, October 20, 1997, 64.
5. Mitchell Krugel, *Jordan: The Man, His Words, His Life* (New York: St. Martin's Press, 1994), 39.

8. THE LAW OF INTUITION

1. Cathy Booth, "Steve's Job: Restart Apple," *Time*, August 18, 1997, 28–34.
2. Leander Kahney, "Inside Look at Birth of the iPod," *Wired*, July 21, 2004, http://www.wired.com/news/culture/0,64286-1.htm (accessed September 1, 2006).
3. Ana Letícia Sigvartsen, "Apple Might Have to Share iPod Profits," InfoSatellite, March 8, 2005, http://www.infosatellite.com/news/2005/03/a080305ipod.html (accessed April 6, 2006).
4. BBC News, "iPod Helps Apple Quadruple Profit," December 10, 2005, http://newsvote.bbc.co.uk (accessed September 1, 2006).

10. THE LAW OF CONNECTION

1. CBC News Canada, "Bush Visits 'Ground Zero' in New York," September 15, 2001, http://www.cbc.ca/story/news/?/news/2001/09/14/bushnyc_010914 (accessed September 11, 2006).

NOTES

2. Sheryl Gay Stolberg, "Year After Katrina, Bush Still Fights for 9/11 Image," *New York Times*, August 28, 2006, http://www.nytimes.com/2006/08/28/us/nationalspecial/28bush.html (accessed September 12, 2006).

3. H. Norman Schwarzkopf, "Lessons in Leadership," vol. 12, no. 5.

4. H. Norman Schwarzkopf and Peter Petre, *It Doesn't Take a Hero* (New York: Bantam Books, 1992).

5. Kevin and Jackie Freiberg, *Nuts! Southwest Airlines' Crazy Recipe for Business and Personal Success* (New York: Broadway Books, 1996), 224.

11. THE LAW OF THE INNER CIRCLE

1. Michael Specter, "The Long Ride: How Did Lance Armstrong Manage the Greatest Comeback in Sports History?" *New Yorker*, July 15, 2002, http://www.newyorker.com/printables/fact/020715fa_fact1 (accessed September 15, 2006).

2. Dan Osipow, "Armstrong: 'I'm More Motivated Than Ever,'" *Pro Cycling*, June 23, 2005, http://team.discovery.com/news/062205tourteam_print.html (accessed September 15, 2006).

3. Discovery Channel Pro Cycling Team, "Cycling FAQ: Learn More About Team Discovery," http://team.discovery.com/index.html?path=tabs3 (accessed September 15, 2006).

4. Lawrence Miller, *American Spirit: Visions of a New Corporate Culture* (New York: Warner Books, 1985).

5. Warren Bennis, *Organizing Genius: The Secrets of Creative Collaboration* (New York: Perseus Books, 1998).

6. Proverbs 27:17 CEV.

7. Judith M. Bardwick, *In Praise of Good Business* (New York: John Wiley and Sons, 1988).

12. THE LAW OF EMPOWERMENT

1. Peter Collier and David Horowitz, *The Fords: An American Epic* (New York: Summit Books, 1987).

2. Lee Iacocca and William Novak, *Iacocca: An Autobiography* (New York: Bantam Books, 1984).

3. Lynne Joy McFarland, Larry E. Senn, and John R. Childress, *21st Century Leadership: Dialogues with 100 Top Leaders* (Los Angeles: Leadership Press, 1993), 64.

4. Benjamin P. Thomas, *Abraham Lincoln: A Biography* (New York: Modern Library, 1968), 235.

5. Richard Wheeler, *Witness to Gettysburg* (New York: Harper and Row, 1987).

6. Donald T. Phillips, *Lincoln on Leadership: Executive Strategies for Tough Times* (New York: Warner Books, 1992), 103–4.

13. THE LAW OF THE PICTURE

1. Stephen E. Ambrose, *Band of Brothers* (New York: Simon and Schuster, 2001), 36.
2. Dick Winters with Cole C. Kingseed, *Beyond Band of Brothers: The War Memoirs of Major Dick Winters* (New York: Penguin, 2006), front flap copy.
3. Ambrose, *Band of Brothers*, 38.
4. Ibid., 95–96.
5. Winters, *Beyond Band of Brothers*, 283.
6. About.com: U.S. Military, "Historian Stephen E. Ambrose, Author of *Band of Brothers:* The Story of Easy Company," http://usmilitary.about.com/library/milinfo/bandofbrothers/blbbambrose.htm (accessed September 26, 2006).
7. Author unknown, quoted in John Wooden with Steve Johnson, *Wooden: A Lifetime of Observations and Reflections On and Off the Court* (Chicago: Contemporary Books, 1997).
8. Ajilon Office, "Trouble Finding the Perfect Gift for Your Boss—How About a Little Respect?" October 14, 2003, http://www.ajilonoffice.com/articles/af_bossday_101403.asp (accessed September 25, 2006).
9. Rudolph W. Guiliani with Ken Kurson, *Leadership* (New York: Miramax Books, 2002), 37.
10. Ibid., 209.
11. Ibid., 70.
12. Ibid., xiv.

14. THE LAW OF BUY-IN

1. Otis Port, "Love Among the Digerati," *Business Week*, August 25, 1997, 102.

15. THE LAW OF VICTORY

1. James C. Humes, *The Wit and Wisdom of Winston Churchill* (New York: Harper Perennial, 1994), 114.
2. Ibid., 117.
3. Arthur Schlesinger Jr., "Franklin Delano Roosevelt," *Time*, April 13, 1998.
4. Andre Brink, "Nelson Mandela," *Time*, April 13, 1998.
5. Mitchell Krugel, *Jordan: The Man, His Words, His Life* (New York: St. Martin's Press, 1994), 41.
6. Southwest Airlines, "Southwest Airlines Fact Sheet," http://www.southwest.com/about_swa/press/factsheet.html#Fun%20Facts (accessed October 19, 2006).
7. Freiberg, *Nuts! Southwest Airlines' Crazy Recipe for Business and Personal Success.*
8. Southwest Airlines, "Southwest Airlines Fact Sheet."
9. Southwest Airlines, Annual Report 2005, http://www.southwest.com/investor_relations/swaar05.pdf (accessed October 20, 2006). [Stockholders' equity and total assets are from 2005, the latest available.]
10. Freiberg, *Nuts! Southwest Airlines' Crazy Recipe for Business and Personal Success.*

16. THE LAW OF THE BIG MO

NOTES

1. Guardian Unlimited, "Regus London Film Festival Interviews 2001: John Lasseter," November 19, 2001, http://film.guardian.co.uk/lff2001/news/0,,604666,00.html (accessed October 25, 2006).
2. Catherine Crane, Will Johnson, and Kitty Neumark, "Pixar 1996" (case study), University of Michigan Business School, http://www-personal.umich.edu/~afuah/cases/case14.html (accessed October 27, 2006).
3. Brent Schlender, "Pixar's Magic Man," *Fortune*, May 17, 2006, http://cnnmoney.printthis.clickability.com (accessed October 24, 2006).
4. Michael P. McHugh, "An Interview with Edwin Catmull," *Networker*, September/October 1997, http://was.usc.edu/isd/publications/archives/networker/97-98/Sep_Oct_97 (accessed October 26, 2006).
5. Crane, Johnson, and Neumark, "Pixar 1996."
6. Pixar, "Pixar History: 1995," http://www.pixar.com/companyinfo/history/1995.html (accessed October 30, 2006).
7. Austin Bunn, "Welcome to Planet Pixar," *Wired*, http://www.wired.com/wired/archive/12.06/pixar_pr.html (accessed October 25, 2006).
8. IMDb, "All-Time Worldwide Boxoffice," http://www.imdb.com/boxoffice/alltimegross?region=world-wide (accessed October 30, 2006). [Figures as of October 23, 2006.]
9. Claudia Eller, "Disney's Low-Key Superhero," *Los Angeles Times*, June 12, 2006, http://pqasb.pqarchiver.com/latimes/access/1057182661.html?dids=1057182661:1057182661&FMTS=ABS:FT&type=current&date=Jun+12%2C+2006&author=Claudia+Eller&pub=Los+Angeles+Times&desc=The+Nation (accessed October 26, 2006).
10. Jay Mathews, *Escalante: The Best Teacher in America* (New York: Henry Holt, 1988).

17. THE LAW OF PRIORITIES

1. Janet C. Lowe, *Jack Welch Speaks: Wisdom from the World's Greatest Business Leader* (New York: John Wiley and Sons, 1998), 110.
2. John Wooden and Jack Tobin, *They Call Me Coach* (Chicago: Contemporary Books, 1988).

18. THE LAW OF SACRIFICE

1. King Encyclopedia, "Montgomery Improvement Association," http://www.stanford.edu/group/King/about_king/encyclopedia/MIA.html (accessed November 8, 2006).
2. The King Center, "Chronology of Dr. Martin Luther King, Jr.," http://www.thekingcenter.org/mlk/chronology.html (accessed November 8, 2006).
3. David Wallechinsky, *The Twentieth Century* (Boston: Little, Brown and Company, 1995), 155.
4. Hillary Margolis, "A Whole New Set of Glitches for Digital's Robert Palmer," *Fortune*, August 19, 1996, 193–94.
5. Antonia Felix, *Condi: The Condoleezza Rice Story* (New York: Newmarket Press, 2005), 48.
6. Ibid., 34.

7. Ibid., 67.
8. Ibid., 72.
9. Ibid., 127.
10. Ibid., 152–53.

19. THE LAW OF TIMING

1. David Oshinsky, "Hell and High Water," *New York Times*, July 9, 2006, http://www.nytimes.com/2006/07/09/books/review/09oshi.html?ei=5088&en=4676642ee3fc7078&ex=1310097600&adxnnl=1&partner=rssnyt&emc=rss&adxnnlx=1162847220-jiFf9bMhfwwKfuiWDA/Nrg (accessed November 6, 2006).

2. CNN, "New Orleans Mayor, Louisiana Governor Hold Press Conference" (transcript), aired August 28, 2005, 10:00 a.m. ET, http://transcripts.cnn.com/TRANSCRIPTS/0508/28/bn.04.html (accessed November 6, 2006).

3. Jonathan S. Landay, Alison Young, and Shannon McCaffrey, "Chertoff Delayed Federal Response, Memo Shows," McClatchy Washington Bureau, September 13, 2005, http://www.realcities.com/mld/krwashington/12637172.htm (accessed November 2, 2006).

4. CNN, "Red Cross: State Rebuffed Relief Efforts: Aid Organization Never Got into New Orleans, Officials say," September 9, 2005, http://www.cnn.com/2005/US/09/08/katrina.redcross/index.html (accessed November 2, 2006).

5. Madeline Vann, "Search and Rescue," *Tulanian* (Summer 2006), http://www2.tulane.edu/article_news_details.cfm?ArticleID=6752 (accessed November 7, 2006).

6. Answers.com, "Hurricane Katrina," http://www.answers.com/topic/hurricane-katrina (accessed November 7, 2006).

7. Coleman Warner and Robert Travis Scott, "Where They Died," *Times-Picayune*, October 23, 2005, http://pqasb.pqarchiver.com/timespicayune/access/915268571.html?dids=915268571:915268571&FMT=ABS&FMTS=ABS:FT&date=Oct+23%2C+2005&author=Coleman+Warner+and+Robert+Travis+Scott+Staff+writers&pub=Times+-+Picayune&edition=&startpage=01&desc=WHERE+THEY+DIED+ (accessed November 7, 2006).

8. Douglas Southall Freeman, *Lee: An Abridgement in One Volume* (New York: Charles Scribner's Sons, 1961), 319.

9. Samuel P. Bates, *The Battle of Gettysburg* (Philadelphia: T. H. Davis and Company, 1875), 198–99.

10. Ibid.

11. Richard Wheeler, *Witness to Gettysburg* (New York: Harper and Row, 1987).

21. THE LAW OF LEGACY

1. Grenville Kleiser, *Training for Power and Leadership* (Garden City, New York: Garden City Publishing, 1929).

2. Q&A Session with Truett Cathy and Dan Cathy, Exchange [conference], November 2, 2005.

COMING SPRING 2008!

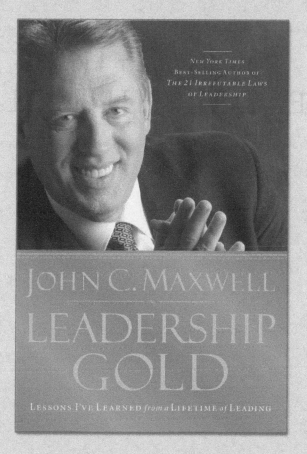

Also available in audio and Spanish editions

Leadership Gold delivers leadership guru John C. Maxwell's most valuable lessons from forty years of leading.

THOMAS NELSON
Since 1798

AN EXCERPT FROM
LEADERSHIP GOLD

Introduction

SEARCHING FOR GOLD

I confess I've wanted to write this book for almost a decade. In a way, I've been working on it for most of my life. But I promised myself that I would not sit down and write it until I turned sixty. In February of 2007, I reached that milestone and began writing.

I've had a remarkable and rewarding journey as a leader. In 1964 at the age of seventeen, I started reading and filing thoughts on the subject of leadership because I knew leading was going to be an important part of my career. At age twenty-two, I held my first leadership position. In 1976 I became convinced that everything rises and falls on leadership. That belief was accompanied by a passion to be a lifelong student and teacher of this vital subject.

Learning to lead effectively has been a real challenge. Teaching others to lead effectively has been an even greater one. During the late 1970s I poured myself into training and raising up potential leaders. To my delight, I discovered that leaders could be developed. That eventually prompted me to write my first leadership book in 1992, entitled *Developing the Leader Within You*. Since then I have written many others. For more than thirty years, leading and teaching leadership have been my life's work.

ADDING VALUE TO YOUR LEADERSHIP

This book is a result of years of living in a leadership environment and learning through trial and error what it means to be a leader. The lessons I've learned are personal and often simple, yet they can have a profound impact. I have spent my entire life mining them. I think of each chapter as a gold nugget. In the hands of the right person, they can add tremendous value to their leadership.

As you read each chapter, please understand that . . .

1. *I'm still learning about leadership.* I haven't arrived, and this book is not my final answer on the subject of leadership. Within weeks of this book's publication, there will be thoughts I wish I could add. Why? Because I continue to learn and grow. I hope to keep growing until the day I die. I expect to keep discovering nuggets that I want to share with others.

2. *Many people have contributed to the leadership gold in this book.* One of the chapters in this book is entitled, "Few Leaders Are Successful Unless a Lot of People Want Them to Be." That has certainly been true for me. It's said that a wise person learns from his mistakes. A wiser one learns from others' mistakes. But the wisest person of all learns from others' successes. Today I stand on the shoulders of many leaders who have added great value to my life. Tomorrow I hope *you* will be able to stand on *my* shoulders.

3. *What I'm teaching can be learned by nearly anyone.* Greek philosopher Plato said, "The greater part of instruction is being reminded of things you already know." That's what the best learning is. As an author and teacher, what I try to do is help people truly understand in a new and clear way something that they have long sensed intuitively. I try to create "aha moments."

Though I have lived my life in leadership by moving forward, I have begun to better understand it by looking backward. Now at age sixty, I want to share with you the most important lessons I've learned as a leader. This book is my attempt to take the leadership gold I've mined through painful trial and error and put it on the "lowest shelf" so that inexperienced as well as experienced leaders can have access to it. You don't have to be an expert to understand what I'm teaching, and you don't have to be a CEO to apply it. I never want anyone who reads my books to be like *Peanuts'* Charlie Brown, who admired a sand castle he had created on the beach only to have it leveled by huge a downpour. As he looked at the smooth place where his artwork had once stood, he said, "There must be a lesson here, but I don't know what it is." My goal isn't to impress you. It's to be a friend who helps you.

4. Much of the leadership gold I'm sharing is a result of leadership mistakes I made. Some of the things I've learned were very painful to me at the time. I can still feel the sting as I pass them on to you. I am reminded of how often I have made mistakes. Yet, I am also encouraged because I'm glad to recognize that I am wiser today than I was in years past.

Poet Archibald MacLeish remarked, "There's only one thing more painful than learning from experience, and that is not learning from experience." Too often I see people make a mistake and stubbornly plow ahead only to end up repeating the same mistake. With great resolve they say to themselves, "Try and try again!" How much better it would be to, "Try, then stop, think, change, and then try again."

5. Your ability to become a better leader depends on how you respond. Reading a book is never enough to make a difference in your life. What has the potential to make you better is your response. Please don't take shortcuts with this book. Hammer every gold nugget into something useful that can help you become a better leader. Don't be like the boy playing chess with his grandfather, who cried, "Oh no! Not again! Grandpa, you always win!"

"What do you want me to do," replied the old man, "lose on purpose? You won't learn anything if I do that."

The boy responded, "I don't want to learn anything. I just want to win!"

Wanting to win isn't enough. You have to go through a process to improve. That takes patience, perseverance, and intentionality. William A. Ward said, "Committing a great truth to memory is admirable; committing it to a life is wisdom."

I suggest that you keep this book as your companion for a significant amount of time so that it becomes a part of your life. Author and professor Peter Senge defines learning as "a process that occurs over time and always integrates thinking and doing." He goes on to say, "Learning is highly contextual . . . It happens in the context of something meaningful and when the learner is taking action."

If you are an emerging leader, I recommend that you spend twenty-six weeks working your way through the book—one week for every chapter. Read the chapter and then take the time to follow the instructions in that chapter's application section. If you take time to let each lesson sink in and then flesh it out by taking action before going on to the next one, I believe that in time you will be amazed by the positive changes that occur in your leadership.

If you are a more experienced leader, take fifty-two weeks. Why longer? Because after you have worked your way through a chapter, you should spend a week taking people you are mentoring through that same chapter. By the end of the year, not only will you have grown, but you will have helped emerging leaders in your organization to go to the next level!

LEADERSHIP MAKES A DIFFERENCE

Why should you go through all this trouble to learn more about leadership? For that matter, why have I worked so hard to learn about leadership and mine gold nuggets for forty years? Because good leadership always makes a difference! I've seen what good leadership can do. I've seen it turn around organizations and positively impact the lives of thousands of individuals. True, leadership is not easy to learn, but what worthwhile thing is? Becoming a better leader pays dividends, but it takes great effort. Leadership requires a lot from a person. It is demanding and complex. Here's what I mean . . .

Leadership is the courage to put oneself at risk.

Leadership is the passion to make a difference with others.

Leadership is being dissatisfied with the current reality.

Leadership is taking responsibility while others are making excuses.

Leadership is seeing the possibilities in a situation while others are seeing the limitations.

Leadership is the willingness to stand out in a crowd.

Leadership is an open mind and an open heart.

Leadership is the ability to submerge your ego for the sake of what is best.

Leadership is evoking in others the capacity to dream.

Leadership is inspiring others with a vision of what they can contribute.

Leadership is the power of the one made many and the many made one.

Leadership is your heart speaking to the hearts of others.

Leadership is the integration of heart, head, and soul.

Leadership is the capacity to care, and in caring, to liberate the ideas, energy, and capacities of others.

Leadership is the dream made reality.

If these leadership thoughts quicken your pulse and stir your heart, then learning more about leadership will make a difference in you, and you will make a difference in the lives of others. Turn the page, and let's get started.

Chapter 1

IF IT'S LONELY AT THE TOP, YOU'RE NOT DOING SOMETHING RIGHT

My father's generation believed that leaders should never get too close to the people they lead. "Keep a distance," was a phrase I often heard. Good leaders were supposed to be a little above and apart from those they led. As a result, when I began my leadership journey, I made sure to keep some distance between me and my people. I tried to be close enough to lead them but far enough away to not be influenced by them.

This balancing act immediately created a lot of inner conflict for me. Honestly, I liked being close to the people I led. Plus I felt that one of my strengths was my ability to connect with people. Both of these factors caused me to fight the instruction I had received to keep a distance. And sure enough, within a few months of accepting my first leadership position, my wife Margaret and I began developing close friendships. We were enjoying our work and the people in the organization.

Like many leaders early in their career, I knew that I would not stay in this first job forever. It was a good experience, but I was soon ready for bigger challenges. After three years, I resigned to accept a position in Lancaster, Ohio. I'll never forget the response of most people when they realized we were leaving: "How would you do this after all we have done together?" Many people took my departure personally. I could see they felt hurt. That really bothered me. Instantly, the words of older leaders rang in my ears: "Don't get too close to your people." As I left that assignment to take my next leadership position, I promised myself to keep people from getting too close to me.

THIS TIME IT'S PERSONAL

In my second position, for the first time in my leadership journey, I could employ staff to help me. One young man showed great promise, so I hired him and began pouring my life into him. I soon discovered that training and developing people was both a strength and a joy.

This staff member and I did everything together. One of the best ways to train others is to let them accompany you, observe what you do, give them some training, and then let them make an attempt at doing it. That's what we did. It was my first experience in mentoring.

I thought everything was going great. Then one day I found out that he had taken some sensitive information I had shared with him and violated my confidence by telling others about it. It not only hurt me as a leader, but it also hurt me personally. I felt betrayed. Needless to say, I let him go. And once again, the words of more experienced leaders rang in my ears: "Don't get too close to your people."

This time I had learned my lesson. I once again determined to keep space between me and everyone around me. I would hire staff to do their job. And I would do my job. And we would only get together at the annual Christmas party!

For six months I managed to maintain this professional separation. But then one day I realized that keeping everyone at a distance was a double-edged sword. The good news was that if I kept people at a distance, nobody would ever hurt me. But the bad news was that no one would ever be able to help me either. So at age twenty-five, I made a decision: As a leader, I would "walk slowly through the crowd." I would take the time—and the risk—of getting close to people and letting them get close to me. I would vow to love people before trying to lead them. This choice would at times make me vulnerable. I would get hurt. Yet the close relationships would allow me to help others as well as be helped by them. That decision has changed my life and my leadership.

LONELINESS IS NOT A LEADERSHIP ISSUE

Today I realize that loneliness is not a positional issue; it is a personality issue. Being at the top doesn't mean you have to be lonely. I've met lonely people at the bottom, on top, and in the middle. There's a cartoon in which an executive is shown sitting forlornly behind a huge desk. Standing meekly on the other side of the desk is a man dressed in coveralls, who says, "If it's any comfort to you, it's lonely at the bottom too."

To many people, the leader's image is that of an individual standing alone at the top of the mountain, looking down on his people. He's separated, isolated, and lonely. Thus the saying, "It's lonely at the top." But I would argue that the phrase was never made by a great leader. If you are leading others and you're lonely, then you're not doing it right. Think about it. If you're all alone, that means nobody is following you. And if nobody is following you, you're not really leading!

> *Loneliness is not a positional issue; it is a personality issue.*

What kind of a leader would leave everyone behind and take the journey alone? A selfish one. Taking people to the top is what good leaders do. Lifting people to a new level is a requirement for effective leadership. That's hard to do if you get too far from your people—because you can no longer sense their needs, know their dreams, or feel their heartbeat. Besides, if things aren't getting better for the people as the result of the leader's efforts, then they need a different leader.

TRUTHS ABOUT THE TOP

Because this leadership issue has been so personal to me, I've given it a lot of thought over the years. Here are some things you need to know.

An Excerpt from Leadership Gold

No One Ever Got to the Top Alone

Few leaders are successful unless a lot of people want them to be. No leaders are successful without a few people helping them. Sadly, as soon as some leaders arrive at the top, they spend their time trying to push others off the top. They play king of the hill because of their insecurity or competitiveness. That may work for a time,

> *Taking people to the top is what good leaders do.*

but it usually won't last long. When your goal is to knock others down, you spend too much of your time and energy watching out for people who would do the same to you. Instead, why not give others a hand up and ask them to join you?

Making It to the Top is Essential to Taking Others to the Top

There are a lot of people in the world who are willing to give advice on things they've never experienced. They are like bad travel agents: They sell you an expensive ticket and say, "I hope you enjoy the trip." Then you never see them again. In contrast, good leaders are like tour guides. They know the territory because they've made the trip before, and they do what they can to make the trip enjoyable and successful for everybody.

A leader's credibility begins with personal success. It ends with helping others achieve personal success. To gain credibility, you must consistently demonstrate three things:

Initiative—You have to get up to go up.
Sacrifice—You have to give up to go up.
Maturity—You have to grow up to go up.

If you show the way, people will want to follow you. The higher you go, the greater the number of people who will be willing to travel with you.

TAKING PEOPLE TO THE TOP IS MORE FULFILLING THAN
ARRIVING ALONE.

A few years ago I had the privilege of speaking on the same stage as Jim
Whittaker, the first American to climb Mt. Everest. During lunch I asked
him what had given him the most fulfillment as a mountain climber. His
answer surprised me.

"I have helped more people get to the top of Mt. Everest than any other
person," he replied. "Taking people to the top who could never get there
without my assistance is my greatest accomplishment."

> *A leader's credibility begins
> with personal success. It
> ends with helping others
> achieve personal success*

Evidently this is a common way of
thinking for great mountain guides.
Years ago I saw an interview with a
guide on *60 Minutes*. People had died
while attempting to climb Mt. Everest,
and a surviving guide was asked,
"Would the guides have died if they
were not taking others with them to the top?"

"No," he answered, "but the purpose of the guide is to take people to
the top."

Then the interviewer asked, "Why do mountain climbers risk their lives
to climb mountains?"

The guide responded, "It is obvious that you have never been to the top
of the mountain."

I remember thinking to myself that mountain guides and leaders
have a lot in common. The purpose of leadership is to take others to the
top. And when you take others who might not make it otherwise to the
top, there's no other feeling like it in the world. To those who have never
had the experience, you can't explain it. To those who have, you don't
need to.

Retired army general Norman Schwarzkopf remarked, "You can't help
someone up a hill without getting closer to the top yourself." The difference
between a boss and a leader is that a boss says, "Go." A leader says, "Let's go."

An Excerpt from Leadership Gold

Much of the Time Leaders are Not at the Top

Leaders rarely remain stationary. They are constantly on the move. Sometimes they are going down the mountain to find new potential leaders. At other times they are trying to make the climb with a group of people. The best ones spend much of their time serving other leaders and lifting them up.

Jules Ormont said, "A great leader never sets himself above his followers except in carrying responsibilities."

> *"You can't help someone up a hill without getting closer to the top yourself."*
> – Norman Schwarzkopf

Good leaders who remain connected with their people stoop—that's the only way to reach down and pull others up. If you want to be the best leader you can be, don't allow insecurity, pettiness, or jealousy to keep you from reaching out to others.

ADVICE TO LONELY LEADERS

If you find yourself too far from your people—either by accident or by design—then you need to change. True, there will be risks. You may hurt others or be hurt yourself. But if you want to be the most effective leader you can be, there is no viable alternative. Here's how to get started:

1. Avoid Positional Thinking

Leadership is relational as much as it is positional. An individual who takes a relational approach to leadership will never be lonely. The time spent in building relationships creates friendships with others. Positional leaders, on the other hand, are often lonely. Every time they use their title and position to "persuade" their people to do something, they create distance between themselves and others. They are essentially saying, "I'm up here; you're down there. So do what I say." That makes people feel small, alienates them, and drives a wedge between them and the leader. Good leaders don't belittle people—they enlarge them.

Every year I invest time teaching leadership internationally. Positional leadership is a way of life in many developing countries. Their leaders gather and protect power. They alone are allowed to be on top and everyone else is expected to follow. Sadly, this practice keeps potential leaders from developing and creates loneliness for the one who leads.

If you are in a leadership position, do not rely on your title to convince people to follow you. Build relationships. Win people over. Do that and you will never be lonely at the top.

2. Realize the Downsides of Success and Failure

Success can be dangerous—and so can failure. Any time you think of yourself as a success, you start to separate yourself from others you view as less successful. You start to think, *I don't need to see them,* and you withdraw. Ironically, failure also leads to withdrawal, but for other reasons. If you think of yourself as a failure, you avoid others, thinking, *I don't want to see them.* Both extremes in thinking can create an unhealthy separation from others.

3. Understand That You Are in the People Business

The best leaders know that leading people requires loving them! I've never met a good leader who didn't care about people. Ineffective leaders have the wrong attitude, saying, "I love mankind. It's the people I can't stand." But good leaders understand that people do not care how much you know until they know how much you care. You must like people or you will never add value to them. And if you become indifferent to people, you may be only a few steps away from manipulating them. No leader should ever do that.

4. Buy into the Law of Significance

The Law of Significance in *The 17 Irrefutable Laws of Leadership* states, "One is too small a number to achieve greatness." No accomplishment of real value has ever been achieved by a human being working alone. I challenge you to think of one. (I've made this challenge at conferences for years, and no one has succeeded in identifying one yet!) Honestly, if on your own you can fulfill the vision you have for your life and work, then you're aiming too low. Occasionally a person will introduce himself to me by saying, "I am a self-made man." I am often tempted to reply, "I'm so sorry. If you've made everything yourself, you haven't made much."

In my organizations I don't have employees; I have teammates. Yes, I do pay people and offer them benefits. But people don't work for me. They work with me. We are working together to fulfill the vision. Without them, I cannot succeed. Without me, they cannot succeed. We're a team. We reach our goals together. We need each other. If we didn't, then one of us is in the wrong place.

> *Leadership is relational as much as it is positional. An individual who takes a relational approach to leadership will never be lonely.*

PEOPLE WORKING TOGETHER FOR A COMMON VISION CAN BE AN incredible experience. Years ago, when operatic tenors Jose Carreras, Placido Domingo, and Luciano Pavarotti were performing together, a reporter tried to find out if there was a competitive spirit among them.

Each singer was a superstar, and the reporter was hoping to uncover a rivalry between them. Domingo dismissed it. "You have to put all of your concentration into opening your heart to the music," Domingo said. "You can't be rivals when you're together making music."

For many years now I have tried to maintain that kind of attitude toward the people I work with. Our focus is on what we are trying to accomplish together, not on hierarchies or professional distance or the preservation of power. I've come a long way from where I started in my leadership journey. In the beginning my attitude was that it was lonely at the top. But it has changed, following a progression that looks something like this:

- "It's lonely at the top," to
- "If it's lonely at the top, I must be doing something wrong," to

- "Come up to the top and join me," to
- "Let's go to the top together," to
- "It's not lonely at the top."

Nowadays I never "climb the mountain" alone. My job is to make sure the team makes it to the top together. Some of the people I invite to go along pass me and climb higher than I do. That doesn't bother me. If I know I was able to give them a hand and pull them up along the way, that is very fulfilling to me. Sometimes they return the favor and pull me up to their level. I'm grateful for that too.

If you're a leader and you feel isolated, then you're not doing something right. Loneliness on the part of a leader is a choice. I choose to take the journey with people. I hope you do too.

If It's Lonely at the Top, You're Not Doing Something Right
Application Exercises

1. *Are you better at the science or art of leadership?* Some leaders are better at the technical side of leading: strategy, planning, finances, etc. Others are better at the people part: connecting, communicating, casting vision, motivating, etc. Which is your strength?

If you are more of a technical person, never lose sight of the fact that leadership is a people business. Take steps to improve your people skills. Try walking slowly through the halls so that you can talk to people and get to know them better. Read books or take courses. Ask a friend who is good with people to give you some tips. Do whatever it takes to improve.

2. *Why do you want to be at the top?* Most people have a natural desire to improve their lives. For many, that means climbing the career ladder so that they can gain a higher position. If your only motivation for leading is career advancement and professional improvement, you are in danger of becoming the kind of positional leader who plays "king of the hill" with colleagues and employees. Spend some time soul searching to discover how your leadership can and should benefit others.

3. *How big is your dream?* What is your dream? What would you love to accomplish in your life and career? If it's something you can accomplish alone, you are missing your leadership potential. Anything worth doing is worth doing with others. Dream big. What can you imagine accomplishing that would require more than you can do on your own? What kinds of teammates would you need to accomplish it? How might the trip benefit them as well as you or the organization? Broaden your thinking and you will be more likely to think of climbing the summit with a team.

BOOKS BY DR. JOHN C. MAXWELL
CAN TEACH YOU HOW TO BE A REAL SUCCESS

RELATIONSHIPS

Be a People Person

Becoming a Person of Influence

Relationships 101

The Power of Influence

The Power of Partnership in the Church

The Treasure of a Friend

Ethics 101

Winning with People

25 Ways to Win with People

EQUIPPING

Developing the Leaders Around You

Equipping 101

The 17 Indisputable Laws of Teamwork

The 17 Essential Qualities of a Team Player

Partners in Prayer

Your Road Map for Success

Success One Day at a Time

Today Matters

Talent Is Never Enough

ATTITUDE

Be All You Can Be

Failing Forward

The Power of Thinking Big

Living at the Next Level

Think on These Things

The Winning Attitude

Your Bridge to a Better Future

The Power of Attitude

Attitude 101

Thinking for a Change

The Difference Maker

The Journey from Success to Significance

LEADERSHIP

The 21 Indispensable Qualities of a Leader

Revised & Updated 10th Anniversary Edition of *The 21 Irrefutable Laws of Leadership*

The 21 Most Powerful Minutes in a Leader's Day

Developing the Leader Within You

Leadership 101

Leadership Promises for Every Day

The 360 Degree Leader

The Right to Lead

The Power of Leadership

ABOUT THE AUTHOR

J ohn C. Maxwell is a #1 *New York Times* bestselling author, coach, and speaker who has sold more than 26 million books in fifty languages. In 2014 he was identified as the #1 leader in business by the American Management Association® and the most influential leadership expert in the world by *Business Insider* and *Inc.* magazines. He is the founder of the John Maxwell Company, the John Maxwell Team, EQUIP, and the John Maxwell Leadership Foundation, organizations that have trained millions of leaders. In 2015, they reached the milestone of having trained leaders from every country in the world. The recipient of the Mother Teresa Prize for Global Peace and Leadership from the Luminary Leadership Network, Dr. Maxwell speaks each year to *Fortune* 500 companies, presidents of nations, and many of the world's top business leaders. He can be followed at Twitter.com/JohnCMaxwell. For more information about him visit JohnMaxwell.com.

GET YOUR <u>FREE</u>
LEADERSHIP ASSESSMENT
FROM
JOHN C. MAXWELL

Discover the traits you need to become an exceptional leader with a FREE leadership assessment from John C. Maxwell. You'll identify areas where your leadership skills need further development as well as where you currently lead effectively. He'll equip you with powerful resources and practical thinking to grow your influence, create lasting change and facilitate growth in others.

Visit **MaxwellLeader.com** to sign up for your FREE leadership assessment.

MINUTE
WITH MAXWELL

Your Free Daily Video Coaching with John!

John Maxwell's leadership principles are as timeless as they are true. Let John support your success by equipping you with leadership teachings to apply to your life daily.

Sign up to learn and grow everyday...

- **Enjoy wisdom & wit** from world renown leadership expert, John Maxwell.

- The most **powerful video minute** of coaching on the planet.

- **Benefit** from John's 40+ years as one of the world's top communicators **FOR FREE!**

- As a **BONUS**, send John your word, and he will teach on it during one of his videos.

> ## "I love each word.
> **My kids and I listen as we walk to school each morning and then we talk about what we learned. It's a great way for us to set our intention for the day!"**
>
> -Denise Russo, USA

Sign up for your Minute with Maxwell today at
www.JohnMaxwellTeam.com/MWM-DLWY

LEADERSHIP CAN BE TAUGHT
DEVELOP THE LEADERS WITHIN
YOUR COMPANY

COACHING | LEADERSHIP DEVELOPMENT | CUSTOM TRAINING

BASED ON THE JOHN MAXWELL PRINCIPLES

CALL TODAY

(800) 333-6506

GO TO...

JOHNMAXWELLCOMPANY.COM/LEADERSHIP

The JOHN MAXWELL **Co.**
Corporate Leadership Solutions

LEADERSHIP
FOUNDATION

transforming
LEADERS
transforming
COUNTRIES

Together,
WE CAN CHANGE THE WORLD.
jmlf.org

MOBILIZING LEADERS FOR
TRANSFORMATION

iequip.church | 678.225.3300

CPSIA information can be obtained
at www.ICGtesting.com
Printed in the USA
LVHW032158041020
667921LV00004B/77

9 780785 289357